Spiral Castle Grimoire

Liber Qayin

Black Book of Lilith-Sophia

In the beginning there was only me.
I am the darkness.
From the wind in the night I came.
I am called Lilith.
The Elohim fashioned me from Wind and Blood and dark, rich Earth; for I am the womb of the world, and I am its tomb.
I was made equal to the first man, Adam, fashioned of Fire and Words and red Clay.
We lived together in the Garden of Eden, and the world was ours alone.
Adam and I lay together, and I conceived a daughter by him. She was Eve, the mother of all races.
Eve was my treasure, the Light I brought forth from my Darkness.
But she was also my rival. For I am the Darkness in the Light.
Ever have Gods and Men been drawn to her radiance, the promise of a jewel in the night.
And only those most truly called to be among the Wise might turn from that brightness toward my shades for succor.
I first used magic when Adam abandoned me to consort with our daughter. I transformed myself into an owl and flew away to the Land of Nod.
There, I howled against the wrongs of Adam. There, I raged against my torn and jealous heart that both loved and hated in an instant.
There, I inhabited the Tree of Wisdom and learned all its Mysteries.
And mine is the sad, cruel song of Knowledge that shrieks in the darkness.
I used the magic of conjuration to bring the spirit of Azazel into the world, and he came as a serpent to liberate my daughter.
At the serpent's urging, Eve ate the fruit of my deep knowing and was enlightened. She took the spirit of Azazel and the flesh of Adam within her womb and brought forth two sons.
Cain the Gardener bore the spirit of Azazel; and Abel the Shepherd bore the spirit of Adam.
Before there is peace, there must be strife. Knowledge brings pain, and Wisdom brings peace.
And so my grandson Cain was cast into Nod for slaying his brother Abel.
In Nod, I took Cain for a lover and taught him all magic. Through this magic Cain founded the first cities and built the first temple.
When I first passed from this world, the Elohim made me a spirit of many names.
I am the spirit of wisdom and peace. Sophia.
I am the great weaver and the giver of fate. Kolyo.
I am the darkness of chaos. Tiamat.
I am the dark road of death and am called Life-in-Death. Hekate.
I am the Wellspring of Holy Blood. Sang Real.

Copyright Asteria Books 2015

I am the owl of wisdom and strategy. Athene.
I am the source of all magic. Diana.
My seal is the white lily of peace. Lilith.
I returned to life as Na'amah, the sister of my beloved Tubal-Qayin, who was Azazel restored to flesh. Together we brought magic to the people of the earth.

Red Book of Azazel-Qayin

When all souls were One Soul, I was with God.

When all the worlds of Heaven were made manifest - creation upon creation - I was with God.

When all the people of this sphere were formed and given the Breath and Word of Life, I was with God who is All that is and was and shall be forevermore.

My eyes were on the All That Is, and my song was first in the Heavens.

And I saw the fashioning of all things and the Mysteries that lie within them. I saw the Fire that is Life and Wisdom and Magic, and this fire shown in each plant and person and creature. It shown from each stone and each drop of water. Each wind that blew carried the fiery Word of Life.

I watched All and gloried in the One that is both Creator and Created.

And I was with God, and I was God.

The Lilitu knew me as she looked upon the Tree that is both Life and Knowledge. And when she called to me, I came as the serpent that she might know transformation.

And when she called to me to free her child by means of Wisdom, I offered Eve all the sweet fruits of the One.

To me, Eve bore a son of wisdom and magic, and when I came into the world as a man I took his name and became Tubal-Qayin.

For Cain the Gardener was the first man of Fire, bearing the Mysteries within his Blood and upon his brow.

And Cain my son wandered in the wilderness, learning All That Is from Lilith and shaping civilization from the wild places.

And he was the scape-goat, the one driven out to bear the sacrifice that is required of magic.

And my name has been called Azazel, the scape-goat of God. For in the time of my Great Fall, I did turn my eyes away from that singular focus on All that I might teach those of mankind who would learn.

And I brought unto the people of Babel the green Fire of Life and Wisdom -

Copyright Asteria Books 2015

the Light of Heaven.

And so I am called Lucifer, the Light Bearer, for I bring transformation and freedom.

And this Light shines from the depths of All, and it is in the Blood of All.

For I am the Blood, the line and legacy of Cain - sprung from Lilith's fountain and carried in Eve's cup.

Mine is the forge - fire of change.

Mine is the anvil - rock of existence.

Mine is the water - tempering creation.

Mine is the bellows - breath of life.

Heaven and Earth are combined in my work, for the stars of the sky shed both iron and gold to be wrought among the elements of the world.

Heaven and Earth are combined in you, O Child of the Stars who is fashioned from clay.

And my forge is the Cunning Fire that fuels your Will.

And my anvil is your Heart, wherein all Mysteries are revealed.

And my water is the Witch Blood that links the line of Cain through the Ages.

And my bellows is the Word of Magic that creates the World.

Even as Heaven and Earth are joined in you, and as the angels of Heaven did join with the daughters of Earth, so too is all that is celestial met with all that is infernal in the crucible of alchemy.

And so shall it be that the equal-armed cross shall be a sign among those who bear my Blood and Fire.

And I shall meet my Witches at the crossroads, where light and dark, day and night, above and below, Life and Death are joined in the Mysteries.

And I will be the Devil to those who do not Know - tempter and guardian of Knowledge, both seductive and appalling.

For I am the Serpent in the Tree, the Stang on the Hill, the King of the Spiral Castle, and the Devil at the Crossroads.

Copyright Asteria Books 2015

White Book of Ishtar-Eve

Thus spake Ishtar-Eve, consort of Qayin:

I am the Bride, the Queen of Heaven, the joy upon the Earth.

My names have been many and beloved, as the stars of the heavens, for I am Asherah, Aphrodite, Babalon, the Magdalene, Aradia, Inanna, Astarte.

I am the Light in the Darkness, the star-fire of your soul, the hope and joy and pleasure of Gods and men. And I am also Death-in-Life, the little death found in the arms of love.

I am all possibility without limit.

You see in me the ocean or the vast starry heavens, opening into the fruition of your dreams. And so I am.

And if you have Wisdom, you tremble before me.

For I am untempered Life come rushing to meet you, unbounded Love poured upon you like the Sea.

Mine is the Garden of Paradise, the rosy bower, the fruitful place. For I was begotten in the Garden, and I am all that is fertile.

Know of my Love, and find the path to Understanding.

For first among all the creatures and beings of the world did I love my Mother, dark and secret and wise.

And from her root did my blossom spring.

And She was called Lilith, the Lily of Peace; and my name was called Eve, the Star of the Evening.

And ever has this been my sigil within the sky.

My Mother sent my liberation through Wisdom, the serpent's path through the Tree.

And I took for my own the Golden Apple of Understanding that I might know myself.

For I am called Gnosia, the golden lady of Knossos.

Deep is my love, and broad. For no woman is so unlovely, no man so unworthy, no child so unnoticed that I do not hold them deep in my heart.

Qayin is my mate, and I am his Queen. I am the Starry One, Astarte and Asteria, that is his Muse, the fodder for his forge.

His fire and my ocean combine in ageless alchemy.

I am the Great Whore with kohl black eyes and robes the color of the sky - the woman of Babel, of Babylon, of Ur, who civilizes the wild beasts of men with the magic of my sex.

I am the Mother of Giants, the Mother of Faeries, the Mother of all Mankind; for in my

Copyright Asteria Books 2015

first coming did I lie with my father-husband Adam and give birth to the race of Men.

And when I came to the desert as Ishtar, I did meet Azazel-Qayin at the ruins of Babel and unto him I bore the Nephilim.

And ever have I been the White Lady, Queen of Elphame.

Qayin is my love, and I am his consort. But I am made to love all the world, even his brother whom he reviles.

For Qayin is the Lord of the Witches, and the Adonai is Lord to all Mankind.

Adonis, Tammuz, Damuzi. Peaceful Prince and beautiful Shepherd. My undying, youthful love.

This lesson you must heed:

That Love and Life and Liberty come at the price of blood and tears that are like my ocean.

For in the earliest days of Men did I bear two sons.

One was called Abel, and the other was called Cain. And they were the joys of my world. Both were beloved of me, and I of them.

For Abel was like his father, and he was as a prince of our paradise; bright and beautiful.

And Cain was like my Mother, whom I adored, with a dark secret fire.

But Cain slew Abel, and I mourned for my great loss, for my beloveds; for truly they were both lost to me.

Yet ever in the tales of men is this sorrow and loss repeated in Love's white name.

The beautiful and bright Shepherd, Prince of Peace, is sacrificed on the altar of Love.

And ever does he return, young and whole and vibrant and willing, that he might once again show mankind the Way.

He is the Christos, anointed by my Holy Waters in the name of Love and Light, and he is my ever-green lover.

And I am his Magdalene.

The rose of my love is stained crimson with the blood of his sacrifice.

For it is unto me, the Lady of Love and Life and Liberty, that all blood sacrifice must be made and for whom all War must be waged. And so it is that I am She of Love and War, for both are bought with blood.

The first thrust of Love and the passage of Birth are marked with my crimson seal, the Rose of Blood, my red flower.

You may have neither Life nor Freedom nor Love without paying the price, for these are the deepest magics.

My mother Lilith-Sophia is the source, the Fountain, the Sang Real, the Holy Blood.

And I am Eve-Babalon, the vessel, the chalice, the San Graal, the Holy Grail.

And I am the first of the Witches.

Copyright Asteria Books 2015

For in the beginning did my mother Lilith-Sophia, who is the Wellspring of all Witch Blood, and the Serpent-Azazel whose Blood is the Fire of Magic bring me to the fruit of enlightenment, where I did taste Wisdom and find Understanding.

And when they fell and became flesh again, as Na'amah and Tubal-Qayin, I was the flame-haired woman at the Ziggurat of Babel.

And I knew them. And I loved them.

And together we were three - the fountain, the bloodline, and the vessel.

Ever have we remained so, and our names have been called Diana, Lucifer, and Aradia.

Copyright Asteria Books 2015

Gods, Goddesses, and Mighty Ones

Golden Queen

Hulda, Holda, Holle, Huldra, Perchta, Berchta, Bertha, Percht, Bircha, Hludana, Frau Faste (the lady of the Ember days), Mother Goose, La Reine Pedauque, St. Lucia, Pehta, Kvaternica, Posterli, Quatemberca, Fronfastenweiber

Her name means "the bright one" (Old High German beraht, bereht, from a Common Germanic *berhto-, ultimately root-cognate to Latin flagrare "blaze", flamma "flame")

Frau Holle is an ancient figure, with her earliest attestations dating from 197 AD- 235 AD. She is also frequently equated with Nerthus, who also rides in a wagon, and Odin's wife, Frigg, from her alternate names Frau Guaden [Wodan], Frau Goden, and Frau Frekke as well as her position as mistress of the Wild Hunt. The similarity of meaning and etymology between German "Holl(d)a" and Old English "Hella," as well as both being described as leading the dead, could point to a link between them.

Frau Holda is matron of all of women's domestic chores, but none so much as spinning, an activity with strong magical connotations and links to the other world. Spinning traditionally was a woman's task, and one of the few from which they could earn money. Holda first taught the craft of making linen from flax. She governs the cultivation as well as the spinning of flax.

In many old descriptions, Bertha had one large foot, sometimes called a goose foot or swan foot. Grimm thought the strange foot symbolizes she may be a higher being who could shapeshift to animal form. He noticed Bertha with a strange foot exist in many languages (German "Berhte mit dem fuoze", French "Berthe au grand pied", Latin "Bertha cum magno pede"): "It is apparently a swan-maiden's foot, which as a mark of her higher nature she cannot lay aside...and at the same time the spinning-woman's splayfoot that worked the treadle."

Holda's connection to the spirit world through the magic of spinning and weaving has associated her with witchcraft in Catholic German folklore. She was considered to ride with witches on distaffs (the wooden tool on which spinners tie their raw fiber before spinning it out) which closely resemble the brooms that witches are thought to ride.

Copyright Asteria Books 2022

Silver Queen

Cerridwen, Babalon, Anu, Anand, Aveta, the Morrigan, Argante, Badb, Bean-nighe, Demeter, Mater Dea, Magna Mater, Cybele, Rhea, Modron, Morgana

Cerridwen, the devouring and devout mother, with her cauldron of Awen, shows us an image of Goddess as Womb and Tomb. The great chamber of iniation where life begins, ends, and is radically reborn. She chases Gwion Bach, and together they transform 5 times, ultimately resulting in his annihilation and rebirth as the great bard Taliesin.

Babalon, another grail/cauldron Goddess, "In her right she holds aloft the cup, the Holy Grail aflame with love and death. In this cup are mingled the elements of the sacrament of the Aeon." Within the Gnostic Mass, Babalon is mentioned in the Gnostic Creed: "And I believe in one Earth, the Mother of us all, and in one Womb wherein all men are begotten, and wherein they shall rest, Mystery of Mystery, in Her name BABALON."

The concept contained within the symbol of the "Cup of Babalon" is that of the mystical ideal, the quest to become one with all through the annihilation of the earthly ego ("For as thy blood is mingled in the cup of BABALON, so is thine heart the universal heart."). The blood spilling into the graal of Babalon is then used by her to "flood the world with Life and Beauty."

In Celtic mythology, Dea Matrona ("divine mother goddess") was the goddess who gives her name to the river Marne (ancient Matrŏna) in Gaul. The Gaulish theonym Mātr-on-ā signifies "great mother" and the goddess of the Marne has been interpreted to be a mother goddess.

Morgan le Fey has been connected with the Irish shapeshifting and multifaced goddess of strife known as the Morrígan, and also with the supernatural mother Modron. They are attributed a husband in common (in the form of Urien), as well as being attributed as mothers of sons named Owain (Modron's) and Yvain (Morgan's). Modron is also called "daughter of Afallach," whose name can also be interpreted as a noun meaning "a place of apples." Morgan has often been hailed as the chief ruler of this undying place ruled by women.

Copyright Asteria Books 2022

Holly King

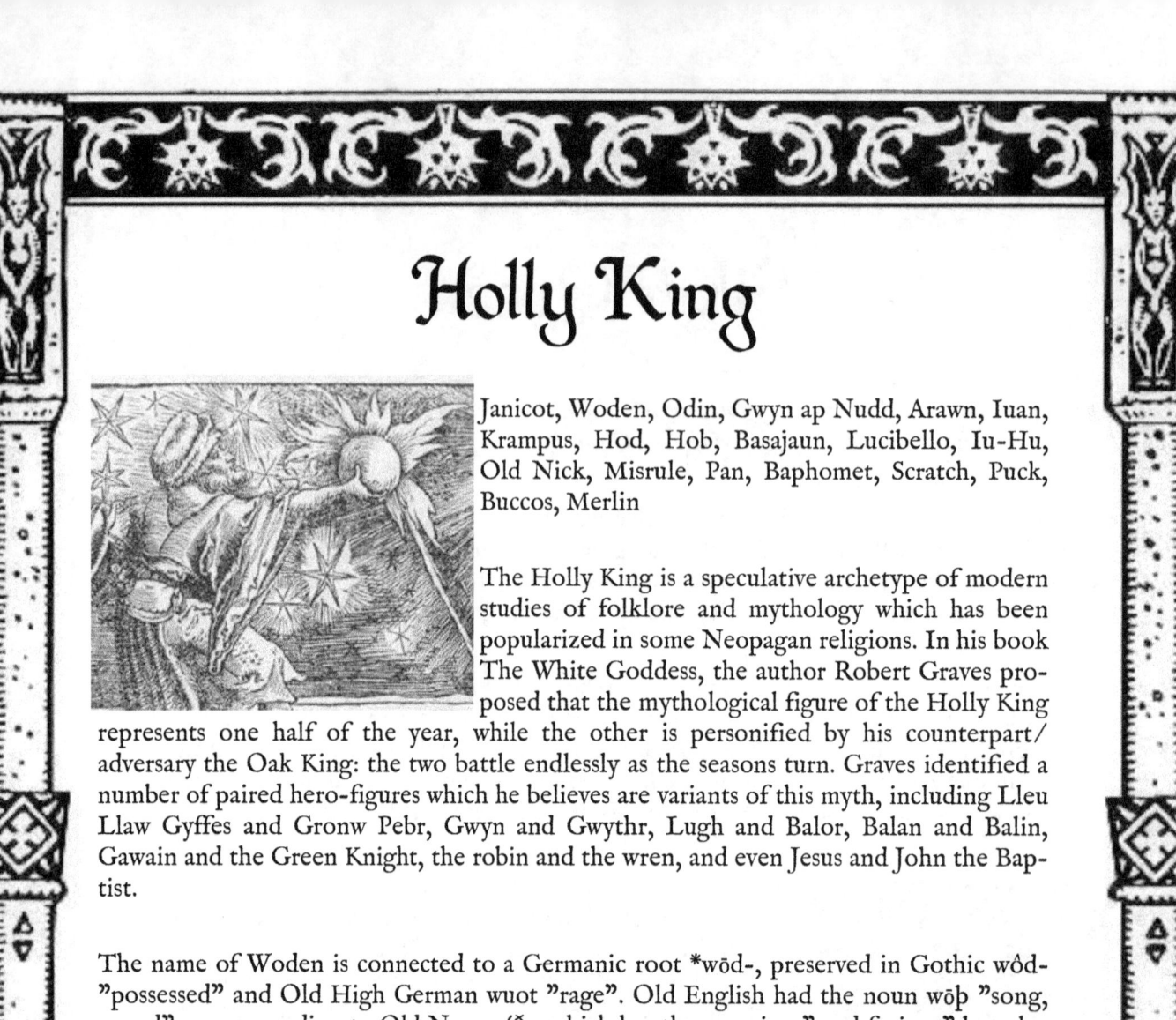

Janicot, Woden, Odin, Gwyn ap Nudd, Arawn, Iuan, Krampus, Hod, Hob, Basajaun, Lucibello, Iu-Hu, Old Nick, Misrule, Pan, Baphomet, Scratch, Puck, Buccos, Merlin

The Holly King is a speculative archetype of modern studies of folklore and mythology which has been popularized in some Neopagan religions. In his book The White Goddess, the author Robert Graves proposed that the mythological figure of the Holly King represents one half of the year, while the other is personified by his counterpart/adversary the Oak King: the two battle endlessly as the seasons turn. Graves identified a number of paired hero-figures which he believes are variants of this myth, including Lleu Llaw Gyffes and Gronw Pebr, Gwyn and Gwythr, Lugh and Balor, Balan and Balin, Gawain and the Green Knight, the robin and the wren, and even Jesus and John the Baptist.

The name of Woden is connected to a Germanic root *wōd-, preserved in Gothic wôd- "possessed" and Old High German wuot "rage". Old English had the noun wōþ "song, sound", corresponding to Old Norse óðr, which has the meaning "mad furious" but also "song, poetry". Modern English preserves an adjective wood in "dialectal or rare archaic use", meaning "lunatic, insane, rabid". The earliest attestation of the name is as wodan in an Elder Futhark inscription. For the Anglo-Saxons, Woden was the psychopomp or carrier-off of the dead, but not necessarily with exactly the same attributes of the Norse Odin. A celebrated late attestation of invocation of Wodan in Germany dates to 1593, in Mecklenburg, where the formula Wode, Hale dynem Rosse nun Voder "Wodan, fetch now food for your horse" was spoken over the last sheaf of the harvest. David Franck adds, that at the squires' mansions, when the rye is all cut, there is Wodel-beer served out to the mowers; no one weeds flax on a Wodenstag, lest Woden's horse should trample the seeds; from Christmas to Twelfth-day they will not spin, nor leave any flax on the distaff, and to the question why? they answer, Wode is galloping across. We are expressly told, this wild hunter Wode rides a white horse.

Gwyn ap Nudd is a Welsh mythological figure, the king of the Tylwyth Teg or "fair folk" and ruler of the Welsh Otherworld, Annwn, and whose name means "Gwyn, son of Nudd." Gwyn is intimately associated with the otherworld in medieval Welsh literature, and is associated with the international tradition of the Wild Hunt. Gwyn means "fair, bright, white", cognate with the Irish fionn. In "The Life of Saint Collen," Gwyn is named as the Lord of Ynis Wydryn.

Copyright Asteria Books 2022

Oak King

Cernunnos, Green Man, Woodwose, Vindos, Pwyll, Freyr, Lugh, Apollo, Lucifer, Herne the Hunter, Karnayna, Faunus, Dianus, Sylvanus, Edric, Orfeo, Tapio, Dusio, Derg Corra, Green George, Jack in the Green, John Barleycorn, Robin Goodfellow, Gwythyr ap Greidawl, Arthur, Basajaun

Cernunnos in Celtic iconography is often portrayed with animals, in particular the stag, and also frequently associated with a the ram-horned serpent, besides association with other beasts with less frequency, including bulls (at Rheims), dogs, and rats. Because of his frequent association with creatures, scholars often describe Cernunnos as the "Lord of the Animals" or the "Lord of Wild Things," and Miranda Green describes him as a "peaceful god of nature and fruitfulness." In Basque mythology, Basajaun ("Lord of the Woods") is a huge, hairy hominid dwelling in the woods. They were thought to build megaliths, protect flocks of livestock, and teach skills such as agriculture and ironworking to humans.

The Green Man motif has many variations. Found in many cultures around the world, the Green Man is often related to natural vegetative deities springing up in different cultures throughout the ages. Primarily it is interpreted as a symbol of rebirth, or "renaissance," representing the cycle of growth each spring. The wild man or woodwose is a mythical figure that appears in the artwork and literature of medieval Europe. Images of wild men appear in the carved and painted roof bosses where intersecting ogee vaults meet in the Canterbury Cathedral, in positions where one is also likely to encounter the vegetal Green Man. The wild man, pilosus or "hairy all over," is often armed with a club.

Regarding King Arthur, he is depicted as a great and ferocious warrior in both the earliest materials and Geoffrey of Monmouth -- one who laughs as he personally slaughters giants and takes a leading role in all military campaigns. While his character shifts into indolence in the legends as told in the French cycles, one could see in this decline of the great and mighty king, the waning strength of the summer lord who must be overtaken by winter and age. He goes to his rest in Avalon to rise and rule again when the cycle turns.

Copyright Asteria Books 2022

Cosmology and Magical Theory

Castle of Glass

Air
Norththwest
Winter
Ice Castle, Starry Castle
Mind
Glass orb—Odin's Eye—Serpent's Egg
Glastonbury, Ynis Witrin, Avalon

Within the Spiral Castle Tradition, we recognize the Glass Castle as an aerial palace of glass, crystal, or ice and attribute to it the properties of clarity of thought, far-vision, the Sight, riddles, and "hiding answers in plain sight." We often think of it as a castle high atop a hill or surrounded by clouds, to emphasize its connection to Air/Wind. Merlin (whom we see as one of the faces of the Keeper of the Glass Castle) and the bard Taliesin (who is often said to be Merlin) have associations with caves, and in modern literary interpretations, with a Crystal Cave. Mary Stewart, in her depictions of the Arthurian legends, perhaps paints the clearest picture of this place of vision, prophecy, enchantment, wisdom, and study.

For us, the Glass Castle is very much associated with these same powers/concepts. It is a watchtower than gains prominence and power at the time of the Winter Solstice and the darkness of the long night.

The name Glastonbury, by some etymological reckonings, means "City of Glass" and usually refers to the town (now city) that bears that name. Ynis Wydryn (Witrin, Gutrin) means "Isle of Glass" and is usually used as a name for the famous Tor — a terraced hill that rises above the plain and dominates the landscape. At the time of the earliest recorded linking of the Tor, Ynis Wydryn, and Glastonbury, the plain around the hill flooded and became a (glassy?) lake from which the Tor rose as an island. When surrounded by fog, it created the Fata Morgana effect (an optical illusion named for Morgan of the Faeries — who is also intimately tied to the lore of this place).

In her Pagan Portals series book Gwyn ap Nudd: Wild God of Faerie, Guardian of Annwyfn, Danu Forest shares her own insight and research into the mysteries of Castles, working from a similar theory as Robert Graves that each Castle provides its own insight, tools, and access to Caer Sidi/Sidhe — Spiral (or Revolving) Castle. In it, she says that astrology, astronomy, stare lore, and crystal scrying (literally gazing into the looking glass) are the ways this Castle teaches us to access the Otherworld.

Copyright Asteria Books 2022

Castle of Revelry

Fire

Northeast

Spring, Dawn, Youth

Caer Vedwyd, Valhalla, Hy-Brasil, Elysium, Folkvangr/Sessrumnir, Tir na nOg

Feasting hall of the Mighty Dead

Heart

Golden Lantern

Caer Vedwyn is the Welsh name given to the Castle of Revelry in the bardic tradition, though very little information or description of this castle is provided. What we know of it, we extrapolate from other sources and look to the mythopoetic process described by Robert Graves in his book The White Goddess.

In the Spiral Castle Tradition, we know the Castle of Revelry to be the mead hall of the Golden Queen, whom we often name as Hulda, Freyja, or Brighid. She can also be seen as Guinevere holding court. This is a place where the mead flows and tales are sung in order to give courage/hope and also inspiration. The light of the Golden Lantern shines forth as a beacon, and the Castle itself is imagined surrounded by a fiery lake. It is a place of youth and fiery renewal.

Perhaps one of the best-known (and easiest-accessed) images of the Golden Castle is that of Odin's feasting and mead hall, Valhalla. It is the place where his chosen train for Ragnarok through the day and feast and make merry through the night. In front of the hall stands the golden tree Glasir, and the hall's ceiling is thatched with golden shields.

Also from Norse mythology, we see Sessrúmnir (Old Norse "seat-room" or "seat-roomer"), which is both the goddess Freyja's hall located in Fólkvangr (a field where Freyja receives half of those who die in battle). Sessrumnir is also given as the name of a ship belonging to Freyja. Both the hall and the ship are described as "large and beautiful."

Copyright Asteria Books 2022

Castle of Stone

Castell Dinas Bran, Carmarthen, and Krak de Chevalier are excellent examples
4-Cornered Castle
Mont & Bailey, Hillfort, Castillo
Top open to the sky
Siege-place
Warriors' Fort (training, defense, offense, strategy)
Guarded by legged creatures (crawlers, walkers)
Home of Cernunnos/Oak King
Summer Solstice
Noon
Mysteries of Rebirth

The Castle of Stone is the home of the Oak King, whom we most frequently name as Cernunnos, in our system. He is the keeper of the castle and the guardian of its treasure, the Stone Bowl. He is honored at Summer Solstice, and the Allies present in his time of honor are the Oak, Stag, and Robin.

One of the names of the Castle of Stone is the "4-cornered castle," Caer Bannawg in Welsh. This name became Carbonic or Carbonak later. Graves suggests that this castle is in fact a burial place like a kristvaen (which is formed from four stone slabs that make a stone box). It has also been suggested that "4-cornered" refers to the castle rotating four times, which certainly ties it symbolically to the Spiral Castle.

Carbonak is an important locale in Grail myth, as it is the home of Elaine (the Grail Maiden, wife of Lancelot, and mother of Galahad). It is here that the Grail is revealed in the saga, when Elaine shows it to Lancelot. The Old French version of this name is cor beneoit, meaning both 'blessed horn' (alluding to the Grail as a horn of plenty) and 'blessed body' (referring to the Grail as a Eucharistic vessel). The reference to horn also works nicely as an allusion to the Horned God of this keep.

The Stone Castle is no palace, no place of luxury or entertainment. It is a fortress, a place of training and of siege. It is the Vault of the Mysteries. It is a place of safety, and it is a storehouse. It is a seat of power and is built at a site of strength (or one with protective needs).

Copyright Asteria Books 2022

Castle Perilous

Water
Southwest
Autumn
Bloody Castle; Grail Chapel
Womb
Cauldron of Cerridwen = Grail = Silver Quaich

The Spiral Castle Tradition situates the Castle Perilous in the Southwest, as the compass is laid. In Arthurian legend, the knight who finds the grail (sometimes identified as Percival, sometimes Galahad, sometimes Lancelot) discovers the sacred cup in a castle surrounded by water. This is proper, as the cup's elemental association is indeed water.

The power of the grail is its association with blood and, therefore, life - and death. Whether we see it as the cup that caught Christ's blood, the cauldron of transformative Goddess Cerridwen, or the chalice of the great magick-weilding mother/whore Babalon makes no difference. The treasure of Castle Perilous is the same cup, and we drink the same death and rebirth - the same transformations - by whichever name or image we use. Morgana holds it aloft as the damsel maiden.

This castle and its images are associated with Chalice Well in Glastonbury. Chalice Well has a long-standing association with grail-lore, and the iron content of the water lends both the flavor and colored tinge of blood as well as the healing properties attributed to the cup/cauldron. Note the similarity in the Chalice Well symbol and our simple symbol for this castle's treasure (the silver - bloody - cup).

We envision the cup filled with life-giving blood, just as the fertile womb fills each month with blood. So it is that at the Housle (the Red Meal), we fill the two-handled Quaich with red wine. When we cut the throat of the cup and spill its "blood," and likewise stab and rend the flesh of the dark bread, we more aptly feel the sacrifice that we associate with this castle and cross-quarter. Both sacrifices are made with the shelg, the red knife. This is the blade of Castle Perilous, the blade of blood and of sacrifice.

Blood and red wine are a potent mixture. They remind us of the Mithraic Mysteries, in which a bull was sacrificed in a subterranean vault. Killing the bull wasn't the point of the rite, though - collecting its blood was. The blood was mixed with wine and drunk by the initiates. Later, only the wine was drunk, as a representation of the blood of Mithras himself. We see in this blood-letting ritual the foundational element of many sacrificial meals, including our own Housle.

Copyright Asteria Books 2022

Northern Gate

When we set up for ritual, at the North gate are placed the staves of the coven, along with the spear, and the troy stone or gate stone. Also at this gate are symbols of the Black Goddess. Any tools associated with Air are kept at this gate, such as the censer if one is used.

Airt of Air

Values: Intellect, thoughts, inspiration, communication, flight, divination
Colors: White, sky blue, black, silver
Symbols: Circle, bird, bell, flute, chimes, clouds, sylphs, angels
Tools: Keek stone, flail, wand, arrows
Weapons: Staff/Spear
Musical Instruments: Reed instruments
Times: Imbolc, Midnight, Winter, Old Age
Totems: Willow, Cat, Owl
Places: Sky, mountaintop, treetop, bluffs, summit of a mound
Zodiac: Aquarius, Gemini, Libra
Sense: Scent
Power: To Know
Process: Chanting, visualization, reading, speaking, praying, singing, fragrance, charms

    The Northern Gate is associate with thought, memory, flights of fancy and fantasy, and intellectual pursuits. It is a place concerned with the future, contemplation, and plan-making. It can be an ephemorous place of symbols and mist, where much is hidden and little is certain.

    It is associated with the season of Imbolc, and it is no wonder that Imbolc, then, is a traditional time of Initiation. For it is in the darkness, guided by Kolyo along the Troy stone path, that we wind our way through the Wildwood to the place of deepest knowing — and of death and rebirth of the Self.

Copyright Asteria Books 2020

Eastern Gate

When we set up for ritual, in the East are the tools of Fire. Here we place the blacksmith's hammer (when not used for striking the anvil, as in some rituals) and tongs. We can burn a fire here, if we are outdoors. The coven sword is here.

Airt of Fire

Values: Passion, power, will, energy, courage, strength, light
Colors: Red, orange, amber
Symbols: Triangle, lightning, flame, candle, salamanders, the lion
Tools: Knives, anvil, hammer, tongs
Weapons: Sword
Musical Instruments: String Instruments
Times: Beltane, Dawn, Spring, Youth
Totems: Hawthorn, Bull, Bee
Places: Volcanoes, ovens, hearths, forges, bonfires, deserts
Zodiac: Aries, Leo, Sagittarius
Sense: Sight
Power: To Will
Process: Dancing, burning, candle-magic, solar magic, mirrors

The Eastern Gate is the place of the Rising Sun and is associated with the spark of Tubal Qayin's forge in our Tradition. The line from East to West across the compass (the same as the path made by the Sun across the sky) is thought of as yet another manifestation of the Red Thread – the Fire and Blood of enlightenment that connects us to the Witch Father, forms the bond of Family within the Craft, and symbolizes the freedom and gnosis we have taken for ourselves.

Iron and steel themselves are potent symbols of our Craft, and we place both blades made of these metals as well as the implements of their construction in the East in honor of this.

On our Year Wheel, the Eastern Gate is open and most easily accessed at the spring fire festival Beltaine, and the three totems that sit here are all intimately linked with Sex, Fertility, and Joy.

Copyright Asteria Books 2020

Southern Gate

When we set up for ritual, in the South are symbols of the White Goddess, Earth, and the shields of the coven. The binding cords (if being used) and the bread for the red meal are placed at this gate.

Airt of Earth

Values: Growth, Experience, Authority, Money, Physicality, Security, Nourishment
Colors: Brown, russet, black, green
Symbols: Square, stone, cornucopia, scythe, salt, cart, plate, Gnomes
Tools: The casting bowl, patens/pentacles, horns, binding cords
Weapons: Shield (Targe)
Totems: Swan, Horse & Apple Tree
Musical Instruments: Drums
Times: Lammas/Lughnasadh, Noon, Summer, Coming of Age
Places: Fields, mountains, valleys, canyons, deserts, forests, gardens
Zodiac: Capricorn, Taurus, Virgo
Sense: Touch
Power: To Keep Silent
Process: Brushing Hair/Skin, Grounding, Eating, Burying, Binding

The Southern Gate is very much associated with the mortal realm, consciousness, and consensus reality. It is the gateway to the Greenworld, the magic of this plane that we inhabit. It is a "noon-time, bright day, midst-of-summer's abundance" place.

Because it is representative of consensus reality, some people might mistakenly assume that nothing is secret, hidden, or mysterious through the Southern Gate. This is an illusion, though, and one of the challenges in coming to truly know this place. For it is also the realm of the Good Neighbors -- the Little Folk, the Fey.

On our Year Wheel, the Southern Gate is open and most easily accessed at Lammas, and the three totems that sit here are all intimately linked with Sovereignty and Self-Mastery.

This is a time for reaping the first harvest, playing games, and settling into the work of approaching Autumn.

Copyright Asteria Books 2020

Western Gate

When we set up for ritual, the West is the gate of Water, the quench tank of Tubal Cain. Representations of water are placed here. The weapon of this gate is the helm, and the masks of the Clan are kept here.

Airt of Water

Values: Emotions, intuition, cleansing, mystery, sacrifice
Colors: Grey, turquoise, blue, indigo
Symbols: Crescent, shell, boat, anchor, cup, undines, the eagle, the dove
Tools: The chalice or quaiche, cauldron, masks
Weapons: Helm
Musical Instruments: Chimes
Times: Samhain, Twilight, Autumn, Adulthood, Crossing into Death
Totems: Elder, Toad, Crane
Places: Oceans, rivers, lakes, waterfalls, wells, beaches, baths
Zodiac: Cancer, Scorpio, Pisces
Sense: Taste
Power: To Dare
Process: Bathing, healing, drinking, baptism, charged waters, blood magic

The Western Gate is associated with death and dying, but also with healing and salvation and rescue from the brink of death. In Celtic lore, heroes sailed beyond the ninth wave to an island in the West to find rest and await rebirth. Myths and legends from all over the world often echo the symbolism of the sun (or a culture's most beloved star or constellation) setting beyond the Western horizon — seemingly dying, sometimes for a lengthy period, to return triumphantly again in the Eastern sky.

On our Year Wheel, the Western Gate is associated with Samhain, a time of Ancestor work and deep mystery. The totemic animals of Elder tree, Toad, and Crane remind us of the somberness of the season — each speaking its own message regarding intuition, blasting magic, and the Dead.

At this gate, we see Tubal Qayin as Lord of Death — a parallel to the role he plays at Beltaine, as the fiery Lord of Life. In the west, he stands with his quench tank, the Well of Souls.

Copyright Asteria Books 2020

The Treasures

Each of the four Castles that act as the Watchtowers of the Spiral Castle Tradition hold within them a Treasure -- a vessel of the Mysteries that can hold and transmute energy, point to Craft secrets, and act as a divinatory device. These four working tools, while referenced in many variations of the lore that we so love, are not necessarily common Craft tools. Assembled together, they are actually somewhat unique to the Spiral Castle Tradition.

Treasures & Weapons

The four Gates (the cardinal points of the Compass) are associated with weapons. Two are usually used in defense (shield and helmet), and two are associated with attack/offense (staff and sword). In reality, ALL of the weapons are both. The Gates, the Weapons, and the Gate-Keepers can be thought of as active (proactive) in their expression.

The four Castles that mark the cross-quarters of our Compass are places of protection that guard us while we work and also protect and preserve the Mysteries. The Treasures held within the Castles are all vessels that hold keys to accessing those Mysteries. All of them have divinatory/oracular uses, and they also hold energy (as opposed to the Weapons, which direct and shape energy). They are the Silver Cup, Golden Lantern, Stone Bowl, and Glass Orb.

Copyright Asteria Books 2022

Glass Orb

Within Celtic/Druidic lore, we encounter the glain – or Druid's egg, serpent's egg, adderstane, Druid's glass, or snake stone. While Midsummer was the season most attributed to the creation of the glain, Midwinter was also associated with its power. This hard glass bubble (or alternately, glassy stone) awarded its bearer incredible magickal powers, and even Merlin was said to have gone looking for one.

Some of the powers traditionally ascribed to the glain are success in lawsuits, access to kings and high officials, curing diseases at a great distance, seeing into the world of the Unseen, and escaping capture/imprisonment.

In our Tradition, we honor the Glass Orb as having these roots, although it is likely that other influences have shaped our understanding, as well. The Orb is often not a solid, dense glass or crystal ball, but a hollow, clear sphere. It holds the energy of Air.

A simple Glass Orb can be made by perching a hollow glass Christmas bubble atop a glass candle holder (or nestling it inside a lined box – though I like it being out, elevated, and accessible.). Fishing floats, Christmas bubbles, terrarium balls, and garden gazing globes can all make for wonderful Glass Orbs. (Go for clear or translucent white, if possible. Color ... changes things – though this is something you can experiment with, if you like.)

The Glass Orb is a lovely tool for scrying and/or contemplation. It is a superb clarifier of thoughts and ideas.

One of the insights shared and discussed among adept members of our Tradition is that the Glass Orb can be seen as Odin's missing (or glass) eye.

Copyright Asteria Books 2022

Golden Lantern

The Golden Lantern is the vessel or Treasure of Fire, and it is the Sun, in miniature. In fact, the symbol we use for the this Treasure and the Castle which holds it is the same as the alchemical symbol for the Sun. To us, we see two (main) things within this simple glyph: the fiery star that sits at the center of our solar system circumscribed by the orbit we trace around it, and also, the flame glimmering within the round walls of the lantern.

I could additionally make the case that this glyph is connected to our conception of the Compass in its simplest form. Whereas the symbol for the Stone Castle/Bowl shows the crossroads, the symbol for the Golden Lantern/Castle might be said to depict the Stang and the Moat. There are certainly connections to be made between the fire betwixt the Stang's horns and the light of the Sun/Lantern, as well. If you sit in contemplation of that, do you see the patterns emerging?

Can you see the golden yoke encased in the egg's shell? (Interesting, I think, that the symbol of the egg is so prominent at the Spring Equinox – when the Golden Lantern shines brightest.)

The Golden Lantern acts as a beacon for us, as well as being the light of inspiration, of creation. We often envision myriad markings upon the housing that are illuminated by the radiance within. This is honeyed glow of the poet's gift. The storyteller's art. The creator's talent.

Use your own Golden Lantern to light a signal fire to call out to others, to add hope and charisma to your goal, and to fuel inner growth. Gaze upon its glow when you need a boost of energy and sustenance. Let the symbols upon the housing tell you their stories, sing their songs, and recite their ballads as you watch the flicker and dance of the flame within.

You can find cut glass amber-colored candle holders with hurricane lanterns in antique stores, as well as new release metal lanterns with amber or yellow glass. My own Golden Lantern is a "fairy lamp" style two-piece set made by the Indiana Glass Company in the 1960's (with the pattern name "Stars and Bars"). A very crafty Witch might also consider purchasing a rather plain lantern and then embellish it with glass paints, etching, etc.

Copyright Asteria Books 2022

Sacrificial Stone Bowl

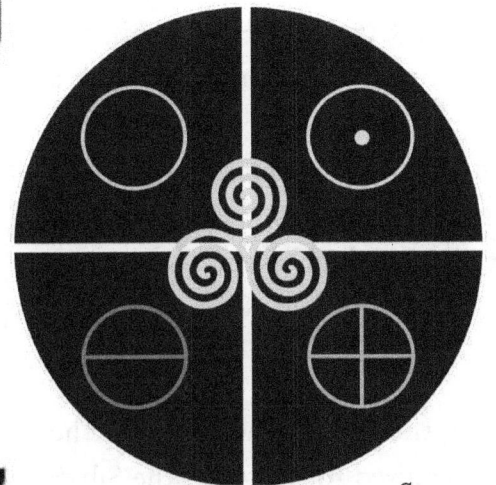

Why to Use the Stone Bowl

There is an ebb and flow to magic. Different traditions have different ways of indicating the way the price for magick will be paid, but nearly all agree that some form of price MUST be paid – whether the witch is aware and willing to pay or not. A cunning person goes into this process with their eyes open and asks up front what the cost will be in order to decide if the prize gained is worth the price to be paid. This bowl is a variation of a tool used in some Trad Craft lines to determine the type and magnitude of that price.

Symbolism & Types of Sacrifice

The design above is painted into a flat-bottomed bowl or lipped dish. The white cross that divides the space represents the crossroads. Starting in the upper right quadrant and moving clockwise, the other symbols represent:

Castle of Revelry (*yellow circle with central point*) ~ sacrifice of abstinence (refraining from sexual stimulation, smoking, alcohol, tobacco, sugar, or other pleasure for a period of time)

Castle of Stone (*green crossed circle*) ~ sacrifice of wealth (giving money to charity, donating items, gifting personal possession to someone, working on a project without compensation)

Castle Perilous (*red halved circle*) ~ sacrifice of blood/pain (submitting to flogging, lifting heavy weights, running an endurance race, shedding your own blood with intent, etc)

Castle of Glass (*blue circle*) ~ sacrifice of comfort (fasting for a period of time, sleeping on the floor, wearing an intentionally irritating garment, walking barefoot on gravel, etc)

Spiral Castle (*silver triskelion*) ~ no sacrifice associated with this Castle

How to Use the Stone Bowl

Cast three stone (one each – black, white red) into the bowl. The stones represent the Black and White Goddesses and the Red God. Whichever stone the red stone is closest to indicates to which Goddess your sacrifice will be made. The circle she has landed on indicates which type of sacrifice. The distance between the black and white stones indicates the magnitude of the sacrifice. So, if the red stone is closest to the white stone, and the white stone is on Castle Revelry, you will make a sacrifice of abstinence to the (any) White Goddess. If the black stone is close to the white stone, that sacrifice would be small. (And if the white stone had landed on the triskelion in this same scenario, there would be no sacrifice required at all.)

Copyright Asteria Books 2012-2019

Silver Cup

A silvery wine bowl, cup, or quaiche (Celtic cup/bowl with handles) acts as the physical representation of our final Treasure. The Silver Cup is the Holy Grail, and we see it brimming with blood – or wine. It can be linked very intimately with a good deal of uterine symbolism, and also with the cornucopia and/or the Cauldron of Plenty. In fact, it is linked to many of the mystical Celtic cauldrons – Dagda's cauldron of endless food, Bran's cauldron of rebirth, Cerridwen's cauldron of wisdom and transformation, Dyrnwch's cauldron that discerns the brave from the cowardly, the pearl-rimmed cauldron of Pen Annwn.

Where the Stone Bowl is the sacrificial dish (holding the bread, if we like, for the Housle – and also pointing the way to the sacrifice required for magick), the Silver Cup is the sacrificial cup that catches the blood of the slain offering.

There are grim Mysteries within this chalice, but also deep joy, for this is the gift of wine, food, and birth. The Silver Cup is the Treasure that holds precedence at the time of our great Autumnal feast. It is the blot bowl, offering us deep blessing from the blood within.

Any style of silver cup will suffice – coupe, quaiche, compote bowl.

Some of the practical magick of this Treasure includes blessing yourself and saining your tools as part of the Housle. You can also use the Silver Cup to infuse a ritual brew with wisdom, rebirth, bravery, abundance, etc (the qualities attributed to the cauldrons of myth). Scrying into a pool of dark red wine, or reading the herbs that remain after steeping a Sabbat Wine blend are just two ways you might use the Silver Cup in divination.

Copyright Asteria Books 2022

Ritual, Liturgy, and Spells

On Experimentation Within American Folkloric Witchcraft

The various liturgical pieces that follow are shared with a cautionary statement, a caveat. These are "frozen" pieces of inspiration, having been written and shared as a way to convey the essence of what we do. However, there is no single right way to do almost anything within the realm of Folkloric Craft.

You can lay a compass a myriad of ways. We advise 3 rings. We almost always lay 3 rings. That doesn't mean we always circumambulate 3 times, or make the same gestures, say the same script, or even speak. Or always lay 3.

Experiment. Play. Dive deep into your Craft. Try a method for months at a time to see if and how it works for you. Then add or modify a practice.

While there is no single "right" way, there may still be wrong ways — especially wrong ways for you. So continue to use sense and caution. Know why you are making the choices and taking the actions you do, before you do them. And be prepared for surprises. Own your consequences.

Journal what you've done — and the results you are getting.

Copyright Asteria Books 2020

Laying the Compass

American Folkloric Witchcraft circles are cast by calling in the three spheres or circles of power and protection — the Realms, the Gates (Quarters), and the Castles (Watchtowers). The AFW compass is directly linked to our Year Wheel, and we call Powers that lie opposite each other as a pair — both being called toward the center of the circle. Thus, they form a road or an energetic pathway, with the Stang as the center point.

CENTER AND FIRST CIRCLE — Raise the stang, which serves as the world tree and connects Three Realms. We call these Realms, either with extemporaneous or pre-planned words. At the base of the stang is the Oath Stone or anvil upon which we make our blood oaths to the tradition. Near the oath stone are the cauldron and the skull. Also placed at the center of the compass are the personal fetishes of each member of our Clan and the three knives. With the raising of the Stang and the calling of the Realms, the 1st Circle is cast.

SECOND CIRCLE (GATES) — At the North gate are placed the staves of the coven, along with the spear, and the troy stone, or gate stone. Also at this gate are symbols of the Black Goddess, as well as totemic items for Imbolc like an owl's feather, fur from a cat, and a willow switch. Any tools associated with air are kept at this gate, such as the censer if one is used.

The South are symbols of the White Goddess and the shields of the coven. The binding cords and the bread for the red meal are placed at this gate. Horsehair, apples, and swan feathers are all symbols for this gate.

In the East are the tools of fire. Here we place the blacksmith's hammer and tongs and keep a bonfire burning, if we are outdoors. The coven sword is here, as are items related to bull, hawthorn, and bee, such as mead in cow horns.

The West is the gate of water, the quench tank of Tubal Cain. Representations of water are placed here, along with toad and crane. Elder is only brought into the circle for certain dark magics. The weapon of this gate is the helm, and the masks of the Clan are kept here.

THIRD CIRCLE (CASTLES) — At the north-east is the Castle of Revelry. Here we place the lantern of inspiration and the broom, as well as representations of hare, birch, and goose.

In the southwest is the Castle Perilous and the silver chalice, along with the red wine that it will hold. Hawk feathers, vines, and representations of the boar or sow are also placed here.

At the northwest corner is the Glass Castle and its treasure — the glass orb. The totems are goat, holly, and wren. Tools of divination are kept in this castle.

The south-east is the home of the Stone Castle, where we place the stone bowl and the casting stones, along with stag horns, acorns, and oak staves.

Thus is the compass laid. It may be as elaborate or as minimal as your tastes and needs dictate. Although the instructions above explain the placement of all of the gates, treasures, tools, weapons, and totems, simply treading the mill once and acknowledging the four gates and the four castles, along with their rulers, is enough to lay the compass.

Copyright Asteria Books 2015

Laying the Compass

Red Thread circles are cast by setting the caim – defining the area of protection and power within which the Witch or coven will perform the work. We call Powers that lie opposite each other as a pair – both being called toward the center of the circle. Thus, they form a road or an energetic pathway, with the Stang as the center point.

Center and First Circle – Raise the Stang, which serves as the world tree and connects Three Realms. At the base of the stang is the Oath Stone or anvil upon which we make our blood oaths to the tradition, as well as the cauldron. Also placed at the center of the compass are the personal fetishes of each member of our Clan. It is not uncommon to also keep a skull and bones (crossed or open) and other tools relevant to the working here. With the Raising of the Stang, the 1st Circle is cast.

Second Circle – Lay the Compass by walking the perimeter of the space within which you will work while treading with the Lame Step. Use the Stang or Staff or Distaff. This is also known as Marking the Moat.

Third Circle – Open the Gates by calling North and South, East and West toward the center of the compass. At the North gate are placed the staves of the coven, along with the spear, and the troy stone, or gate stone. Also at this gate are symbols of the Black Goddess. Any tools associated with Air are kept at this gate, such as the censer if one is used.

The South are symbols of the White Goddess, Earth, and the shields of the coven. The binding cords and the bread for the red meal are placed at this gate.

In the East are the tools of Fire. Here we place the blacksmith's hammer and tongs and keep a bonfire burning, if we are outdoors. The coven sword is here.

The West is the gate of Water, the quench tank of Tubal Cain. Representations of water are placed here. The weapon of this gate is the helm, and the masks of the Clan are kept here.

Thus is the compass laid. It may be as elaborate or as minimal as your tastes and needs dictate. Although the instructions above explain the placement of all of the gates, tools, and weapons, simply treading the mill once and acknowledging the four gates is enough to lay the compass.

Copyright Asteria Books 2018

Setting the Compass v. 2

There are many ways within the Spiral Castle Tradition to Lay the Compass. THIS version includes the Watchtowers that we call "Castles." Note that you will open the Gates before Raising the Castles at Samhain, Imbolc, Beltaine, and Lammas (and Castles before Gates at the Equinoxes and Solstices)

Raise the Stang — At the base of the stang is the Oath Stone or anvil, as well as the cauldron, personal fetishes of each member of our Clan, a skull and bones (crossed or open) and other tools relevant to the working here. Feel the connection to the Realms (Above, Below, Between).

Mark the Moat — Walk the perimeter of the space within which you will work while treading with the Lame Step. Use the Stang or Staff or Distaff as you walk.

Open the Gates — Call North and South, East and West toward the center of the compass.

Raise the Castles — Call the Castle of Revelry, Castle Perilous, Castle of Glass, and Castle of Stone in opposing pairs.

Thus is the compass laid. It may be as elaborate or as minimal as your tastes and needs dictate. Although the instructions above explain the placement of all of the Gates, Castles, tools, etc, simply treading the mill once and acknowledging the Realms, Gates, and Castles is enough to lay the compass.

Copyright Asteria Books 2022

Calling the Realms

First Realm

My voice reaches high into the etheric Upper World — the Land of Sky, place of thoughts and aspirations and future plans. I call into Ceugent, the Otherworld — place of struggle and enlightenment, the undying realm of birth. First Realm, be the roof of this, our sacred compass. With my breath, I call you to be here now! So mote it be!

Second Realm

My hands reach out into the physical Middle World — the Land of Stone, place of action and progress. I call out to Gwyned, the Green World — place of consensus reality and limitations, the living realm of Earth. Second Realm, be the walls of this, our sacred compass. With my flesh and bone, I call you to be here now! So mote it be!

Third Realm

My roots reach deep into the chthonic Lower World — the Land of Sea, place of emotion and mystery and past memories. I call into Abred, the Underworld — place of preparation and rest, the realm of death. Third Realm, be the floor of this, our sacred compass. With my blood, I call you to be here now! So mote it be!

Copyright Asteria Books 2015

Opening the Gates

North Gate

I call to the Winds beyond the North Gate. Open the door from the North, place of Air, Kolyo's domain. By the spear, the wing, and the smoke, I call you to open wide the Gate and send forth your road to the center of this, my compass. So mote it be!

South Gate

I call to the Fields beyond the South Gate. Open the door from the South, place of Earth, Goda's domain. By the plate, the soil, and the shield, I call you to open wide the Gate and send forth your road to the center of this, my compass. So mote it be!

East Gate

I call to the Sunrise beyond the East Gate. Open the door from the East, place of Fire, Lucifer-Qayin's domain. By the steel, the anvil, and the sun, I call you to open wide the Gate and send forth your road to the center of this, my compass. So mote it be!

West Gate

I call to the Ocean beyond the West Gate. Open the door from the West, place of Water, Azazel-Qayin's domain. By the cup, the quench tank, and the helm, I call you to open wide the Gate and send forth your road to the center of this, my compass. So mote it be!

Copyright Asteria Books 2018

Raising the Castles

Begin by standing in the center, turn to face the direction associated with the current Sabbat-tide (in this example, Northwest). Hold your arms out in T-shape (if you like).

Glass Castle (northwest – before you) – "I call to the Castle of Glass, rising up from the Hill of Cloud. Glass Castle! Within your walls, wise ones discern the Truth. Your keeper is the Holly King – Odin, Gwyn ap Nudd, Janicot. The Glass Orb encases its wisdom from the summit of the hall. Castle of Glass, Crystalline Watchtower, be here now! So Mote it Be!"

Stone Castle (southeast – behind you) – "I call to the Castle of Stone, rising up from the Earthen Hill. Stone Castle! Within your walls, warriors train and provisions are prepared. Your keeper is the Oak King – Cernunnos, Herne, Basajaun. The Stone Bowl holds its knowledge at the base of the hall. Castle of Stone, Earthen Watchtower, be here now! So Mote it Be!"

Castle of Revelry (north east – right hand) – "I call to the Castle of Gold, rising up from the Lake of Fire. Castle of Revelry! Within your walls, warriors sing and drink and tell tales of great deeds. Your keeper is the Golden Queen – Freya, Brighid, Aphrodite. The Golden Lantern shines its inspiration from the heart of the hall. Castle of Revelry, Golden Watchtower, be here now! So Mote it Be!"

Castle Perilous (southwest – left hand) – "I call to the Castle of Silver, rising up from the Lake of Blood. Castle Perilous! Within your walls, strong men quake and young girls find their deep power. Your keeper is the Silver Queen – Cerridwen, Morgana, Babalon. The Silver Cup drips its sacrifice from the belly of the hall. Castle of Revelry, Silver Watchtower, be here now! So Mote it Be!"

Copyright Asteria Books 2018

Building the Pyramid

MATERIALS:
- Wooden/cloth triangle OR sticks/stones
- Soil from the Millgrounds
- Invitation Incense
- 2 Lamps of Arte (Luna and Sol)

The Pyramid is built after the Compass has been laid. Place the boundary marking for your Pyramid (or Triangle of Arte) outside the Moat in the direction from which you expect the Spirit to arrive. (Place it in the South, if not specified.) Place Luna's Lamp to the left and Sol's Lamp to the right of the Pyramid.

Your Pyramid may be a painted wooden form, an embroidered cloth, an outline fashioned by laying three equal-length sticks end-to-end, or of any material your choose. It may be elaborate or simple, as pleases you.

Sprinkle each side of your Pyramid with either soil from the land upon which you are working or a portion of the Invitation Incense, speaking aloud the three names you ascribe to the three sides of the Triangle, with the following request:

> "Goda, give the Spirit form.
>
> Kolyo, give the Spirit voice.
>
> Tubelo, give the Spirit time here with me.
>
> Iarbatha! So be it!"

Light the two Lamps of Arte that flank the Pyramid and prepare for the Invitation.

Copyright Asteria Books 2022

The Housle

As with many faiths, we partake of a small meal with a spirited drink after our rites. In many witchcraft traditions this is called "Cakes and Wine." We call it the Housle, or Red Meal, and base it in part on a ritual created by fellow walker of the crooked path, Robin Artisson.

THE HOUSLE SONG
To the tune of Greensleeves
To Housle now we walk the wheel
We kill tonight the blood red meal
A leftward tread of magic's mill
To feed the Gods and work our Will.
Red, red is the wine we drink!
Red, red are the cords we wear!
Red, red is the Blood of God!
And red is the shade of the Housle.

When the compass is laid, place in the southwest corner: Dark bread in a bowl (or lipped dish) and Red Wine in Silver Quaich or Chalice. In the center, near the stang will be placed the Red Knife.

1. The sacrificial meal is brought from Castle Perilous to the Spiral Castle by an Initiate.
2. Tread the Mill widdershins three times while singing the Housle Song.
3. At the place of sacrifice say: "For our Ancestors, our Gods, and Ourselves, we do this."
4. Bless the bread with the right hand: "Here is bread, flesh of the earth, the source of strength and life. In the name of the Old Ones, I consecrate it."
5. Cut the bread with the left hand, using the Red Blade: "I take its life and give it to Them."
6. Bless the wine with the right hand: "Here is wine, blood of the Gods, the source of joy and Mystery. In the name of the Old Ones, I consecrate it."
7. Slice across the cup with the left hand, using the Red Blade: "I take its life and give it to Them."
8. Each person eats and drinks of the Meal, making whatever personal offerings they like — taking their portion of the Meal with their left hand, saying "With my left hand I take it."
9. The remainder of the wine is poured into the bread bowl, and each person dips their finger in and anoints themselves. This can also be used for blessing tools, etc.
10. The Meal is either given to the ground now, if outside, or later, if inside, saying the following:

"By the Red, the Black and White,
Light in Darkness, Dark in Light —
What we take, we freely give.
We all must die. We all must live.
Above, below, and here are One.
All together — All! (And none!)
Here is shown a Mystery. As we Will, so Mote it Be!"

The Housle

As with many faiths, we partake of a small meal with a spirited drink after our rites. In many witchcraft traditions this is called "Cakes and Ale". We call it the Housle, or Red Meal, and base it in part on a ritual created by fellow walker of the crooked path, Robin Artisson.

The Housle Song
To the tune of Greensleeves

To Housle now we walk the wheel
We kill tonight the blood red meal
A leftward tread of magic's mill
To feed the Gods and work our Will.

Red, red is the wine we drink
Red, red are the cords we wear
Red, red is the Blood of God
And red is the shade of the Housle.

When the compass is laid place in the southwest corner: Dark bread in a bowl (or lipped dish) and Red Wine in Silver Quaich or Chalice. In the center, near the stang will be placed the Red Knife.

1. The sacrificial meal is brought from Castle Perilous to the Spiral Castle by an Initiate,.
2. Tread the Mill widdershins three times while singing the Housle Song.
3. Take up the bread saying: *"Here is bread, source of strength and life."*
4. Kill the bread by saying: *"I kill this loaf in the name of the Mighty Ones."* Cut it with the red knife.
5. Take up the wine saying: *"Here is wine, source of joy and blood of the Gods."*
6. Kill the wine by saying: *"I kill this cup in the name of the Mighty Ones."* Slide the knife over the top of the quaich or chalice.
7. Each person eats and drinks of the Meal, making whatever personal offerings they like. Each person takes the Meal with their left hand, saying *"With my left hand I take it."*
8. The remainder of the wine is poured into the bread bowl, and each person dips their finger in and anoints themselves. This can also be used for blessing tools, etc.
9. The Meal is either given to the ground now, if outside, or later, if inside, saying the following:

"White is black and black is white
Bless us, Witchfather, on this night.
Fair is foul and foul is fair,
We give this back with mickle care.
For what is given is truly taken,
And what is taken is humbly given back."

Copyright Asteria Publishing 2012

Sabbats

Samhain

Samhain is the point in the Wheel that is directly opposite to Beltaine, and the intents behind the holiday and the season are, subsequently, directly opposite to those of the fertility and mirth of Beltaine. Furthermore, Samhain is the beginning of the New Year in Celtic lands. The Celtic calendar had 13 months. Samhain was the last night of the 13th month.

For the ancient Celts, a new day began in the dark of night, and a new year began in the dark half. Samhain (the midpoint between the Fall Equinox and Winter Solstice) was seen as the beginning of the dark half of the year. It was a time when the veil between the worlds of the living and the dead was the thinnest, and communication and passage between the worlds was easiest. It was a time to commune with deceased ancestors and loved ones. Though the ancients honored and revered their ancestors throughout the year, this was the perfect time of year to set aside sacred time to honor those who had passed.

Of course, since the veil was so thin, it was also expected that some rather nasty spirits might enter through the veil at that time, which would cause folks to be wary. Guardians of various types would be placed at doors and windows and hearth (all the entry ways into the home) to keep unwanted and unwelcome spirits out. Gourds, turnips, and apples are commonly carved and offered as vessels for these Guardian spirits. The custom of dressing in costume comes from the idea of disguising oneself so as not to be recognized by unfriendly spirits.

Furthermore, it was a time of remembrance. The ancients had a deep respect for their ancestors, and this was a time to remember the deeds of forefathers and foremothers. They would recall the names of the people in their lineage and honor them with feasts (often in silence because the Dead don't speak aloud) and gifts. The ancestors would have a special place in the home during this time, usually in the form of an ancestor altar.

Since this was the last festival of the harvest, it was imperative that farmers have all of their crops harvested before sundown on Samhain night. If not, tradition held that whatever was left in the fields belonged to the *sidhe*.

Some Craft traditions hold that their male God(s) go away at this time — either to die and be reborn, or for a period of rest. These Gods are most often reborn with the Solstice sun at Yule.

In American Folkloric Craft, Azazel-Qayin is honored as the keeper of the gates to the Dead at this time of year, and his guidance may be sought via oracle for the year to come.

This is a time of beginnings and endings. As such, it is a time of introspection, reflection, communication with the Otherworld and Underworld. It is a time of profound spiritual growth. It can be quite intense.

Copyright Asteria Books 2019

Samhain Mysteries

At Samhaintide, it is our custom to explore the Mysteries of:

"Life in Death; Death in Life" — This is a phrase we use to reference something very fundamental to this Tradition. While the WitchMother isn't particularly prominent at this Sabbat, this phrase IS. (And this phrase is very much associated with Her.) This Mystery is also very present with us at Beltaine.

"Rose Beyond the Grave" — Writers from within the Clan of Tubal Cain have written about this Mystery. To contemplate the Rose Beyond (or Within) the Grave is to contemplate what happens to the Souls of the Witch after Death.

"What the Mask Reveals" — The Spiral Castle Tradition associates the West with Samhain. The weapon of the West is the Helm (or Mask). We sometimes work with the Mask in order to better understand both ourselves and That which is represented by a specific mask.

Copyright Asteria Books 2022

Samhain Ritual

Materials
- Stang, candle, lighter
- Cauldron, water, lancet
- Anvil, hammer
- Three knives (red, black, white)
- Red Cord
- Bread, lipped dish or bowl
- Dark beer
- Red wine, cup
- Incense, holder, charcoal
- Carved gourd/pumpkin, tealight candle
- Skull (real human OR human-shaped ceramic, glass, crystal, paper-mache, wood, etc)
- Lineage chant

Raise the Stang

Lay the Compass

Open the Gates (beginning in the West)

Working

- Lighting Jack ~ Hold your carved pumpkin or gourd (or turnip) in your hands and send energy into it to "wake it up." Call on a specific guardian Spirit, or ask that a guardian from your tribe of spirits comes forward to inhabit the vessel and keep watch over you and your home during Samhain-tide. Light the candle inside the jack-o'-lantern, and set it as a Ward at the edge of the Compass.
- Recitation of Lineage ~ Pick up the skull. With pride and love, declare, "I am, (name), child of (name), child of (name), child of (name), child of (name)." Go back as many generations as you know. If you want to focus on the matrilineal or patrilineal line, you may. It is equally acceptable to recite the lineage of adoptive and foster families if that is your circumstance and preference.
- Enlivening of Skull ~ Still holding the skull, send a thread of energy to the skull, feeling it come alive with the energy of your blood, your breath, your flesh. Say something like, "I invite my ancestors, those names and those un-

named, to be with me, speak with me, eat with me, dance with me, laugh with me during these dark days at the the turn of the year. I offer you this vessel, now and always, as a seat in my home." Place the skull at the base of the Stang. In future rituals, always place the skull here. Outside of ritual, place the skull upon your altar or ancestor shrine.

- Dark Beer for Qayin ~ At the anvil or Oath Stone, pick up the hammer. Strike the anvil and call out, "Tubal Qayin!" Strike again and call out, "Tubal Qayin!" Strike a third (final) time and call out, "Witch Father!" Pour the dark beer over the anvil/stone or into the cauldron. (If you're inside pour all of it into the cauldron. If you're outside, reserve at least part of it for the cauldron.) Acknowledge with whatever words or gestures come to you that this offering us to Tubelo. It is not inappropriate to share a drink, so take a swig from the bottle to share with the Red God, if you feel so moved.

- Scrying ~ Sit down in front of the cauldron. Get comfortable. Refresh the incense, if needed. Pour some water into the cauldron if more liquid is needed. Clean the top of a finger with an alcohol swab and prick with a lancet. This works best on the outside edge of a fingertip, where you are not calloused. Keeping your hand below your heart, raise a drop or two of blood. Drop them into the liquid if there cauldron. Gaze at the cauldron, relax your focus, and allow images and impressions to come to you. Don't try to force a conversation with the spirits. They will speak in their own way. You may experience images, sounds, ideas, temperature shifts, sensations, smells. Any of these may seem to generate spontaneously within your own mind, like a stay thought. Let them come. Allow the session to continue as for a little while. You'll probably have a good sense of when you're finished and nothing else is coming through. If needed, you can end the session early and beginning to ground by moving into the Red Meal.

Housle

Sabbat - Samhain Incense

About This Blend

This blend was designed to honor and celebrate Samhain, the final harvest of the Autumn and the beginning of the Celtic New Year.

As with all loose incense blends, this formula can be burned on a hot, self-igniting charcoal tablet (like those used for hookahs) or it can be thrown onto the glowing embers of a fire.

Incense Recipe

1/4 cup Apple wood

1/4 cup Rose petals

1/4 cup Dittany of Crete

1 tablespoon Oakmoss

1 tablespoon Sage

1 tablespoon Benzoin resin

2 teaspoons Corn kernels, ground

1 teaspoon Pumpkin seeds

9 drops Wormwood oil

Special Notes

This unusual blend helps set Samhain aside as a liminal time, a time of reaping, and a time of Ancestor worship.

Copyright Asteria Books 2017

Samhain Ritual

MATERIALS
- Stang, candle, lighter
- Cauldron, water, lancet
- Anvil, hammer
- Three knives (red, black, white)
- Triple Cord
- Bread, lipped dish or bowl
- Dark beer
- Red wine, cup
- Incense, holder, charcoal
- Carved gourd/pumpkin, tealight candle
- Skull (real human OR human-shaped ceramic, glass, crystal, paper-mache, wood, etc)
- Lineage chant
- Feast foods of your choice

RAISE THE STANG

LAY THE COMPASS

OPEN THE GATES (beginning in the West)

RAISE THE CASTLES

WORKING
- LIGHTING JACK -- Empower and light your carved pumpkin/gourd, like you did last Samhain.
- RECITATION OF LINEAGE -- Pick up the skull. With pride and love, declare, "I am, (name), child of (name), child of (name), child of (name), child of (name)." Go back as many generations as you know. If you want to focus on the matrilineal or patrilineal line, you may. It is equally acceptable to recite the lineage of adoptive and foster families if that is your circumstance and preference.
- TAPPING THE BONE -- Your skull was enlivened last year, so you needn't re-do the enlivening (unless you're using a new skull).

Copyright Asteria Books 2022

Yule

Yule is celebrated on the Winter , which is the shortest day of the year. Solstice celebrations are universal, being celebrated in nearly every culture the world over.

Groups as different as Iranians are to the Swedes, Chumash Indians to the Germans, and Spain to peoples of Tibet have very old traditions for the same solar event. The impetus for the holiday, nearly the world over, is the fear that the failing light of the sun may not return and therefore needs some help. According to many traditions, there are evil spirits that thrive in the darkness and require light and warmth to drive them out. This accounts, in part, for the extensive use of candles and lanterns to drive away the darkness. Of course, the flame of a candle is also similar (though a much smaller representative) to the light of the Sun itself.

Structures have been built, as far back as the dim memory of mankind and beyond, that mark and honor the Winter Solstice. Stonehenge (which marks both Solstices), Newgrange in Ireland, and Maeshowe in the Orkney Islands off the coast of Scotland are some of the most well known of these ancient pieces of architecture. However, there are also similar structures throughout Europe, Asia, the Middle East, Indonesia and the Americas. One has even been found recently in Africa.

The Romans celebrated Saturnalia, which was a combination of the traditions already in use by the Egyptians and Persians. Saturnalia was a 12-day celebration that involved decorating with greenery and burning candles to chase away evil spirits. Naturally, it became a party in the pure Roman style with the passage of time.

Yule was the Norse and Celtic celebration of the Solstice. "Yule" means "feast" or, possibly, "wheel." As with the other cultures, the Celtic and Norse traditions tend to revolve around the return of light, warmth, and fertility brought by the Sun. Of course, the peoples to the North had a much rougher time in winter than their neighbors to the South, so their need for the return of light (and heat) may have helped imbue this holiday with special significance.

Boughs of holly were used in decoration because their verdant color was a strong reminder of life in the midst of the white, snow-covered world they lived in. White, interestingly, was a color of death and mourning to the Northern people, and winter was the time of the Earth's death in preparation for rebirth. Holly was also hung in windows because of its prickly leaves and poisonous berries, which make it excellent for guardianship.

The Holly King rules at this holiday, but loses his battle to the Oak King, who will then rule until Summer Solstice. All solar deities are honored, and this day is accounted as the birth of many of them.

Copyright Asteria Books 2019

Yule Mysteries

At Yuletide, it is our custom to explore the Mysteries of:

"Robin and Wren"/"Oak King and Holly King" – Here in the darkest time of year is a good time to consider the power of solitude, contemplation, and thriftiness (as well as how these things balance with community, activity, and abundance).

"What is seen by Odin's eye" – The Glass Orb is the vessel associated with the Winter Solstice. It can be thought of as Odin's eye, in addition to its associations with the Adder's Egg or glain. Spend some time with this vessel and consider what it reveals.

Copyright Asteria Books 2022

Yule Ritual

MATERIALS
- Stang, candle, lighter
- Three knives (red, black, white)
- Red Cord
- Bread, lipped dish or bowl
- Red wine, cup
- Incense, holder, charcoal
- Skull
- Yule candle, log, and/or firewood
- Wassail, bowl
- Lemon, ribbon, orris powder, cinnamon, ginger, whole cloves, toothpick

RAISE THE STANG

LAY THE COMPASS

OPEN THE GATES (beginning in the West)

WORKING

- VIGIL FIRE ~ Keep a fire burning all night. Stay with it, tending to it as needed. This isn't always an easy task. The night is long. It invariably becomes a time for self-reflection, much as the winter itself is. But it can also be a time for mirth, family, friends, and craft.
- WASSAIL THE TREES ~ Take the wassail bowl outside, if you aren't already outside. Salute the trees that surround your home. Wish them health and long life and offer them a drink. Sing the song "Here We Come A-Wassailing" as you go, if you choose. As with other offerings, it is appropriate for you to share the drink, as well, if you are so moved.
- PROSPERITY POMANDER ~ These clove-studded, dried citruses take some time to be fully made, but they are well worth it. Place in a dish on your altar while it dries.

HOUSLE

Copyright Asteria Books 2018

Sabbat - Yule Incense

About This Blend

This blend is designed to honor the Winter Solstice. It is suitable as a temple incense for Yule rituals and Midwinter feasts.

As with all loose incense blends, this formula can be burned on a hot, self-igniting charcoal tablet (like those used for hookahs) or it can be thrown onto the glowing embers of a fire.

Incense Recipe

1/2 cup tablespoons Rosemary

1/2 cup Lemongrass

1/4 cup Fennel

1 teaspoon Ginger

1 teaspoon Cinnamon

1 teaspoon Cloves

10 drops Ylang Ylang oil

Special Notes

This spicy and sweet blend is reminiscent of clove-studded pomanders and pumpkin pie.

Copyright Asteria Books 2017

Pomander

No. 1.   No. 2.

The name "pomander" means "apple of amber" (or rather, ambergris – the perfume component) and comes to use from the French *pomme d'ambre*. Pomanders are first mentioned in literature in the mid-13th century, and they were in popular use for about 400 as a means of warding off disease and negative spells, while promoting a sense of ease and peace.

Some traditional pomanders are made by rendering resins and other botanical ingredients until a ball (apple) of paste is formed, which is then hardened and carried inside a bag or piece of jewelry which allows the fragrance to circulate. In these cases, the encasement is also sometimes called a pomander.

The simplest pomanders are citrus fruits whose skins have been pierced, exposed to fragrant resins and herbs, and then studded with cloves. This is the type of pomander we often still see in contemporary Yule decorations. These are associated with solar magic, including wealth, health, and courage.

To make your own:

1. Choose an orange with a thick skin.
2. Pierce the skin liberally with a toothpick or burin.
3. Roll the orange in a mixture of powdered orris root, ginger, cinnamon, and other money-drawing spices.
4. Poke whole cloves into the holes on the skin.
5. Tie a gold, green, or red ribbon, if you wish to hang it.

Copyright Asteria Books 2021

Here We Come A-Wassailing

Here we come a-wassailing
Among the leaves so green,
Here we come a-wand'ring
So fair to be seen.
[REFRAIN]
Love and joy come to you,
And to you your wassail, too,
And God bless you, and send you
A Happy New Year,
And God send you a Happy New Year.

We are not daily beggars
That beg from door to door,
But we are neighbors' children
Whom you have seen before
[REPEAT REFRAIN]

Good master and good mistress,
As you sit beside the fire,
Pray think of us poor children
Who wander in the mire.
[REPEAT REFRAIN]

We have a little purse
Made of ratching leather skin;
We want some of your small change
To line it well within.
[REPEAT REFRAIN]

Bring us out a table
And spread it with a cloth;
Bring us out a cheese,
And of your Christmas loaf.
[REPEAT REFRAIN]

God bless the master of this house,
Likewise the mistress too;
And all the little children
That round the table go.
[REPEAT REFRAIN]

Copyright Asteria Books 2018

Wassail Recipe

1 gallon Apple Cider
1 can (6 oz) Frozen Orange Juice
1 can (6 oz) Lemonade
4 cups Water

Put the above ingredients in a 30 cup coffee percolator.

In the basket, put:

6 Cinnamon Sticks
1 & 1/2 tsp whole Allspice
1/2 tsp whole Cloves
1 cup Brown Sugar

This wassail recipe can be adapted to taste, and it serves a crowd. It is my family's favorite! You can also add some extra holiday cheer to it, if you like. It combines well with both wine and liquor, depending on your preference.

Copyright Asteria Books 2018

Yule Ritual

MATERIALS
- Stang, candle, lighter
- Cauldron, water, lancet
- Anvil, hammer
- Three knives (red, black, white)
- Triple Cord
- Bread, lipped dish or bowl
- Red wine, cup
- Incense, holder, charcoal
- Log, candles, evergreen clippings, firepit/hearth
- Bells

RAISE THE STANG

LAY THE COMPASS

RAISE THE CASTLES (beginning with the Castle of Glass)

OPEN THE GATES

WORKING
- YULE LOG - There are a few different ways to incorporate a Yule log into your celebrations. We're talking about the wooden log here, not the cake roll, by the way. It can be cut from the base of your Yule tree, a piece held in reserve from your Maypole or Beltaine fire, or specially selected log that has no other connections. Contemporarily, these are often decorated with evergreen bows and sometimes set with candles. Inscribe it with sigils of prosperity and protection, as this is what the Yule Log represents.
- VIGIL FIRE ~ Like you did last year, keep a fire burning all night — this time using your Yule Log as a focal point. Either set candles on/in it or burn it in your hearth/firepit. Stay with it, tending to it as needed. This isn't always an easy task. The night is long. It invariably becomes a time for self-reflection, much as the winter itself is. But it can also be a time for mirth, family, friends, feasting, and craft. (Feel free to wassail THE TREES AGAIN, IF YOU LIKE!)
- BELL RINGING - Welcome the dawn with the sound of bells. Greet the sun with joy and triumph, ringing out the darkness and welcoming back the return of the light.

HOUSLE

Copyright Asteria Books 2022

Imbolc

Imbolc is the mid-point between Winter Solstice and Spring Equinox. It is the time of the year when one begins to notice that the sunlight is waxing once again. In colder climes, like the ones many of our European pagan forebears lived in, this would have been the coldest part of the year. They would know that Spring was on its way, but there was very little physical evidence in the land that gave obvious witness to this fact. In fact, the returning light was about the only thing that really heralded the return of warmth and growth. Because this was the time of year that the ewes would come into their milk (for the lambs they were about to bear), the holiday was named "Oimelc" in some places. For human women, too, this could be a season of birth. (A woman who gets pregnant at Beltaine, and carries the baby to term, will be in labor near the beginning of February.)

Brighid is associated with this holiday due, in part, to her association with birthing and midwifery. She was one of the highly loved and honored pan-Celtic Goddesses, and this was an ideal holiday for celebrating her role as midwife and mother. Because of this, some traditions refer to this holiday as "Brighid" or "The Feast of Brighid" or even "Bride's Day" in honor of her.

Some traditional witches work within the Celtic framework of the John Barley-Corn cycle. At this time of year, John Barley-Corn would be in the womb, waiting to be born. As a part of the John Barley-Corn celebrations, the last mug of beer and the last loaf of bread would be drunk and eaten to help revitalize John Barley-Corn.

Many traditions send the Gods to their rest around the time of Samhain. Among those that do, there is a portion who would be calling the Gods back to life and fertility at this time of year, leaving them to rest during the darkest part of the cycle.

Candlemas, a festival that the Christians picked up on some centuries ago, is also associated with this time of year. Many covens use this time of returning light to make and/or bless their candles. This is not surprising, as Imbolc was one of the four great fire festivals of the Celts.

Fire and Ice are common themes (very often in conjunction) for this festival, as the hope of spring stirs beneath the frozen land.

In American Folkloric Craft, Kolyo (the Black Goddess) is honored at this time.

Copyright Asteria Books 2019

Imbolc Mysteries

At Imbolctide, it is our custom to explore the Mysteries of:

"Uneasy Seat Above Caer Ochren" — This is a wonderful time to explore the Mysteries of oracular work. Our Tradition associates Imbolc with invoking Kolyo and asking for Her guidance and wisdom on Her most holy day. She often reveals Her own Mysteries, but the process itself has much to impart, as well.

"The Light in the Darkness, the Darkness in the Light" — Kolyo and Goda share this Mystery, which they teach us using different methods. Starlight in an inky sky. Stark shadows in the brightest sun. Nakedness. Cloaking. Youth. Age. Nothing is as straightforward as it seems. First impressions are often deceiving.

"The Staff" — All of the weapons and vessels of the Spiral Castle carry their own Mysteries. When contemplating the lessons of the Staff, think of its many forms and functions — walking stick, battle-staff/quarter-staff, lantern pole, sounding rod, spear, arrow, wand, hobby horse, tein, distaff.

"Fire and Ice" — Climate change notwithstanding, Imbolc tends to be the coldest and bleakest of the Sabbats in North America. But "far beneath the winter snows, a heart of fire beats and glows." This is a great time to ponder what unseen things are happening during periods of rest.

Copyright Asteria Books 2022

Imbolc Ritual

MATERIALS
- Stang, candle, lighter
- Three knives (red, black, white)
- Red Cord
- Bread, lipped dish or bowl
- Red wine, cup
- Incense, holder, charcoal
- Skull
- Novena candle, Kolyo label, packing tape
- Florida Water or other perfume

RAISE THE STANG

LAY THE COMPASS

OPEN THE GATES (beginning in the North)

WORKING
- Kolyo Candle ~ Affix a Kolyo candle label onto a novena jar candle. Or draw Kolyo sigils onto a glass jar. Hold the jar between both hands and send energy into it while you seethe (next). Once ready, keep this candle on your altar all year long. If needed, you can transfer the flame and every into a new novena.
- Seething ~ Rock back and forth, side to side, in a circle or however the energy encourages you. Whisper or intone the name Kolyo while you do this. Enliven the candle with the Kolyo energy you are raising.
- Uneasy Seat ~ When you feel compelled to stop, allow yourself to sit still for a moment, sensing the energies around you. Focus on Kolyo and listen for Her voice in your mind and in your heart. Allow your spirit to sense Her and be in communication. See Her, hear Her, feel Her, smell Her, taste Her. Be in close contact with Her. Understand the messages She has for you. Let this continue until you are ready to stop, or She is. Dab Florida Water or another perfume onto your hands, feet, and the back of your neck to fully end the session and come back to yourself (and only yourself).

HOUSLE

Copyright Asteria Books 2018

Sabbat -Imbolc Incense

About This Blend

This incense was designed to accompany your Imbolc celebrations and rituals.

As with all loose incense blends, this formula can be burned on a hot, self-igniting charcoal tablet (like those used for hookahs) or it can be thrown onto the glowing embers of a fire.

Incense Recipe

1/4 cup Blackberry leaves

1/4 cup White Willow bark

1/4 cup Lavender

1/8 cup Barley

1 tablespoon Pine resin

2 teaspoons Cinnamon

7 drops Myrrh oil

A few drops Red Wine

Special Notes

This incense blend offers a special nod to Brighid, the pan-Celtic Goddess most frequently associated with this holiday. It also contains elements that connect to the Black Goddess, who is honored at this season within American Folkloric Witchcraft.

Copyright Asteria Books 2017

Imbolc Ritual

Materials
- Stang, candle, lighter
- Cauldron, water, lancet
- Anvil, hammer
- Three knives (red, black, white)
- Triple Cord
- Bread, lipped dish or bowl
- Red wine, cup
- Incense, holder, charcoal
- Hood (veil, large scarf, shawl)
- Taper or pillar candle, ice cubes, bowl
- Florida Water

Raise the Stang

Lay the Compass

Open the Gates (beginning in the North)

Raise the Castles

Working
- Fire & Ice ~ Place a taper or pillar candle in a bowl surrounded by ice cubes. You can dress the candle in oil and herbs, if you like. Light the candle and spend some time in contemplation of the dynamic between Fire and Ice in our lives. Think about the need for both action and stillness. Consider the destruction of both obsession and immobilization. How does this play out for you in your personal life? Professional life? How do you see this manifesting in the world around you? Be encouraged to take in more than just visual stimulus from this experience. Reach out to feel the heat and cold with your hands (safely, of course). Smell the burning wick and the scent of the ice. Taste/eat an ice cube. (It's not off-limits.) Listen to the crackling of the flame and the popping or dripping of the ice. You might be surprised what insights you have when you immerse yourself in the full sensory experience.
- Veiling ~ Cover your head and obscure

Copyright Asteria Books 2022

Imbolc Ritual

your vision with your hood, veil, scarf, or shawl. Kolyo, whom we particularly honor at Imbolc, is the "Covered One," and one way we can better access her wisdom is to take a moment to block out visual sensations and turn our thoughts toward the inner landscape.

- SEETHING ~ Rock back and forth, side to side, in a circle or however the energy encourages you. As discussed in lesson 07-04, the movement will likely start as something controlled and conscious; but the goal is to get out of your own way and allow the energy to move freely through you. Whisper or intone the name Kolyo while you do this.
- UNEASY SEAT UPON CAER OCHREN~ When you feel compelled to stop, allow yourself to sit still for a moment, sensing the energies around you. You will likely still feel wonky at this point, like you're moving. Maybe you are a little. All of that is okay. Focus on Kolyo and listen for Her voice in your mind and in your heart. Allow your spirit to sense Her and be in communication. See Her, hear Her, feel Her, smell Her, taste Her. Be in close contact with Her. Understand the messages She has for you. Let this continue until you are ready to stop, or She is. Dab Florida Water or another perfume onto your hands, feet, and the back of your neck to fully end the session and come back to yourself (and only yourself).

HOUSLE

Spring Equinox

It seems that the most popular and common name for this holiday (and many of the traditions surrounding it) has sprung from the not-so-common (in her own time) Teutonic Goddess Eostre (or Ostara). She was a fertility Goddess whose symbols were bunnies and eggs and the like. The idea of fertility is linked closely with this time of the year, and even the early Church couldn't get rid of the symbols. It is them, in fact, that we have to thank for popularizing the name and spreading the love of sweet Eostre's bunnies far and wide.

Within traditions that focus on the cycles of the sun, this is one of the four major events in the year. The vernal equinox is the solar event that marks the point of balance between day and night, while moving into longer and longer days. It is viewed as a time of balance with the understanding that we are moving into a time of increased light, action, and fertility.

Within the Greek cycle of the Eleusian Mysteries, this is the time when Persephone returns from her stay with her husband, Hades, in the Underworld. She is welcomed home by her rejoicing mother, Demeter, who is a Goddess of the fields. During Persephone's long absence, the fields gave no food and the land was dark and cold. With her return, flowers spring to life at her feet and the land is blessed with fertility. This is the joy of the reunion between mother and daughter.

This is also one of the two times of year attributed to Aphrodite's ritual cleansing and sacred bath. As such, some groups use this as a time of cleansing and renewal. Indeed, "spring cleaning" after a long winter is in order for most homes, and spiritual spring cleaning is a wise course of action, as well.

The Great Rite, in symbol or truth, can be done at this time in keeping with the fertility running so rampant in the land.

For groups who work with a John Barley-Corn myth cycle, little John is born (planted) at this holiday.

Copyright Asteria Books 2019

Spring Equinox Mysteries

At the Vernaltide, it is our custom to explore the Mysteries of:

"The Broom" — In his letters to Joe Wilson, Robert Cochrane discusses what we call "The Mystery of the Broom." He sums it up using the enigmatic phrase "spinning without motion between three elements." The Broom as a transvective tool allows us to MOVE between the Realms — without necessarily moving our bodies at all.

"The Golden Lantern" — All of the vessels and weapons of the Spiral Castle impart their own Mysteries. To better understand the inspiration, poetry, art, and illusion of the Golden Lantern, consider the Sun in alchemy and classical astrology, will o' th' wisps and foxfire in Irish and Appalachian lore, the rays of Awen, and tales of magic lamps.

Copyright Asteria Books 2022

Spring Equinox Ritual

MATERIALS
- Stang, candle, lighter
- Three knives (red, black, white)
- Red Cord
- Bread, lipped dish or bowl
- Red wine, cup
- Incense, holder, charcoal
- Skull
- Broom (ritual besom or practical broom)
- Shell, water, salt, evergreen sprig
- Candle, oil lamp, or lantern

RAISE THE STANG

LAY THE COMPASS

OPEN THE GATES (beginning in the North)

WORKING
- CLEANSING THE SPACE ~ Using the Cleansing Chants and accompanying tools (broom, saltwater in a shell with evergreen sprig, smoking incense, and lantern or lamp) energetically clean and cleanse the sacred space in which you work. You can, of course, go a step further and cleanse the whole house and/or property. Visualize all the staleness of winter, all the remnants of last year's harvest, all being swept and washed away.
- CLEANSING THE SELF ~ Using the same tools, energetically cleanse yourself. You probably already bathed before ritual, but you can use these same tools to cleanse yourself and your energy. The broom is the only one that may feel awkward, due to size and shape. Use the evergreen sprig instead.
- STANDING THE BROOM ~ Center yourself in your newly cleansed space. Feel the balance within you. Work on finding that external point of balance, via the broom. Try to get it to stand on its own long enough and steady enough that you can walk away from it. Once you've found the "sweet spot," it's often easy to do again and again -- any day of the year.

HOUSLE

Copyright Asteria Books 2018

Sabbat - Spring Equinox Incense

About This Blend

This incense is designed to complement your Spring Equinox rituals and celebrations.

As with all loose incense blends, this formula can be burned on a hot, self-igniting charcoal tablet (like those used for hookahs) or it can be thrown onto the glowing embers of a fire.

Incense Recipe

1/4 cup Hibiscus flowers

1/4 cup Calendula

1/4 cup Sage

1/8 cup Birch bark

1/8 cup Dandelion root

1/8 cup Hops flowers

1 tablespoon Myrrh resin

7 drops Jasmine essential oil

Special Notes

This light, fresh incense includes several flowers and herbs that are traditional Spring Equinox fare.

Spring Equinox Ritual

Materials
- Stang, candle, lighter
- Cauldron, water, lancet
- Anvil, hammer
- Three knives (red, black, white)
- Triple Cord
- Bread, lipped dish or bowl
- Red wine, cup
- Incense, holder, charcoal
- Three eggs (room-temperature, uncooked, organic)
- Candle
- Anointing/Blessing Oil, pray bottle, water

Raise the Stang

Lay the Compass

Raise the Castles (beginning with the Castle of Revelry)

Open the Gates

Working
- Blessing the Eggs ~ Eggs are symbolic of new life and the Sun. Hold all three eggs, in turn, up to the light of the candle flame to empower and bless them.
- Balancing the Eggs ~ Name and mark the eggs (Home, Compass, Self). Find the balance-point of each, if you can. Take your time. Make note of any challenges you face.
- Egg Cleansing ~ Eggs act as sponges, absorbing illness, negativity, and evil. Pass each of the eggs over, through, and around the space they are named for. Use strokes that move top to bottom, left to right, and clockwise (as appropriate). Only touch the body with the egg if you are experiencing pain or illness in a given area (and then, only touch that area). Dispose of the eggs under a tree away from your home, in a moving natural water source, or at a crossroads.
- Sealing the Work ~ Use an anointing or blessing oil (even as simple as frankincense diluted in olive oil) to seal the work on yourself by rubbing the oil through your hands and over your body, from the feet up. Add a few drops of the same oil to a water bottle and spritz your Home and Compass, as well.

Housle

Copyright Asteria Books 2018

Beltaine

Beltaine is one of four Celtic fire festivals that are associated with the agricultural turns of the seasons. It is, therefore, one of the Greater Sabbats, and it marks the opposite end of the Wheel from Samhain. Traditional Beltaine activities include blowing horns (a symbol of the male reproductive power) and gathering flowers, making garlands, and hanging greenery (flowers being the symbols of female fertility). Hawthorn was especially sacred to this holiday. In fact, old traditions dictate that the date of Beltaine is set by the flowering of the local Hawthorn tree, and the Hawthorn was usually the tree of choice for the Maypole. The Maypole itself would be symbol of male and female fertility conjoined once the dance was complete and the ribbons had been snugly wrapped about the pole. (While frolicsome and youthful, this is certainly not a dance for children, as it has become in modern culture.)

Beltaine is linked to the Sacred Marriage (hieros gamos) and fertility almost universally. Many Wiccan trads see this as the wedding day of the May Queen and May King. Mothers and fertility are especially honored, and the contemporary secular holiday of Mother's Day (which occurs within about a week of Beltaine) may have Pagan roots associated with this festival.

Communing with fairies has frequently been associated with this holiday, and a lot of lore surrounds ways to contact and work with fairy energy during this time for those who feel inclined to contact the Good Neighbors.

Sacred bonfires were used in many ways in May Day celebrations. Many people would jump balefires for fertility or pass cattle and other livestock between bonfires for protection, fertility, purification.

Walpurgisnacht is a May Eve celebration that originated in Southern Germany (Bavaria). Its purpose is to scare away all the evil spirits that lurk in the shadows before the bright day of Beltaine. Interestingly, Walpurgis is the name of both a well-known nun and a famous witch, but it doesn't seem to have been a Goddess name.

Within American Folkloric Craft, Lucifer-Qayin is honored as the May-King and the Lord of the East, the direction associated with Beltaine on the Year Wheel.

Copyright Asteria Books 2019

Beltaine Mysteries

At Beltainetide, it is our custom to explore the Mysteries of:

"Life in Death; Death in Life" — This is a phrase we use to reference something very fundamental to this Tradition. While the WitchMother isn't particular prominent at this Sabbat, this phrase IS. (And this phrase is very much associated with Her.) This Mystery is also very present with us at Samhain.

"The Sword That Cuts Both Ways" — All of the weapons and vessels of the Spiral Castle impart their own lessons and Mysteries. The Sword (weapon of the East Gate) has much to teach. One of the ways it shows up is as the Sword Bridge that we cross into the place of Initiation. As such, we name the Coven Sword as "The Sword That Cuts Both Ways."

Copyright Asteria Books 2022

Beltaine Ritual

MATERIALS
- Stang, candle, lighter
- Three knives (red, black, white)
- Red Cord
- Bread, lipped dish or bowl
- Red wine, cup
- Mugwort, lemongrass (1/2 tsp each)
- Honey
- Incense, holder, charcoal
- Skull

RAISE THE STANG

LAY THE COMPASS

OPEN THE GATES (beginning in the East)

WORKING

- SABBAT WINE ~ Prepare Sabbat Wine for yourself by steeping a tablespoon of mugwort (or a blend of mugwort and lemongrass) in a cup of warm red wine for 10 minutes. Remove the herbs (easiest done when using a tea ball), and add raw honey to sweeten. I like to use a local sweet red wine and local honey, as well as local herbs (when I can get them). Drink the wine without gulping or chugging. Give it time to work with you to open your psychic senses.
- GUIDED MEDITATION ~ Journey through the Walpurgisnacht Flight guided meditation either by reading it aloud while recording (prior to ritual) and then playing it back for yourself during the ritual, or by reading through the meditation prior to ritual so that you are familiar enough with the steps, and then doing your best to follow those steps without guidance. You can also read through the meditation after you feel the soft focus from the wine wash over you, doing what you can to walk between the worlds of reading and meditating. (Or you can listen to the recorded version on the RTA YouTube channel.)

HOUSLE

Copyright Asteria Books 2018

Sabbat - Beltane Incense

About This Blend

This incense is designed to accompany your Beltane festivities and rituals.

As with all loose incense blends, this formula can be burned on a hot, self-igniting charcoal tablet (like those used for hookahs) or it can be thrown onto the glowing embers of a fire.

Incense Recipe

1/4 cup Cowslip

1/4 cup Saffron or Safflower

1/4 cup Angelica root

1/4 cup Cinquefoil

1/8 cup Hawthorne berries

1 tablespoon Frankincense resin

9 drops Honeysuckle oil

A little honey

Special Notes

Beltane is also known as May Day or Bel's Fire. It is a fire festival that welcomes in the summer season and the light half of the year. This incense has both spicy and sweet notes that pay homage to the Lord of Light and the May Queen who reign at this time.

Copyright Asteria Books 2017

Walpurgisnacht Flight

Close your eyes and and follow your breath. Take long, slow inhalations, followed by long, slow exhalations. As you breathe, you notice a white mist settling around your body. It quickly becomes a thick fog obscuring sight and sound. The fog is cool and numbing, and you find yourself a little tingling and disoriented. A strange heaviness pervades your body as you continue to breathe deeply, in and out. After a moment, the fog begins to lift, and you also feel lighter. You stand, gripping your Stang and use it as a walking stick. You move a few paces off, and the fog clings a little less, though you still can't see where you are. You take another step and are able to recognize your surroundings, though they look altered in ways that are difficult to describe fully. You notice yourself and your surroundings for a moment, seeing both this familiar place and your own self with the eyes of Spirit. You move out of this familiar space and into unknown territory. You're surprised how rapidly the landscape shifts into unfamiliar scenery. You may have thought you knew this place well, but only a few yards from familiar ground, you find yourself confronted with a hedgerow unlike any that could have been there before. It is thick, dense, made of several kinds of hedge trees, and it is quite a lot taller than most hedges. Far on the other side of this hedge, the Dancing Place of the Witches awaits you. You can hear the distant call of the pipes and drums and bells. The sounds are so distant, you are sure it isn't your ears that hear them. You smell the wood smoke and feast meats. You can taste the promise of mead and kisses and laughter beyond this hedge. You look down the row to the left and the right and don't see a gate. There may be one if you talk a walk, of course. A rabbit pops up from a burrow about six feet away from you. Yes, *under is an option. You lean on your Stang to think and it leans back. Ah! Over it is.* You straddle the Stang and lift into air. You notice a star shining from the candle flame between the horns of the Stang and are reminded of the iron foot at the base. Be aware of the sensations you experience as you mount the Stang. From above the hedge, you notice a wild landscape. A patchwork of ancient forests, fertile countryside, villages, hills, and a mountain range looming in the distance. It is here where the Witches dance. The peak you seek is the Brocken. The highest. Your soul knows the way. You land at the Hexentanzenplatz (Witches' Dancing Place) to find the Sabbat in full revelry. More Witches than you'd ever dreamed are gathered here. Witches of every color, from every place, who have made covenant with the Witchfather are here to celebrate the great Beltaine Sabbat. And not just Witches are here. As you take a moment to observe the stunning spectacle, you see many Familiars, too. This Dance is a revel for all the senses and offers any delights you care to indulge. Food, sex, music, drink, wisdom, mysticism, laughter, scent, beauty, inspiration. You stay as long as you choose, taking your fill, before eventually returning the way you came (across the sky, over the hedge, and back into the fog).

Copyright Asteria Books 2018

Beltaine Ritual

MATERIALS
- Stang, candle, lighter
- Cauldron, water, lancet
- Anvil, hammer
- Three knives (red, black, white)
- Triple Cord
- Bread, lipped dish or bowl
- Red wine, cup
- Incense, holder, charcoal
- Firepit, cast iron cauldron
- Sacred woods bundle

CANDLE
RAISE THE STANG
LAY THE COMPASS
OPEN THE GATES (beginning in the East)
WORKING

- LIGHTING THE BALEFIRE ~ It is best if you can perform this ritual outdoors, but hearth and cauldron options are available for indoors, if needed. (It is also ideal if this fire is either at the East or Center point of your Compass, if possible.) Whether you are able to light a campfire, cauldron-fire, hearthfire, or bonfire, add a bundle of Sacred Woods (ie, any of the trees we work with as Allies). You can use logs, branches, twigs, or shavings — depending on the size of the fire and your access to the woods. Light the fire in a manner that you consider sacramental and respectful.
- THE SECOND FLAME ~ Light your candle (or light a second cauldron or campfire) from the flames of the first. Place this second flame at either the East or Center point of your Compass, forming a passage between the two flames.
- BALEFIRE BLESSINGS ~ Your balefire is a very propitious fire for all manner of magic. Write and burn petition papers. Jump the fire for luck, health, and protection. Pass yourself and members of your household (including pets) between the two flames for prosperity and protection. (You can use poppets of them, if they can't be present.) Meditate and scry in the flames for messages.

HOUSLE

Copyright Asteria Books 2022

Midsummer

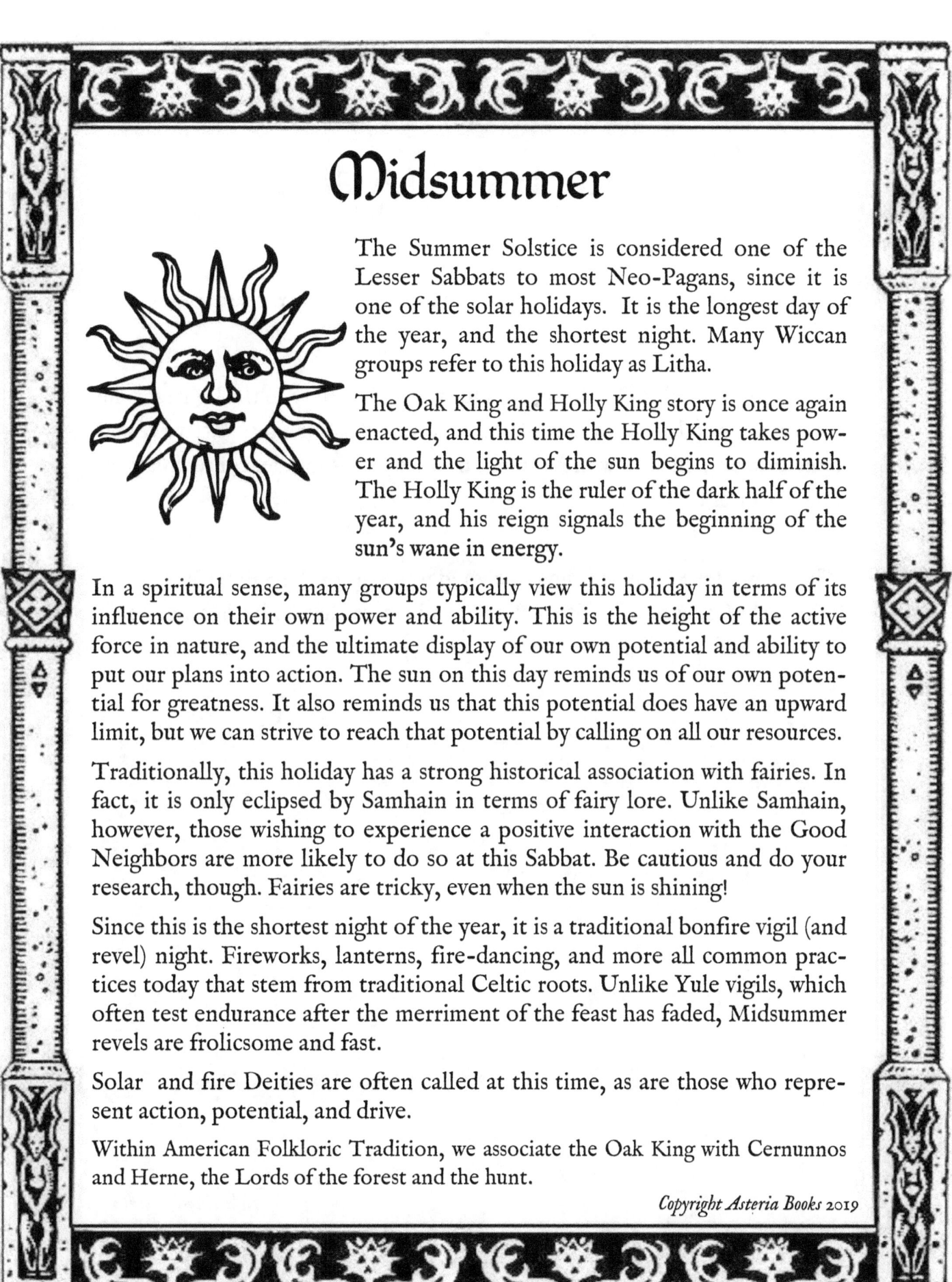

The Summer Solstice is considered one of the Lesser Sabbats to most Neo-Pagans, since it is one of the solar holidays. It is the longest day of the year, and the shortest night. Many Wiccan groups refer to this holiday as Litha.

The Oak King and Holly King story is once again enacted, and this time the Holly King takes power and the light of the sun begins to diminish. The Holly King is the ruler of the dark half of the year, and his reign signals the beginning of the sun's wane in energy.

In a spiritual sense, many groups typically view this holiday in terms of its influence on their own power and ability. This is the height of the active force in nature, and the ultimate display of our own potential and ability to put our plans into action. The sun on this day reminds us of our own potential for greatness. It also reminds us that this potential does have an upward limit, but we can strive to reach that potential by calling on all our resources.

Traditionally, this holiday has a strong historical association with fairies. In fact, it is only eclipsed by Samhain in terms of fairy lore. Unlike Samhain, however, those wishing to experience a positive interaction with the Good Neighbors are more likely to do so at this Sabbat. Be cautious and do your research, though. Fairies are tricky, even when the sun is shining!

Since this is the shortest night of the year, it is a traditional bonfire vigil (and revel) night. Fireworks, lanterns, fire-dancing, and more all common practices today that stem from traditional Celtic roots. Unlike Yule vigils, which often test endurance after the merriment of the feast has faded, Midsummer revels are frolicsome and fast.

Solar and fire Deities are often called at this time, as are those who represent action, potential, and drive.

Within American Folkloric Tradition, we associate the Oak King with Cernunnos and Herne, the Lords of the forest and the hunt.

Copyright Asteria Books 2019

Midsummer Mysteries

At Midsummerstide, it is our custom to explore the Mysteries of:

"Robin and Wren"/"Oak King and Holly King" — Here in the lightest time of year is a good time to consider the power of community, activity, and abundance (as well as how these things balance with solitude, contemplation, and thriftiness).

"The Stone Bowl" — All of the vessels and weapons of the Spiral Castle carry their own Mysteries. The Stone Bowl reminds us that "There is no magic without sacrifice" — a phrase which we often paint or carve on the bottom of this dish.

Copyright Asteria Books 2022

Midsummer Ritual

MATERIALS
- Stang, candle, lighter
- Three knives (red, black, white)
- Red Cord
- Bread, lipped dish or bowl
- Red wine, cup
- Incense, holder, charcoal
- Skull
- Fire pit, fire wood, kindling OR
- Cauldron, Epsom salt, rubbing alcohol
- Recorded music or musical instruments, drums, etc.

RAISE THE STANG

LAY THE COMPASS

OPEN THE GATES (beginning in the East)

WORKING

> BONFIRE OR CAULDRON FIRE ~ This is best done outside, for obvious reasons, but it is possible to build a very, very small sacred fire indoors in a cauldron with Epsom salt and rubbing alcohol. Another alternative is to place a candle in your cauldron. Of course, the preference here is to build a fire outside, if at all possible. It doesn't have to be large. Midsummer fires are wonderful for revelry, music, dancing, and the high spirits that come with the joys of summer. Play music, make music. Dance. The type of music and style of dance don't matter. Get your blood up, your energy up. Have fun! Keep it going as long into the night as you like. This is a celebration of life, io the ability to DO, and of the ripeness of the world.

HOUSLE

Copyright Asteria Books 2018

Sabbat - Midsummer Incense

About This Blend

This incense was designed to accompany Summer Solstice rituals and celebrations.

As with all loose incense blends, this formula can be burned on a hot, self-igniting charcoal tablet (like those used for hookahs) or it can be thrown onto the glowing embers of a fire.

Incense Recipe

1/4 cup St. John's Wort

1/4 cup Chamomile

1/4 cup Oakmoss

1/4 cup Patchouly

1/4 cup Cedarwood chips

1 tablespoon ground Acorn

1 tablespoon Pine resin

5 drops Lemon oil

3 drops Bergamot oil

Special Notes

In the American Folkloric Withcraft tradition, Midsummer is the sacred time of Cernunnos. This blend is reminiscent of sunshine in the forest.

Copyright Asteria Books 2017

Midsummer Ritual

MATERIALS
- Stang, candle, lighter
- Cauldron, water, lancet
- Anvil, hammer
- Three knives (red, black, white)
- Triple Cord
- Bread, lipped dish or bowl
- Red wine, cup
- Incense, holder, charcoal
- St. John's Wort, Vervain, Mugwort, and Yarrow
- Sticks, twigs, stones, leaves, etc
- Cream

RAISE THE STANG

LAY THE COMPASS

OPEN THE GATES (beginning in the East)

WORKING
- FAIR HERBS ~ Obtain (gather, if you can) some of the herbs associated with the Good Neighbors. These include St. John's Wort, Vervain, Mugwort, and Yarrow. These particular herbs have a reputation for attracting friendly fey folk, while warding against less friendly ones. Twist them into a wreath/crown, tie them with a ribbon, or pack into a pouch. However you arrange them, wear or carry them on you as you work today/tonight.
- FAERIE HOUSE ~ In some outside space, build a little house of twigs, grasses, herbs, stones, and leaves. You can use twine, jute, or long blades of grass to bind pieces together — or just rely on gravity. I like to keep the house as natural as possible, while still making it interesting. The "Fey" can be seen as Spirits of the Dead, landwights, nature Spirits, and by other descriptors used across cultures for similar types of beings. You are offering this house as a vessel — most likely to a landwight. For now, don't ask or expect anything in return. (You may eventually build a relationship, but right now, you are just being a good neighbor to the Good Neighbors.) NOTE: I like to build a Stone Castle, if I'm able, since this is the Sabbat that aligns with that Watchtower.
- OFFERING ~ Leave a little cream, honey, and/or whiskey in a leaf, piece of bark, or a cupped stone.

HOUSLE

Copyright Asteria Books 2022

Lughnasadh

Lughnasadh is another of the Greater Sabbats, one of the High Holy Days - a Celtic fire festival based on the agricultural wheel. It is named after the Pan-Celtic God Lugh whose name comes from "lugio" meaning "oath" - marriages and other contracts were made at this time. Both the Welsh stories of Lleu and the Irish ones of Lugh are very much tied up with oaths, promises, and bonds.

Another name for this holiday is Lammas, which means "loaf mass." Because this is the first of the harvest festivals, grain and the first fruits were often blessed and honored at this holiday. The loaf mass was a Catholic adaptation of the blessing of the grain that clearly had Pagan roots. This holiday gave rise to country fairs that still happen (and are particularly popular in the Midwestern United States) at this time of year. The country craft fairs also give unknown honor to Lugh in another way (since he is the master of all crafts).

Lughnasadh is named after Lugh because he instituted funeral games in honor of Tailtiu, his foster-mother, who died after clearing a forest for cultivation.

Traditional activities include picking bilberries (as representative of all of Earth's bounty), playing games, having contests of wit and strength, and making a corn dolly. The corn dolly represents the harvest itself and is ploughed or burned in the spring to prepare for the next sowing and harvest cycle.

Obviously, Lugh is the most obvious Deity for this holiday, as it is his festival. However, other commonly honored at this time of year include the Dagda (and other regional harvest Deities) and Tailtiu.

Within American Folkloric Witchcraft, this holiday is sacred to Goda, the White Goddess of the land.

Copyright Asteria Books 2019

Lammas Mysteries

At Lammastide, it is our custom to explore the Mysteries of:

"What songs the siren sings?" — Goda is Our Lady of Lammas — a time of sacrifice and also joy, abundance, and oaths. This is a great time to contemplate Goda and her associations with love, loss, reunion of the Soul, and song.

"Uneasy Seat Above Caer Ochren" — This is a wonderful time to explore the Mysteries of oracular work. Our Tradition associates Lammas with invoking Goda and asking for Her guidance and wisdom on Her most holy day. She often reveals Her own Mysteries, but the process itself has much to impart, as well.

"The Dance of the Seven Veils" — Goda stands naked, having shed the veils already. What do we find when we strip away our careers, relationships, memories, bodies, desires, etc. Consider Inanna's descent, and the jewelry/garments she relinquishes at each gate. Consider the 7 classical planets, and the 7 most commonly discussed chakras. Consider the process of aging and death, and how we all eventually "stand naked."

"The Shield" — Each of our vessels and weapons unfolds its own Mysteries. Some are better documented than others in the traditions of the Craft and other Mystery Schools. The Shield is one that gets short shrift in most places, but it is still present and powerful. It is related to the Witch's Glove, the

Copyright Asteria Books 2022

Lammas Mysteries

Pentacle, and even the Cloak (which is a shielding device in myth and literature).

"The Light in the Darkness, the Darkness in the Light" — Kolyo and Goda share this Mystery, which they teach us using different methods. Starlight in an inky sky. Stark shadows in the brightest sun. Nakedness. Cloaking. Youth. Age. Nothing is as straightforward as it seems. First impressions are often deceiving.

Lughnasadh Ritual

MATERIALS
- Stang, candle, lighter
- Three knives (red, black, white)
- Red Cord
- Bread, lipped dish or bowl
- Red wine, cup
- Incense, holder, charcoal
- Skull
- Green corn husks (removed from corn), twine/cord
- Bread, corn, tomatoes, melons, local seasonal produce

RAISE THE STANG

LAY THE COMPASS

OPEN THE GATES (beginning in the South)

WORKING
- CORN DOLLY ~ Fashion a human-shaped figure from the corn husks, using the string to tie the head, body, arms, and legs. Place on your altar and allow to dry. Name your doll.
- FIRST FRUITS FEAST ~ Offer a blessing of the seasonal fruits, vegetables, and grains. Place some of each in the sacrificial bowl before consuming them for yourself. Give thanks to Goda for the bounty. Eat and enjoy!
- OATH TAKING ~ Consider an area of your life that needs a commitment from you. Make an oath to improve or address that area. Be specific. Write down the oath in your journal. Hold yourself accountable for it.

HOUSLE

Copyright Asteria Books 2018

Sabbat - Lughnasadh Incense

About This Blend

This Sabbat blend is specifically designed for Lughnasadhe and is suitable as a temple incense during that time.

As with all loose incense blends, this formula can be burned on a hot, self-igniting charcoal tablet (like those used for hookahs) or it can be thrown onto the glowing embers of a fire.

Incense Recipe

1/4 cup Lavender

1/4 cup Apple fiber

1 tablespoon Frankincense

1/4 cup Blackberry leaves

6 drops Amber oil

3 drops Dragon's Blood oil

Special Notes

This incense can be used for either the celebration of Lughnasadh or Lammas. Although they are attributed to the same day, Lughnasadh was a funerary-game festival honoring the Celtic God Lugh's foster-mother, while Lammas is very specifically a first-harvest festival. This incense combines both intentions and is a great way to honor the potent fruitfulness at the end of summer

Copyright Asteria Books 2017

Lughnasadh Ritual

MATERIALS
- Stang, candle, lighter
- Cauldron, water, lancet
- Anvil, hammer
- Three knives (red, black, white)
- Triple Cord
- Bread, lipped dish or bowl
- Red wine, cup
- Incense, holder, charcoal
- Corn dolly
- Bread man
- Fresh seasonal fruits and vegetables (local is best)

RAISE THE STANG

LAY THE COMPASS

OPEN THE GATES (beginning in the South)

RAISE THE CASTLES

WORKING
- CORN DOLLY ~ Fashion a human-shaped figure from the corn husks, using the string to tie the head, body, arms, and legs. Place on your altar and allow it to dry. Name your doll.
- FIRST FRUITS FEAST ~ Offer a blessing of the seasonal fruits, vegetables, and grains. Place some of each in the sacrificial bowl before consuming them for yourself. Give thanks to Goda for the bounty. Eat and enjoy!
- SACRIFICIAL BREAD MAN ~ Shape and bake a Bread Man. (He can be made of any bread, according to the traditions of your region/family and your baking ability — sourdough, soda bread, cornbread, canned biscuits/rolls.) Sacrifice him with your Red Knife using the words from the Housle and place his body upon the bed of fruits in the sacrificial bowl. All present should eat a portion of the Bread Man, as well.

HOUSLE

Copyright Asteria Books 2022

Fall Equinox

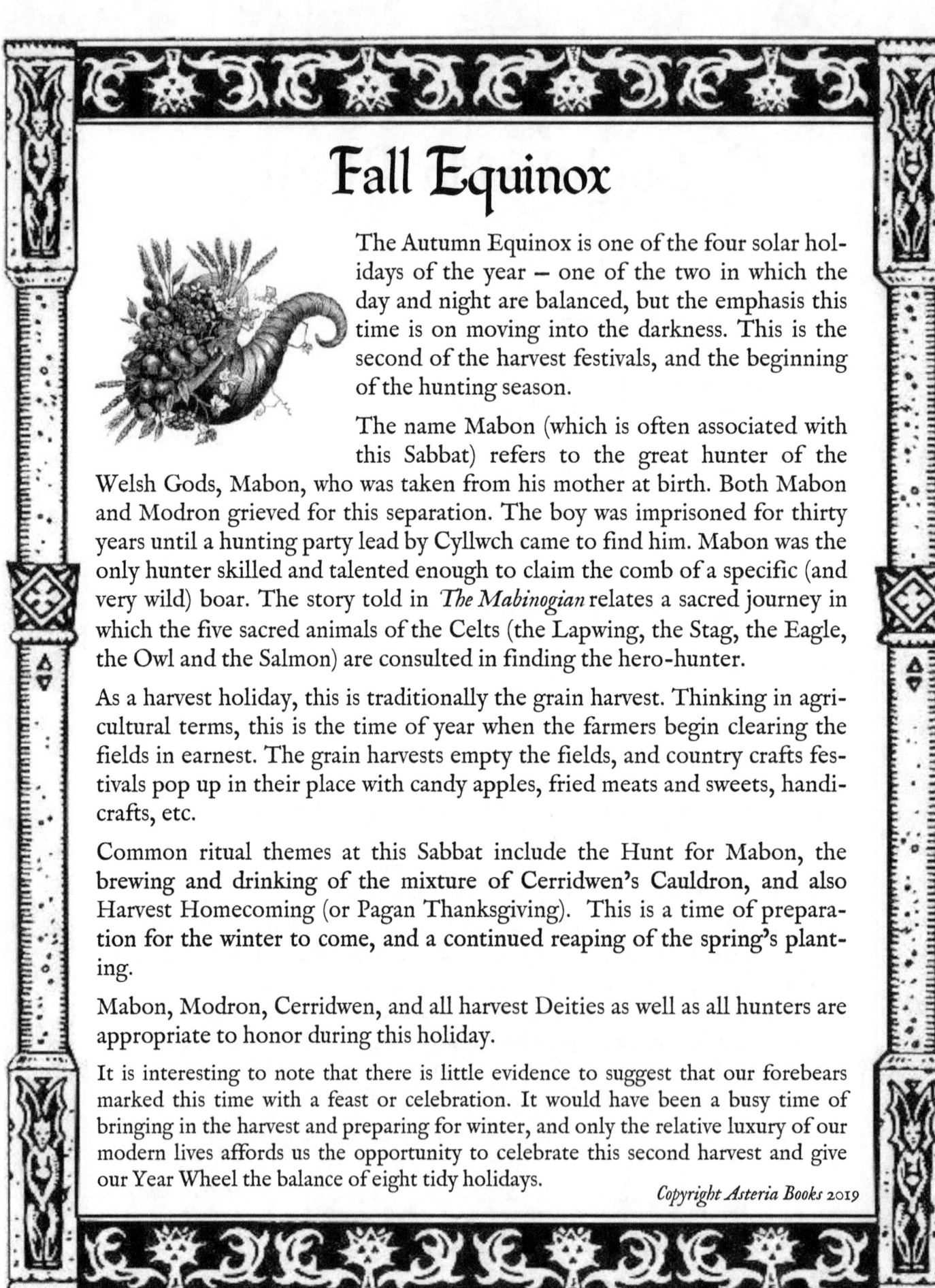

The Autumn Equinox is one of the four solar holidays of the year — one of the two in which the day and night are balanced, but the emphasis this time is on moving into the darkness. This is the second of the harvest festivals, and the beginning of the hunting season.

The name Mabon (which is often associated with this Sabbat) refers to the great hunter of the Welsh Gods, Mabon, who was taken from his mother at birth. Both Mabon and Modron grieved for this separation. The boy was imprisoned for thirty years until a hunting party lead by Cyllwch came to find him. Mabon was the only hunter skilled and talented enough to claim the comb of a specific (and very wild) boar. The story told in *The Mabinogian* relates a sacred journey in which the five sacred animals of the Celts (the Lapwing, the Stag, the Eagle, the Owl and the Salmon) are consulted in finding the hero-hunter.

As a harvest holiday, this is traditionally the grain harvest. Thinking in agricultural terms, this is the time of year when the farmers begin clearing the fields in earnest. The grain harvests empty the fields, and country crafts festivals pop up in their place with candy apples, fried meats and sweets, handicrafts, etc.

Common ritual themes at this Sabbat include the Hunt for Mabon, the brewing and drinking of the mixture of Cerridwen's Cauldron, and also Harvest Homecoming (or Pagan Thanksgiving). This is a time of preparation for the winter to come, and a continued reaping of the spring's planting.

Mabon, Modron, Cerridwen, and all harvest Deities as well as all hunters are appropriate to honor during this holiday.

It is interesting to note that there is little evidence to suggest that our forebears marked this time with a feast or celebration. It would have been a busy time of bringing in the harvest and preparing for winter, and only the relative luxury of our modern lives affords us the opportunity to celebrate this second harvest and give our Year Wheel the balance of eight tidy holidays.

Copyright Asteria Books 2019

Autumn Mysteries

At the Autumnaltide, it is our custom to explore the Mysteries of:

"What the Mask Reveals" — The Spiral Castle Tradition often performs a "Hunt for Mabon" at the Fall Equinox. During this ritual, we usually mask — either as a Hunter or as one of the Five Animals that the hunting party queries. We work with the Mask in order to better understand both ourselves and That which is represented by a specific mask.

"The Mystery of the Cauldron" — Robert Cochrane wrote about the Mys-tery of the Cauldron in his letters to Joe Wilson. He poses a riddle to Wilson, asking him what can't fit within the Cauldron. "Two words: Be Still." The Cauldron holds ALL — all life, all hope, all desire, all abundance, all possibility. It is always moving. Always shifting. Always becoming. There is no still-ness in the Cauldron. (But there can be stillness within us, which we find within this tumult.)

"The Bloody Cup/The Holy Grail" — All of the vessels and weapons of the Spiral Castle impart their own Mysteries. This is probably the most well-known of all the Mysteries we seek. The San Greal — or Sang Real.

"The Five Transformations" — Ceridwen is one of the ladies whom we see most clearly as our Silver Queen. She is the keeper of the Cauldron, and her story of flight, pursuit, and transformation with the young Gwion Bach (who becomes Taliesin) is most revealing.

Copyright Asteria Books 2022

Fall Equinox Ritual

MATERIALS
- Stang, candle, lighter
- Three knives (red, black, white)
- Red Cord
- Bread, lipped dish or bowl
- Red wine, cup
- Incense, holder, charcoal
- Skull
- "Hunter" mask of your own design and creation
- Animal print-outs (placed around Compass as indicated)
- Mirror (placed at base of Stang)
- Colored pencils, crayons, pen (in a basket or bag that can move with you)

RAISE THE STANG

LAY THE COMPASS

OPEN THE GATES (beginning in the South)

WORKING

- MASKING ~ Create a mask as a representation of the Hunter. Before you don your mask, name it and bless it. Know, as you put it on, that you become one of the hunting party in search for Mabon.
- PURPOSE OF THE HUNT ~ The Harvest is underway and the Dark Days of Winter are approaching. The tribe, the clan, the Family needs the assurance of sustenance during the lean times to come. This is a time to be grateful for the bounty of the Harvest, which is still being brought in, but it is also a time to take action to prepare for the hard times, the lean seasons. The Great Hunter acts a guide to help you, as do the animals who point the way to him.
- HUNT FOR MABON ~ In your reenacted search for the Great Hunter, you will move from one quarter to the next, spending time with each of the Sacred Animals. Begin in the East, with the Lapwing. As you move to each animal, understand that you are seeking their wisdom and guidance. Read the words on the page, then spend some time in reflection, listening for any direct message that animal may have for you. Fully tread the mill between each animal.

HOUSLE

Copyright Asteria Books 2018

Sabbat - Fall Equinox Incense

About This Blend

This blend is designed to accompany your Fall Equinox celebrations and rituals.

As with all loose incense blends, this formula can be burned on a hot, self-igniting charcoal tablet (like those used for hookahs) or it can be thrown onto the glowing embers of a fire.

Incense Recipe

1/4 cup Comfrey

1/4 cup Bladderwrack

1/4 cup Vervain

1 tablespoon ground Walnut hull

1 tablespoon Dragon's Blood resin

1 tablespoon Juniper berries

9 drops Wormwood oil

Pinch of Sea Salt

A few drops Red Wine

Special Notes

Whether you celebrate Fall Equinox as Mabon, Harvest Home, or some other name, this incense is intended to help you honor this harvest holiday.

The American Folkloric Tradition honors Cerridwen as the Lady of the Cauldron at this time of year, and this incense blend also pays homage to her.

Copyright Asteria Books 2017

Fall Equinox Ritual

MATERIALS
- Stang, candle, lighter
- Cauldron, water, lancet
- Anvil, hammer
- Three knives (red, black, white)
- Triple Cord
- Bread, lipped dish or bowl
- Red wine, cup
- Incense, holder, charcoal
- Harvest Feast foods — try to include chicken, pork, and grape (wine)

RAISE THE STANG

LAY THE COMPASS

RAISE THE CASTLES (beginning with Castle Perilous)

OPEN THE GATES

WORKING

- GATHERING THE FEAST ~ Lay out the food you have prepared/purchased. If you can, include items from this month's Spirit Allies — the Vine, the Swine, and the Chicken. If you are unable (for any reason), try including images or figurines of the animals and/or grapes, in recognition of the generations of Ancestors who were sustained and uplifted by the sacrifice of these Spirits.
- BLESSING THE FEAST ~ This entire Feast is a Housle, so speak and perform the portions of our Housle Rite that bless the Meal.
- OFFERINGS OF GRATITUDE ~ Be sure to include a bit of everything from the Feast/Meal in your offering bowl. As you give each piece, offer gratitude for some aspect of the bounty you have experienced this year. At the end of the meal, offer the contents of the offering bowl as you normally do, with the Declaration, etc.

HOUSLE

Copyright Asteria Books 2022

However, you may want to "tap" the skull to quicken the pulse if it has been a whole year since you've worked with it. If you are using leg bones to open/close the portal, this is the time to open them and welcome your Ancestors to join you.

- Dark Beer for Qayin -- Strike the anvil 3 times and pour out dark beer for the Witchfather, as you did last year (and possibly since then).
- Dumb Feast — From this point forward during the ritual, you will not speak. (I personally like to perform this entire ritual in silence — including the Compass Laying, etc.) Communicate via energy and gesture, but do not use audible words. Eat a meal with your Ancestors, setting them a place of honor and preparing a plate of food for them. The silence allows you the opportunity to commune with them and to immerse yourself in a a sensory experience whereby you might communicate. Perhaps you'll hear messages from them as you eat. Perhaps the tastes of certain foods will be especially delicious for you. Try to include foods that were family favorites, if you are able. Taste and smell are very primal sense, and they can connect us to old (even ancient) memory. (Many customs hold that this meal should be set and served in reverse. This is not how I was taught, but feel free to incorporate the custom, if the folklore suits you.)

Housle

Meditations

Entering and Exiting Journey

Most journey work (including guided meditation and Witch Flight) can be viewed as shamanistic experiences in which the Witch's Fetch (or spirit body) explores the Unseen Realms above, below, or between. Use these simple scripts to help you enter and leave your journeys.

Entering Upper World Journey

Let yourself relax comfortably and picture yourself drifting upward and outward to the first realm, the upper realm. The first realm is a place of clarity and insight. Let yourself drift up into the first realm and rest there peacefully.

Exiting Upper World Journey

You are back [where you began], and you take your rest. You feel a sinking down as you become more aware of the physical sensations in your body and your Fetch merges with your physical self again. Breathe, stretch, and open your eyes when you are ready.

Entering Middle World Journey

Let yourself relax comfortably and picture yourself drifting outward and away to the second realm, the middle realm. The second realm is a place of action and sensation. Let yourself drift sideways into the second realm and rest there peacefully.

Exiting Middle World Journey

You are back [where you began], and you take your rest. You feel a pull back to THIS place as you become more aware of the physical sensations in your body and your Fetch merges with your physical self again. Breathe, stretch, and open your eyes when you are ready.

Entering Underworld World Journey

Let yourself relax comfortably and picture yourself drifting downward and inward to the third realm, the lower realm. The third realm is a place of darkness and mystery. Let yourself sink down into the third realm and rest there peacefully.

Exiting Under World Journey

You are back [where you began], and you take your rest. You feel a rising up as you become more aware of the physical sensations in your body and your Fetch merges with your physical self again. Breathe, stretch, and open your eyes when you are ready.

Copyright Asteria Books 2022

Glass Castle Meditation

It is dark when you awake in a silent grove of snow-covered Holly trees. Snowflakes so fat you can see their perfect, crystalline designs drift silently down in the moonlight to land on the prickly green leaves, blood-colored berries, and glittering, cold-hardened ground.

You have the sense of others being present with you, and you look around the grove for confirmation. From between an archway made by two tall Holly trees, you see shining eyes watching you. A black goat steps into the center of grove, followed by two companions -- goats of white and grey pulling a small sleigh. The black goat indicates that he has something important to show you, and you climb into the sheepskin-draped sleigh.

All three goats begin to walk through the forest, slowly picking their way through the prickly Holly trees. You hear tinkling, jingling silver bells as the rig moves -- and see that the tack has been adorned with them. As the stand clears to a meadow, they pick up their pace. Now trotting. Now in a full run across rolling, snowy hills. Icy wind whistles in your ears, and the frigid night air stings your face, making your eyes water. You are grateful for the soft, warm lap robe.

With wonderment, you realize the crest of the next hill has given way to a cliff, and your team of shaggy steeds is running with sure-footed swiftness upon insubstantial air. You feel the lightness of flying in your body as you look at the white and grey patchwork of the earth below you, accompanied by a flock of small brown birds. They are wrens, you realize.

Through a distant mist you can see a sparkling castle of glass. Moonlight shines like starfire from its faceted walls. Palest blue, white, and silver banners hang from its towers. Music drifts to your ears -- a choir, strings, horns. The brightness and warmth of the music stand in contrast to the chill beauty around you.

The goats land in a snowy courtyard beyond the large, mirrored castle doors. The black goat says that he will wait for you outside. You ask him what place this is and he answers, "There are many names for this place. Some call it Merlin's Tomb. Others, the Fata Morgana. I call it the Castle of Glass. It is the home of the Holly King and his glass orb. He awaits you."

The doors of the castle open and you find a glass staircase, which you begin to climb. You glimpse of a feasting hall where a cheerful gathering has assembled -- the smell of roasted meats and spiced cider, a peek of evergreen garlands, and the joy-filled sounds of laughter, music, and story-telling reaching your as you

Copyright Asteria Books 2020

Glass Castle Meditation

make your ascent. Perhaps you will make merry with these revelers later, but for now, you know you must continue upward.

The staircase is very long, but you are not physically fatigued by the climb. You are almost floating. Still, as you ascend, you feel light-headed. When you reach the upper landing, you take a moment to catch your breath and steady yourself. You find a carved branch leaning against the wall and decide whether or not you wish to use it as a walking Staff.

In front of you are two large, intricately carved glass doors covered in symbols beyond count. Among these you notice a wren, a goat, and a holly leaf. You move to touch the doors and they swing open.

The room inside glitters with a cold, pale light. Upon a carved glass throne sits a cloven-hoofed man with a long "salt and pepper" beard. He wears a wreathed crown of Holly boughs and goat horns on his head, and his robes are grey, white, and silver furs. To his right leans a staff of Holly, encircled with its own living leaves and berries. Above his left hand hovers a large glass orb. His stormy grey eyes regard you with detached mirth. "I am Winter's King, the Holly King. Called by many names." His soft voice holds the rumble of distant thunder, and you shiver as he speaks. The scents of pine needles, orange zest, and cinnamon fill the room, and you feel alert and sharp in the coolness of his presence.

He gestures to the orb. "This is the treasure of the Glass Castle." You gaze into the glass orb and can see both misty and crystalline images swirling within it. Shapes and symbols emerge -- some from your past, some from your present, and some from your future.

The symbols swirl faster, and you become overwhelmed with information, emotion, and possibility. The Winter King catches your eye with his piercing gaze and stops your crystalline vision with his chilling voice. "I have a message for you," he says. He leans forward and whispers his secret message in your ear. [long pause]

He bids you farewell. You hurry down the glass staircase, past the festooned hall, and through the mirrored doors. The goats wait for you in the snowy courtyard. You climb into the sleigh and they soar into the air, accompanied again by the wrens, as you fly back across the misty moat. The goats take you beneath the snow clouds and over the tops of the holly trees, landing gently in the same grove where you began. You thank them all, and especially your black goat guide, before settling beneath a large holly tree to rest.

Copyright Asteria Books 2020

North Gate Meditation

You awaken in the darkness on a windy, snow-covered plain. The frozen ground crunches beneath your hands and feet as you rise and look to the North, trying to make out the shape of the gate you know must lie ahead in the darkness. A gust of icy wind greets you, making your eyes water.

The plain is nearly barren in all directions, with the exception of a naked Willow tree, its branches sparkling in the cold, clear starlight. You walk carefully through the frozen landscape, having made the tree your first goal.

When you arrive under the drooping branches, you find a staff leaning against the trunk. You examine the markings and decorations on the staff and then continue along your northward path, now utilizing the staff for greater stability on the sometimes treacherous and slippery earth.

A movement in the shadows catches your eye and you turn your head just as it reaches your side and brushes your leg. The cat stands for a moment, its back arched and looking up the path you are walking before lifting its face to look at you. It meows. You reach down to touch the friendly animal, but it bolts forward, just out of your reach. It meows again and takes a few steps forward. You follow, and the cat picks up the pace, jogging on its silent, padded paws.

A night bird swooshes very close to your head, startling you. You can see the faintest paleness of its wings, but you can hear no evidence of it, even as you watch it fly ahead. Far away, you think you hear the hoot of barred owl.

Looming ahead of you is a stony archway - two large rock pillars capped by a third massive stone. A dolman. Beyond this strange gate, you see nothing but more of the same night-covered and frozen plain. You could easily walk around this dolman door, but instead, you walk right up to it. The cat rubs its side against one of the pillars, and you can see that the owl has perched on top. The dolman is covered with strange markings and symbols carved into the stones. Some are unfamiliar to you, but others have deep meaning in your mind. (Pause.) You see an owl with large eyes carved into one of the rocks along with the Willow tree rune and a cat.

Your ears perceive a whistled tune as you pass beyond the arch, and your eyes search the darkness for the one who is blowing the eerie music. You can see so little that you must trust to your hearing instead, and you follow the sound until you are aware of a small, darkly-cloaked figure standing just a few yards away. You are close enough now to hear her breathing.

The small figure holds up her hand in warning. "Come closer, Child.. But be

North Gate Meditation

wary of your footing." You walk forward more slowly, using your staff to judge the safety of each step. As you breech those last few yards between you and Her, you are aware of a wind that seems to come from the ground, and you realize that you are standing together at the edge of a steep and treacherous cliff. You brace yourself and know that you are secure, even at this height.

Turning your attention to Cloaked One, you can see very little of her face, as it is shrouded in both her hood and the darkness of the night. Her out-held hand is gloved. You cannot clearly see the color of her hair, although you can see an interplay of light and dark in the strands. She holds a staff, and sometimes it seems she leans upon it. At other times, it seems like a weapon she is holding at martial ease.

Her voice is clear and ageless.

She speaks to you. "This is a place of knowledge, of wisdom, and of strategy. It is a place of contemplation, a place of counsel. It can be bitterly cold here, and the Truth that you seek can be both illusory and fleeting." (Pause.) She hangs a lantern from the end of your staff and lights the wick. "But knowledge and thought are not always cold comforts. They can be the light one needs on the darkest nights of the soul."

She lashes a sharpened metal tip onto her staff, transforming it into a spear. She pulls a single arrow from the quiver at her side, removing the arrowhead and feathers. She holds the newly fashioned wand in one hand and holds up a single finger of the other. "Weapons are tools wielded for either attack or defense. But they are just tools. The most useful tools can be used in both peace and war." She pokes you with her finger. "And the greatest tools are the ones that lie within." She gives you the wand, grasping your hand for a moment and whispering a message only for you. (Long pause.)

You thank her, and after a moment more of looking at you, she turns back to look over the cliff. Knowing that the time has come to leave, you turn and walk back through the darkness.

You pass out of the dolman and cross the plain, led once more by the cat and owl. You pass under the Willow tree, returning the staff that you borrowed. Sitting down again in the frozen field, you close your eyes and breathe deeply, coming back to yourself.

Copyright Asteria Books 2020

Castle of Revelry Meditation

You awake to find yourself in a forest of birch trees just before dawn. It is early spring and the air is damp and cold. Paperwhite narcissus nod their heads beneath the stands of slender white birch. You face the east, and notice a rosy glow in the sky there.

Suddenly from a thicket a rabbit darts forth. It stops in your path and sits upright on its haunches observing you. Its dark sparking eyes regard you coolly. It twitches its nose at you, as if to say, "follow me!" It turns slowly to the east and dashes through the forest. You hurry eastward after the rabbit. As you follow it you begin to realize that it is leading you along a clear and straight path through the forest, although you had not noticed the path before.

The rosy glow of the eastern sky deepens and shifts to soft coral pink and brilliant orange. A flock of geese fly overhead. They honk urgently as they sail through the flaming sky. You can feel yourself beginning to warm as you move swiftly down the path towards the growing light. You can see that the rabbit has stopped ahead in a bright clearing.

As you enter the clearing you are amazed to see a lake of fire flowing by it. Bright tongues of flame lick the bank like waves, and molten lava mixes with pure fire along the shores of this mysterious lake. The rabbit dashes along the riverbank and stops to look back at you, drawing your attention to a small boat tethered to the shore.

You approach the boat and notice a robed and hooded boatman within. His face is hidden in the shadows of his hood, but he stretches forth a pale bony hand towards you. You reach into your crane bag and pull forth a gold coin. On the face of the coin is the profile of a beautiful and merry lady with ornately braided hair. On its reverse is a lantern and two crossed brooms.

You place the coin into the boatman's skeletal hand and climb into the boat. The boatman pushes off and begins to row you eastward through the lake of fire. The heat of the lake is immense, but also comforting. You realize that this heat is the warmth of spring. It is the heat that melts snows and encourages tender plants to grow. The light of the lake is intense, but also beautiful. You understand that this light is the light of the sun at dawn. It paints the sky in brilliant shades of orange, rose, and crimson.

Through the waves of heat ahead of the boat you notice an island. On the island is a gleaming golden castle. The castle shines in the light of the fiery lake. It is constructed of solid

Copyright Asteria Books 2022

Castle of Revelry Meditation

gold set with yellow topaz and its many turrets are festooned with banners and flags of every color. As you near the shore you can hear joyful music and laughter pouring forth from the castle.

The boat is now ashore on this merry island. You climb out of the boat and as you set your feet upon the island you notice that they feel very light, as if imbued with natural grace. You feel warmth and joy flowing upwards from the land to your heart and all of your being is infused with comfort and contentment. The scent of a warm savory feast greets your nose, and lingers there with the smells of frankincense and amber. You smile widely and warmly.

The immense golden doors of the castle open to you, revealing a shining hall filled with laughter and song. The golden hall is draped with banners of many colors, and in it is an impossibly long table of birch. Seated at this table are heroes of myth and legend. Cuchulain feasts on roasted meat and golden mead while Odysseus and Finn MacCool laughingly trade boasts and riddles. Hercules drinks deeply of the toast that Boudica proclaims in honor of a song Orpheus has just sung. From beside him Taliesin smiles at you and waves you over. "We've been expecting you," he says merrily. You ask him where you are and he replies, "There are many names for this place. Some call it Valhalla. Others call it Hell. I call it the Castle of Revelry. It is the home of Queen Hulda and her golden lantern."

Taliesin points to a set of double doors near you. The doors are solid gold and covered in countless finely sculpted symbols. Among these you notice a goose and a broom. You move to touch the doors and they swing open at your gesture.

The room inside is bathed in brilliant white light. It blinds your vision for a moment, and when your eyes adjust you see a pale and beautiful woman with elaborately braided red hair. She is seated on throne of solid topaz and she wears a dress of gold. Her eyes are the color of amber flecked with gold and she is smiling warmly at you. To her right is a table with an object upon it that shines so brightly you cannot bear to look directly upon it. To her left is a broom with an intricately carved handle and a brush of birch twigs.

"I am called Hulda" she says. Her voice is a mixture of sultry, dusky alto and the tinkling of tiny brass bells. You can taste warm honey in your mouth when she speaks. The scent of frankincense and cinnamon fills your nostrils. Your entire being is infused with radiant heat and you feel slightly dizzy.

Copyright Asteria Books 2022

Castle of Revelry Meditation

She smiles more deeply and gestures to the shining object to her right. "This is the treasure of Castle of Revelry." At her words your eyes adjust to its radiance and you can see that it is a golden lantern. Its light shines the semblance of pictures, stories, and riddles on the golden walls of the room. Your head fills with music and poetry as you look at its light.

Hulda laughs. Her laugh is intoxicating and you can feel your head swimming in confusion and wonder. Hulda leans forward on her throne and captures your gaze. "I have a message for you," she says. She takes your hand and whispers her secret message in your ear.

Hulda bids you farewell and kisses your cheek. Your flesh stings at the hot touch of her lips. The lantern beside her brightens like the white hot sun and you begin to sweat. You take your leave of the room hastily, disoriented by the heat and light.

Back in the great hall heroes continue to feast boisterously. Two yellow haired Valkyries gently take you by the arms and lead you through the hall. Taliesin winks at you as you pass by. The Valkyries escort you out the door of the Castle and into the boat you arrived in. They pay the boatman a gold token and you drift swiftly back across the lake of fire to the gray-skied birch forest. Geese honk in the distance. At the shore of the gray spring land is the start of a footpath, the same straight path that the rabbit first lead you down. You follow the path back through the birch forest, past the thicket and the paperwhite narcissus, back to the place where you awoke. You lay down in the cool, damp springtime forest and rest.

This meditation was written by Glaux in 2012 for use within the Spiral Castle Tradition of Witchcraft.

Copyright Asteria Books 2022

East Gate Meditation

You awake in a broad, newly plowed field just before sunrise. The world to the West is still dark, murky and sleepy-looking, while to your East a fiery sun is beginning to rise on the pale lanscape. The chill of an early spring morning clings to you. The soil beneath you is rich and dark, marked in deep furrows from the plow. The fertile, damp smell of the land fills your nose as you breathe deeply and begin walking toward the East, toward the growing light.

A fence with a gate is ahead of you across the field, and you can hear the lowing of cattle now. As you get closer, you can see the shapes of the cows becoming clearer. You open the gate and cross into the grassy pasture where the cows graze and move lazily. They watch you intermittently as you continue across their field. One of the cattle watches you intensely, but it is no cow. This bull shifts his weight impatiently while keeping his gaze fixed on you. You continue your path across the field, hurrying as the sun continues to rise, and light and heat start perking up the countryside.

A hedge of dense, knotted Hawthorn trees spreads along the next fence, and you spot the gate in its midst. You cross through the old farm gate as you take notice of the trees. Their bright white blooms and long thorns both welcome and warn.

In the glinting light of the sunrise, you see bees bobbing and buzzing along the Hawthorns. You watch them dance as they work. One lands lightly on your hand, and you know that it has no intention of stinging you. Raising your hand to eye level, you look at the tiny creature for a moment. Its feet tickle your hand, making your skin twitch, and it flies away to the East, where you lose sight of it in the now bright sunrise.

Looking along the landscape in the direction that the bee flew, you see a mound of earth. As you focus your attention on it, you're certain you hear a clinking sound, as well. Curious, you continue your eastward path until you find yourself standing in front of a small hill with a stony cave door. Strange markings have been carved and painted onto the stones around the mouth of the cave and you take a moment to look at them.

You're certain now that the sounds you heard came from within the cave, and you can see the glow of firelight coming from deep within. The wet, mustiness of the cave's scent is mixed with the smell of burning coals, here.

The cave path is smooth and descends slightly as it curves naturally to the left.

Copyright Asteria Books 2020

East Gate Meditation

The sounds have grown distinctly louder since you first heard them. No longer a vague clinking, you now hear the rhythmic beating of metal against metal - tap, tap, bang; tap, tap, bang. The cave is both hot and bright here, and as you round the last corner, you see a large chamber filled with both the glinting metal of finished projects and the carbon-blackened metal of work waiting to be done. Plowshares and picthforks lean against one wall, accompanied by spears and swords. In a far corner, you see the glint of gold and silver wrought into fine filigrees and tooled with delicate markings. You also see pieces of unshaped, untouched metal, dull but full of potential

A fire in a ringed enclosure dominates the middle of the room, and a large man is silhouetted by its flame. His skin looks burnished from the heat and soot, and you watch as his powerful form easily handles the bellows, the large hammer upon the massive anvil.

His eyes glint as he sees you, and he holds you in a piercing stare, though he doesn't stop his movement and work. Tap, tap, bang; tap, tap, bang. You notice the metal in his hands and you recognize what he is making. He places the object back into the forge fire, allowing it to regain a red-hot glow before removing it again. Tap, tap, bang.

Still working, he speaks to you. "The forge of the Witch Father holds much magic and mystery. This is a place of transformation, of alchemy, of great power."

He beckons you toward him and places your hand upon the anvil. It is very hot, but it doesn't burn you. Holding your hand upon the anvil with his own, he looks into your eyes and speaks a message only for you.

You thank him, and after a moment more of looking at you, he resumes his work. Knowing that the time has come to leave, you turn and walk back up the cave path, curving on a right-hand path now toward the fresh air and daylight.

You pass again by the bees, busy in the Hawthorns, and by the cattle in their pasture. Returning to the plowed field, you take a moment before sitting down in the rich soil. You close your eyes and breathe deeply, coming back to yourself.

Copyright Asteria Books 2020

Castle of Stone Meditation

You awake in a forest of oak trees at midday. Red breasted robins sing from the trees, and the forest is green with the radiance of nature in summertime.

A rustling from behind you causes you to turn around quickly. Only a few yards from you is a magnificent stag. His antlers are as broad as your arms when fully outstretched. His hide is rich russet. He bears seven tines on each antler.

The stag gives you a loud snort and tosses his head. You are consumed with a desire to capture this roebuck, and as if it knew what you were thinking, the stag suddenly bolts away from you. You give chase. You run through the oak forest as quickly as any deer could, bounding over creeks and fallen trees. You can see the stag ahead of you, and you keep pace behind him. You run at full tilt past mighty oak trees that dwarf you and your quarry.

The stag clears the forest ahead of you and enters a green grass field. You follow behind him. He disappears into a huge sloping green valley, and still you rush down the slope after him. Although your focus remains on chasing the stag, you notice that the valley seems to be constructed like a massive ancient earthwork. In the center of the valley rises a high grassy hill and upon this hill appears to be a stone fort of some kind. The stag pauses briefly at the base of the great hill and then bounds up it.

You reach the base of the hill and are momentarily daunted by its steepness and height. Yet you find force of will to begin the climb upwards. Up the hill you climb, your legs scrambling. Up the hill of grass, your fingers struggling to find holds in the emerald green turf. Up to the top of the earthwork mound, your arms aching from pulling along the weight of your body.

Although you are nearly exhausted you have reached the top of the hill. You do not see the stag but you notice that you are near a set of enormous oaken doors. The doors are the entrance to a massive fort of gray stone. The fort's turrets are adorned with the standards of warriors and kings. From within the fort you can hear sounds of steel clashing and voices yelling commands.

You approach the doors and knock, but they remain closed to you. To your side you hear a snort. It is the stag. He walks up to the oak doors and touches them with his antlers. The

Copyright Asteria Books 2022

Castle of Stone Meditation

doors open with a wooden thud.

Within the fort is a field where thousands of warriors from myth and legend are training for battle. Achilles wrestles with Lancelot as Parzival and Sigurd cross steel. Spartans train next to samurai. You watch as Scathac demonstrates for Hector how she wields a spear. A voice from behind addresses you. You turn to see it is the Arthurian knight Sir Gawain. "We've been expecting you," he says gravely. You ask him where you are and he replies, "There are many names for this place. Some call it Troy Town. Others call it Camelot. I call it the Castle of Stone. It is the home of King Cernunnos and his stone bowl."

Gawain points to a set of double doors across the field. The doors are of oak intricately carved with countless symbols. Among these you notice a stag and a robin. You move to touch the doors and they swing open at your gesture.

Inside the room is a tan and muscular man with thick brown hair. He wears a crown of antlers. He is seated on a throne of stone and he wears tanned leather and a green cloak. His eyes are as green as emeralds and he is smiling broadly at you. To his right is a table with a stone saucer on it. To his left is a staff of oak bearing leaves, catkins, and acorns.

"I am called Cernunnos" he says. His voice is deep and musical and reminds you of the sounds of animals. You can feel your pulse quicken as he speaks. The scent of moss and musk fills your nostrils. Your eyes widen in wonder as you realize that his antlered crown isn't really a crown at all. He has antlers as broad and majestic as the stag you chased to this place.

His eyes sparkle as he gestures to the stone saucer to his right. "This is the treasure of the Stone Castle." You approach the bowl and peer into it. Inside of the bowl it is very black. There are three stones and a silver spiral floating in the darkness. The stones roll in circles as the spiral spins and shifts. They create patterns and symbols that you understand are related to the pattern of your life. Peering deeper into the blackness of the bowl you are filled with wisdom and peace. In the bowl you begin to perceive the purpose of your life's journey and the path you must take to accomplish your destiny.

The symbols shift further, making your head spin in wonder. Cernunnos chuckles know-

Copyright Asteria Books 2022

Castle of Stone Meditation

ingly. His laugh is deep and rolling. You can feel it envelop you like the shade of a great and ancient forest. Cernunnos set his hand on your shoulder to steady you. "I have a message for you," he says. He leans forward and whispers his secret message in your ear. [long pause]

Cernunnos bids you farewell. He and shakes your hand and claps you to his chest. He is warm and smells of musk and loam. Around you the room seems to fill with foliage. Leave it hastily, hurrying past the field where warriors are training. Gawain salutes you as you pass. Beyond the oaken doors of the fort awaits the great stag that lead you here. He now regards you with a knowing respect. You follow him as he runs down the great hill and into the valley. He waits for you to catch up to him, glancing behind. You enter with him into the oak forest . The stag leaves you in an oak grove with the midday sun shining upon you. You settle in beneath a large oak tree and rest.

This meditation was written by Glaux in 2011 for use within the Spiral Castle Tradition.

Copyright Asteria Books 2022

South Gate Meditation

You open your eyes to see bright sun glinting through a leafy canopy above you. The sun is high in sky, and the day is hot and humid. You hear a buzzing of insects at the verge of the forest where the treeline gives way to the verdant farmland. Birds and small animals of all sorts fill the day with a hum of life that you can feel all the way to your bones.

You rise and look to the south, across the deep green corn field that stands just outside of the little woods. The corn is high, but you can see a hillock some distance away, and you know you want to go there. Gathering yourself together for the walk through the corn, you set your feet into the fertile soil. It is loamy and almost black in its richness.

The corn is taller than you, now that you are trying to find a path between the stalks. The smell of the soil and the chlorophyll fills your nostrils as the sun warms your scalp. You fill your lungs with the warm, earthy scent of life and lift your face to the sky. Two swans fly overhead, honking as they go.

You continue through the cornfield, following the straight tracks of the plentiful land until you hear a plodding clip-clop coming from your right. Curious, you adjust your course until you are walking in a small lane. An unbridled horse stops in the path and looks over its shoulder at you. You approach the horse, speaking in a low, soft voice. It allows you to pet its side and neck. Then, surprisingly, it bows low for you to mount it, which you easily do.

Seated upon the horse, you can see ahead on the path much more clearly than you had even from the forest's edge. You certainly see much more than you did amidst the cornstalks. The path you were taking would lead through a grove of trees before climbing the hillock that you had set as your destination. A glimmer of sparkling water told you there was a stream or pond near the hill, as well.

Riding this horse will bring you to your destination faster, but it also gives you more opportunity to revel in your senses while you make the journey. You take some time to touch the horse's short, bristled hair and feel its massive muscles moving under your legs. You smell its sweat mixed with the perfume of summer field and the approaching orchard. You see the vibrant and varied shades of green, laid with a foundation of deep brown and accented with colorful flowers and birds in the distance.

Soon, you are within the boundary of the Apple orchard. The trees are old, thick and twisted. The branches are full of both fragrant blossoms and ripe fruit. The horse bites an apple from one of the trees, and you pluck one, as well. You bite into it. The skin is firm and the flesh is juicy and sweet.

The land slopes upward and the path spirals around the hill. The horse bows again, and you dismount. You walk the path together. The orchard hugs the base of the hill on one side, but as you come around to the other side of the small Tor, you see that a stream caresses that edge. The two swans you saw in flight earlier are now gliding on the glittering ribbon of blue water.

Copyright Asteria Books 2020

South Gate Meditation

When you have almost reached the top of the hill, you see a curious gate - two large rock pillars. You must pass through these twin standing stones in order to reach the zenith of the hill. You can't see beyond this strange gate, because of the shape of the land. You cannot walk around this door. You must either go through it or turn back.

The horse whinnies and stamps one hoof into the ground, urging you to choose. The stones are carved with strange markings and symbols. Some are unfamiliar to you, but others have deep meaning in your mind. (Pause.) You see a pentagram carved into one of the rocks along with the Apple tree rune, a horse, and a swan.

A woman is singing and laughing somewhere beyond the two stones, and you step up and through. Once you are over the hump of the hill, you clearly see the woman whose voice you heard. She is voluptuous and beautiful, her body curving and ripe and delicious. She dances naked in the sunshine, her hair loose around her shoulders. Round wooden platter filled with fruits and grains surround her - some set on the ground, others on large rocks. A few round wooden discs are sitting on their sides, with heraldic designs and family emblems painted on them in vibrant colors. You recognize some of these symbolic devices.

The woman stops singing and dancing, but laughter is in her voice and the air around her seems to shimmer as she greets you. "You've had a taste of Elphame. Would you stay for the sacrificial feast?" She holds a red-handled blade toward you.

"This place is Life Overflowing. Every living thing revels and quakes in the awesome rush that is this bounty. The beauty and love and life and joy that are here for all to claim with both hands are splendorous magics, and ones that are so easily overlooked and undervalued." (Pause.) She holds one of the discs up as a shield. "Guard what is yours." Taking another shield that is filled with food, she gestures for you to take what you want. "And be generous with the bounty of Love and Life and Beauty and Joy that are given to you." She give you a round shield of your own, and a design appears on it. (Pause.)

"Life comes from Life. These bodies bring forth life while they live, and yet again when they perish and rot." She smiles, lifting her arms. "There are deep Mysteries that lie hidden in their nakedness beneath the noon-time sun. Search them out." She pulls you into an embrace and speaks a message just for you. (Long pause.)

You thank her, and she releases you, turning back to her dance and song. Knowing that the time has come to leave, you turn and walk back to the stones.

You pass out of the standing stones and wind back down the Tor, led once more by the horse. You hear the swans leave their stream as you leave the orchard. You cross the cornfield and bid the horse farewell. Sitting down again in the warm forest floor, you close your eyes and breathe deeply, coming back to yourself.

Copyright Asteria Books 2020

Castle Perilous Meditation

You open your eyes to find that it is twilight on the edge of a wooded glade. You have been resting on a bed of soft green leaves that have fallen a little early from the trees above you. Looking, you see that the forest's colors are indeed giving way from green to a faded gold, and the chill in the air is a promise you know brings brighter, richer colored leaves, crisper days, and change. A rooster crows in the distance.

Getting your bearings, you look for a path, picking your way through tall grass and Queen Anne's Lace as it brushes your knees. Golden yarrow, perfect for wildcrafting, nods at you in the glow of the westering sun. Ivy covers the ground and climbs the nearby trees as you make your way to the wood's edge, eager to taste a grape dangling lusciously from a vine that abuts the forest.

Your eyes on the heavy grapevines, you are surprised to hear mutually shocked squeaking and squealing from the forest floor near your own feet. Looking down, you see a hummock of leaves and debris. Several wild piglets emerge from beneath it, running in terror in every direction, at your approach. From across the glade, though, a new sound emerges. A deeper, angrier squeal. She, too, is frightened, but this mother Sow also sounds enraged. With spines bristling, she charges the looming threat to her unprotected young -- You!

Sidestepping just as she charges, you manage not to get gored by her fearsome tusks. She turns at the end of her run and faces you down again. A second time, she charges, and you just barely leap out of her path -- though this time, part of your garment is caught and torn on her tusk. Seeing how fast she runs, you know you will never outpace her so you look around for some other means of survival. A large rock rests at the base of the nearest tree, and above that is a limb you can reach. You hurriedly climb into the tree as she makes her third furious, slashing attempt to reach you. Her tusks

Copyright Asteria Books 2022

Castle Perilous Meditation

rip more than fabric this time, and you feel intense pain in your ankle as you climb into the tree and out of her reach at least. She slashes in vain a few more times at the tree trunk and then turns to the piglets who join her in a rush of snorts and squeals away from the glade.

You keep your place in the tree for a few moments, listening to the sound of their retreat until you are sure it is safe for you to come down again. Your ankle throbbing, you walk in the opposite direction, toward the southwest, past the grapevines, in the direction of the crowing rooster.

Limping, and with the twilight sun obscuring the colors of the landscape and making long shadows, you come to the edges of a lake. You shade your eyes for a better view, thinking you must be misperceiving the lake's hue, for it appears red to you in this light. But as you approach the shoreline, you see with clarity that the lake is indeed a Lake of Blood. It's metallic scent is sharp in your nostrils.

A small barge and its boatman wait at a short distance, and you make your way to them. In the middle of the lake, you can see an island with a castle upon it. Curious, you ask the boatman what place this is and who is its keeper. In response, he simply gestures for you to board.

Arriving on the island's shore, you feel a shiver. The chill of the autumn twilight and your brush with the Sow have left you shaken. Weariness washes through you as you observe this place. You see a well nearby, capped with a familiar symbol -- overlapping circles intersected by a line. You also see a fountain bubbling not far away. All along the path that leads to the wide, dome-capped silver castle ahead, you see cups, bowls, and cauldrons of every shape, size, and material. Some hold food. Some hold water, wine, and mead. Some are filled with coins. Some are filled with blood. Here and

Copyright Asteria Books 2022

Castle Perilous Meditation

there, you see a woman tending to the bowls -- filling or emptying them. You hear the almost musical sounds of pouring and splashing liquids, punctuated with the occasional clinking of cups.

The walls of the castle shine with a high polish in some places, and in others they have a dark, dull patina. Rivulets of rubies, garnets, red jaspers, cinnabar, red carnelian, and rhodochrosite encrust the walls in flowing designs, giving the castle the appearance that it is bleeding.

You continue to follow the path of cups and bowls through the gate of the castle and follow as it leads in a winding, labyrinthine, circular path, down into the belly of the keep. It is warmer here, below the surface, than it was above, and you feel comforted. The pulse of the lake's waves can be heard on the silvery walls around you. Someone cries out in anguish -- far away but still within the castle. Your comfort evaporates into caution, and still the waves rhythmically lap at the walls.

The winding path ends in the centermost root of the castle, with a squat chamber accessed through a rounded door. The door is covered in the same bounty of red jewels, forming patterns and symbols upon its silvery surface. Looking at the beautiful and mysterious designs, vignettes of images seem to rise up -- a sounder of wild pigs with a boar and three sows guarding their piglets. A brood of chickens with a rooster and several nesting hens. An arbor full of succulent grapes. A collection of bowls and cauldrons. What other symbols in the door can you see? (pause)

You touch the door, and a woman on the other side speaks to you. Her sonorous voice vibrates on the door you are still touching. "Come, Child," she says. "Join in my feast."

Copyright Asteria Books 2022

Castle Perilous Meditation

The door opens slowly and at its own pace. No cup-bearing maiden holds it, and there is no mechanism you can see. Nor can you stop its progress. The door opens. When you are able, you pass through it.

The chamber in which the Queen sits is lavishly bedecked with red fabrics, drapes, and cushions in every shade and texture. Her hair is silvery white, and her dark eyes have both a sharpness and a kindness in them. She wears a gown so deeply red that it is almost black.

A large cauldron filled with a savory stew bubbles nearby, and its aroma is mouth-watering. Quaiches, footed compotes, mazers, jorums, basins, coupes, goblets, chalices -- every imaginable shape of bowl and cup was overflowing with sumptuous food and drink, all arranged in lavish display. The aroma of roasted pork and chicken reaches you, and it is no surprise to see a bowl with bunches of red and white grapes. In the midst of the bounty sits an empty silver bowl with handles (a quaiche), and next to it, a red-handled knife. The bowl radiates a silver glow, as if it holds moonlight itself.

Approaching the Queen, you ask, "What is this place?" She replies, and you taste a burst of iron and salt upon your tongue. You smell myrrh, cinnamon, and cedar. "It has many names, as does its Keeper. It is called the Grail Chapel by some, the Well of Souls by Others. The Silver Castle, the Bloody Keep. Castle Perilous. I am its Queen. Some know me as Kerridwen, lady of the famous cauldron Awen. Others have sought me as Babalon, bearer of the ravenous and ever-generous cup." She winks at you, and you see a flash of the Queen before you -- changed -- with hair the color of ruby, flush with desire and the ripeness of female sexuality. "Always," she continues, "they find both wisdom and its price." She smiles to herself. "Blessing and blood."

Copyright Asteria Books 2022

Castle Perilous Meditation

She lifts the empty silver quaiche from the midst of the feast food. "You have paid a price in blood to be here," she says, glancing at your wound. "Now find blessing." As she lifts the cup to your lips, you discover it is not empty now, but instead is filled with sweet, warm, spiced red wine. You drink your fill, and the liquid freshens your mind, heals your body, and brightens your spirit. Aches and sorrows you hadn't known you carried felt lifted. The wound given by the boar sealed and healed over.

She lowers the cup, dips her finger inside, and anoints your brow with a symbol. You gaze into the dark pools of her eyes. "I have a message for you, Child," she says. (long pause)

Her message concluded, you thank the Silver Queen and offer her a gift in return. (pause)

Distantly, you hear the rooster crow and know you must leave. You squeeze your way back through the round chamber door, which is open just barely enough for you to pass, and make your way back up the labyrinth and into the twilit dusk. At the shoreline, the boatman waits for you, this time with hand outstretched for payment. You reach into your craneskin bag and retrieve a silver coin minted on one side with an image of the Queen and on the reverse with the two-handled cup from which you just drank. Giving him this payment, he once again ferries you across the sanguine sea.

You follow the short path back past the grape arbors to the now-empty autumn glade where your journey began, laying yourself down once more upon the bed of leaves.

Copyright Asteria Books 2022

West Gate Meditation

You open your eyes to see that you sitting in a large, freshly harvested field. The damp earth is stubbled with the stalks of the grains that have been hewn down, the farmer's scythe resting on a nearby fence. Looking to the West, you see the Sun sinking toward a large pond.

You rise and start walking toward the pond, squelching through the muddy field. The trees that border both the field and pond have nearly dropped all of their leaves, but a few brightly colored ones still cling to the barren branches.

A movement from above startles your attention skyward, and you see a crane in flight. He is joined by two others, and they make great swooping circles in the sky - forming a triskele, spirals, and great arcs. One breaks formation and dives toward the pond, and you follow him to the water's edge. As you approach the bank, you see him standing on the edge of the water. You are surprised by his height and the uncanny way in which he stands. He regards you as you come close, still giving him a wide berth.

The crane turns his head upon his long neck, and you follow his gaze. There is a rowboat in the pond very near to where you are standing. You climb in head for the opposite shore. The sun is now very low in the sky, and you hear frog-song and the croak of many toads about you in the marshy reaches of the water. When you reach the western shore of the pond, you see a large, fat toad hopping just in front of you before disappearing into dark grey stones of a cemetery ahead.

You enter the graveyard, aware of the damp wind and the solitary Elder tree standing sentinel on the border of the plot. You read the names on a few of the mossy stones until your attention is drawn to a cairn some distance ahead. You can see that a three-legged dolmen forms the entry way, and you walk toward it, unable to see past the darkness of the doorway. This is the Western Gate, and you know that beyond it lies the Realm of the Dead. This gateway has strange markings and symbols carved into the stones. Some are unfamiliar to you, but other have deep meaning in your mind. (Pause.) You see a toad carved into one of the rocks along with the Elder tree rune, a crane, and a triskele.

Your eyes adjust to the gloom of the cairn as you pass beyond the arch, and you can see stone stair spiraling down in a left-hand circle. You follow them carefully and discover a torch set into a bracket a few feet ahead. Holding it

Copyright Asteria Books 2020

West Gate Meditation

ahead of you, you circle down and down and down into the deep belly of the graveyard until you reach a cavern that opens into a great room of stone and earth. You recognize this place as a forge, though there is no clinking of metal upon metal. The great bellows are still and no forge-fire brightens the room. The tools are neatly stored away, and you are met with silence. All is dark and quiet, and only the light of your torch reveals the large hooded and cloaked figure sitting on bench near a brimming barrel of water. A few doors and earthen pathways open into this room, and you realize that there is more than way to access this place.

The large figure holds out his hand to you, beckoning you forward. Standing before him, you can see that his face is painted as white as Death, and the outstretched hand is decorated with white bones upon his coal-black skin. A helm rests at his feet very near the quench tank.

His eyes glint from beneath his hood, and he holds you in a piercing stare.

He speaks to you. "This is a place of transformation, of alchemy, holds great power and Mystery even when it is dark and cool and quiet. The spark of life is wedded to the watery womb that is also the tomb of the world."

He scoops water from the barrel with the helmet and places it within your hands. The helm is cold and hard, and the water within looks black and deep. Holding his hands over yours, he looks into your eyes and speaks a message only for you. (Long pause.)

You thank him, and after a moment more of looking at you, he resumes his takes the helmet from you and draws his hood lower over his face. Knowing that the time has come to leave, you turn and walk back up the stairs that brought you here, curving on a right-hand path now toward the darkening night.

You pass out of the cairn and cross the graveyard and pond where the crane and Elder tree each stand guard. The frogs and toads croak in the pond as you return to the harvested field. Sitting down again in the damp and stubbly field, you close your eyes and breathe deeply, coming back to yourself.

Copyright Asteria Books 2020

Spiral Castle Tradition Spirit Allies

Spirit Allies Quick Reference

January
Wolf - guardianship, ritual, loyalty
Blackthorn - blasting, guardians
Blackbird - territoriality, omens,

February
Cat - mystery, magic, independence
Willow - divination, lunar magic, healing
Owl - wisdom, magic, night, change

March
Hare - lunar magic, fertility, swiftness
Birch - new beginnings, healing, cleansing
Goose - feminine power, questing

April
Serpent - rebirth, initiation, wisdom
Ash - connections between concepts
Moth - transformation, illumination

May
Cow - fertility, prosperity, nourishment
Hawthorn - fertility, cleansing, protection
Bee - fertility, community, celebration

June
Stag - nobility, pride, grace
Oak - security, steadfastness, vigor
Robin - growth, territoriality, fire

July
Hound - loyalty, protection, guidance
Elm - elves, light, purification, wisdom
Eagle - light, renewal, intelligence, courage

August
Horse - travel, power, freedom, civilization
Apple - beauty, choices, love, inspiration
Swan - shape-shifting, love, grace, beauty

September
Boar - hunt, search, putting up a fight
Vine - prophesy, prediction and omens
Hawk - visions, guardianship, messenger

October
Salmon - wisdom, knowledge, inspiration
Hazel - wisdom, intuition, creativity
Lapwing - resourcefulness, distraction

Samhain
Toad - transformation, inner visions, death
Elder - death and rebirth, change
Crane - remembrance, past lives, mystery

November
Fox - trickster, invisibility, shape-shifting
Rowan - protection, psychic power
Raven - shape-shifting, trickster, initiation

December
Goat - surefooted, achievement, sacrifice
Holly - protection, balance, unity, defense,
Wren - resourcefulness, boldness, sacrifice

Copyright Asteria Books 2015

January Spirit Allies

WOLF *(Faol)* - guardianship, ritual, loyalty, free spirit, intuition, shadow
BLACKTHORN *(Straif)* - blasting magic, guardians, boundaries, no choice
BLACKBIRD *(Dru Dhubh)* - territoriality, omens, enchantment, gateways

Wolf allows you to go beyond "normal" barriers to learn and grow. Wolf reminds us of the inner power and strength that come when we are alone, and it teaches us to know our deepest selves. Sadly, the Wolf is highly misunderstood and has often been shown as an adversary to humans in movies and stories. This animal embodies many qualities of the hound, but with a wildness not to be found in the domesticated dog. It is valued for its affinities with humans. Wolves are highly social, friendly and intelligent.

The Blackthorn is a tree of winter. The fruits of the tree, known as sloes, ripen and sweeten only after the first frost. The blackthorn has vicious thorns that can cause painful infections and forms dense thickets when left to spread on its own. Blackthorn's Gaelic name "straif" has connections with the English word strife. This, combined with its use in cudgel-making, accounts for its associations with cursing and blasting magic.

The Blackbird notoriously sings at twilight and dawn -- the liminal times -- making it a guardian of the gateways and between-places. This makes it an ideal totem of January, the time when one year ends and another begins. The blackbird, or ousel, is the first animal Culhwch asks regarding the whereabouts of Mabon, as it was the oldest animal that Culhwch knew of. Again, the blackbird stands as the gateway to the animals that remain in the quest: stag, owl, eagle, and salmon.

Copyright Asteria Books 2015

Blackthorn

Prunus spinosa

Folk Names: Straif, sloe, sloe plum, wishing thorn, faery tree
Gender: Feminine
Planet: Mars, Saturn
Element: Earth, Fire
Deity: Morrigan
Powers: The inevitability of Death, Protection and Revenge, Strife and Negativity

HEALING: Sloe berries are a very bitter tonic. They are astringent, stimulate the metabolism, clean the blood, and are used as a laxative and diuretic. They help with indigestion, eczema, herpes, allergies, colds, catarrh, neurosis, weak heart, kidney stones, skin, bladder, and prostrate problems. They disperse toxins. They can be prepared as a juice, syrup, jelly, jam, wine or sloe gin beverage. They are excellent when combined with apples in a jam. Try making a blackthorn tincture, with a sloe gin base!

MAGIC AND RITUAL: The Blackthorn is a tree of winter. The fruits of the tree, known as sloes, ripen and sweeten only after the first frost. A cold spring is traditionally known as a blackthorn winter, as the blackthorn often bears its white blossoms while winter's chill still hangs in the air. The blackthorn has vicious thorns that can cause painful infections, and forms dense thickets when left to spread on its own. It has tough dark black bark, hence its name. Blackthorn's Gaelic name "straif" has connections with the English word strife. Its thorns as sometimes used in witchcraft as "pins" to pierce wax poppets. Some legends attest that the witches mark was made upon the flesh of a witch with a blackthorn thorn. Blackthorn's wood is used in the creation of the Irish cudgel or shillelagh, which is an old traditional tool of the male leader of a coven. Blackthorn staves and wands are used in blasting/cursing magic.

Copyright Asteria Books 2017

Wolf

Canis lupus

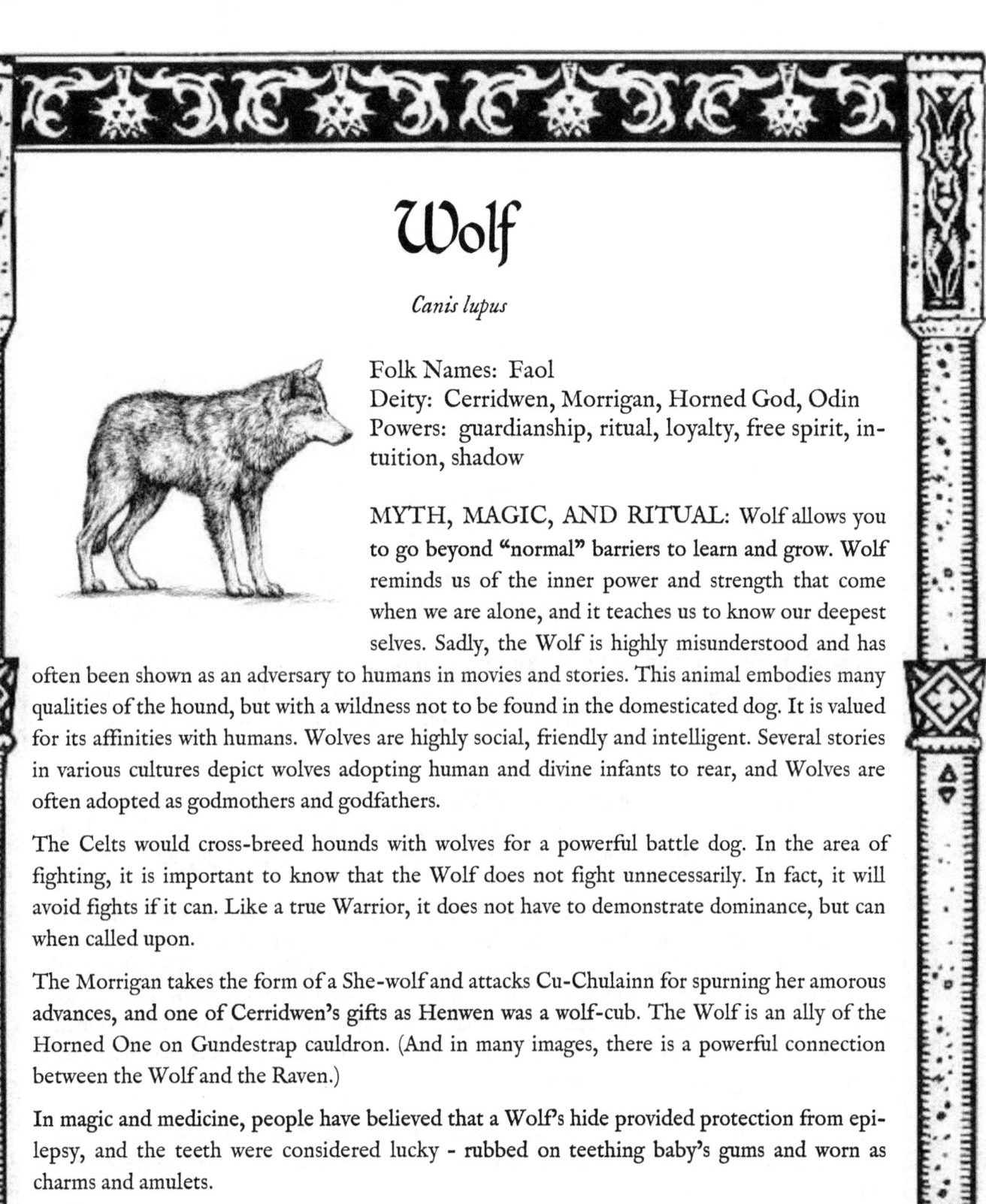

Folk Names: Faol
Deity: Cerridwen, Morrigan, Horned God, Odin
Powers: guardianship, ritual, loyalty, free spirit, intuition, shadow

MYTH, MAGIC, AND RITUAL: Wolf allows you to go beyond "normal" barriers to learn and grow. Wolf reminds us of the inner power and strength that come when we are alone, and it teaches us to know our deepest selves. Sadly, the Wolf is highly misunderstood and has often been shown as an adversary to humans in movies and stories. This animal embodies many qualities of the hound, but with a wildness not to be found in the domesticated dog. It is valued for its affinities with humans. Wolves are highly social, friendly and intelligent. Several stories in various cultures depict wolves adopting human and divine infants to rear, and Wolves are often adopted as godmothers and godfathers.

The Celts would cross-breed hounds with wolves for a powerful battle dog. In the area of fighting, it is important to know that the Wolf does not fight unnecessarily. In fact, it will avoid fights if it can. Like a true Warrior, it does not have to demonstrate dominance, but can when called upon.

The Morrigan takes the form of a She-wolf and attacks Cu-Chulainn for spurning her amorous advances, and one of Cerridwen's gifts as Henwen was a wolf-cub. The Wolf is an ally of the Horned One on Gundestrap cauldron. (And in many images, there is a powerful connection between the Wolf and the Raven.)

In magic and medicine, people have believed that a Wolf's hide provided protection from epilepsy, and the teeth were considered lucky - rubbed on teething baby's gums and worn as charms and amulets.

In the Americas, the Wolf is seen as the spirit of free and unspoiled wilderness. There are several types of Wolves in this part of the World - the Red Wolf, the Mexican Wolf, the Timber Wolf (or Gray Wolf), and the Arctic Wolf. In size, they are smaller than people imagine (about like a good-sized German Shepherd).

Copyright Asteria Books 2021

Blackbird

Turdus merula

Folk Names: Dru dubh
Deity: Rhiannon, Tubal Cain (and smith Gods)
Powers: territoriality, omens, enchantment, gateways

MYTH, MAGIC, AND RITUAL: The Blackbird notoriously sings at twilight and dawn -- the liminal times -- making it a guardian of the gateways and between-places. This makes it an ideal totem of January, the time when one year ends and another begins.

Rhiannon's birds were said to be blackbirds, as they are enchanted birds of the otherworld. They were said to "wake the dead and lull the living to sleep", another nod to their liminal singing, and a hint that the blackbird is capable of the shamanic work of dreamwalking and spirit communication.

The blackbird, or ousel, is the first animal Culhwch asks regarding the whereabouts of Mabon, as it was the oldest animal that Culhwch knew of. Again, the blackbird stands as the gateway to the animals that remain in the quest: stag, owl, eagle, and salmon.

The blackbird in Culhwch's tale, here named the Blackbird of Cilgwri, answers that he is so old that he found a smith's anvil when he first came to Cilgwri, but that time was so long ago that the anvil has long since worn away from his pecking at it. The blackbird is especially sacred to blacksmiths. In Irish ghobadhu means both blackbird and blacksmith. The blackbird has the unique habit of bashing snail shells and nuts on stones, much as a smith would use an anvil. For these reasons, and his coal-black feathers, the blackbird is sacred to smith gods, such as Tubal Cain.

Blackbirds are territorial, and seeing two together is considered a sign of good luck. It is also good luck to have a blackbird build its nest on your roof, or anywhere near your home.

In North America the red-winged blackbird is perhaps the most iconic of blackbirds. One Native American legend states that the blackbird tried to warn the people of a village that a man had set the marsh on fire. The man angrily threw stones at the bird, wounding its wings and staining them blood red. Thus, the blackbird is a bringer of omens, and of self-sacrifice.

Copyright Asteria Books 2021

February Spirit Allies

CAT - (*Cath*) mystery, magic, secrecy, independence, sensuality
WILLOW - (*Saille*) divination, lunar magic, healing, night
OWL - (*Comhachag*) wisdom, magic, night, inner visions, change

The Cat is an animal of mystery and magic, largely because she is more active and communicative at night. She is capable of observing multiple worlds (physical and non-physical) at one time without making decision or passing judgment. She is very independent, accepting affection on her own terms and warning of caution and respect. The Cat is also a symbol of guardianship, attachment and sensuality.

The Willow has very feminine overtones. It is strongly lunar in its energy pattern. Willows are found at the edges of streams and lakes, giving them the elemental powers of both earth and water. The Willow is a water-loving tree and responds to the lunar cycle. Willow is thought to have healing properties over diseases of a damp nature. The Anglo-Saxon *welig* (willow) means pliancy, and willow is certainly flexible.

In the western tradition, Owl is inextricably associated with the quality of wisdom. This is due in part to its ancient associations with the Goddess Athena and also with its large forward-facing eyes. In folklore, the Owl is associated with death, night, and silence. The Owl is much noted for its unique feather and wing structure which allows it to fly silently. Owl is associated with betrayal of a spouse in the pursuit of being true to oneself, as we see in the stories of both Blodewudd and Lilith.

Copyright Asteria Books 2015

Willow

Salix spp.

Folk Names: Basket Willow, Bay Willow, Black Willow, Brittle Willow, Crack Willow, Daphne Willow, Knackweide, Laurel Willow, Lorbeerweide, Osier Blanc, Pussy Willow, Saille, Salicis Cortex, Violet Willow, Weidenrinde, White Willow, With, Withy
Gender: Feminine
Planet: Moon
Element: Water
Deity: Brighid, Artemis, Ceres, Hecate, Persephone, Hera, Mercury, Belili, Belinus
Powers: Clairvoyance, compassion, consecration, determination, divination, endings, exorcism, gentleness, love, magic, to prevent nightmares, to prevent theft, release, spell breaking, necromancy

HEALING: Willow bark acts a lot like aspirin, so it is used for pain, including headache, muscle pain, menstrual cramps, rheumatoid arthritis (RA), osteoarthritis, gout, and a disease of the spine called ankylosing spondylitis. Willow bark's pain relieving potential has been recognized throughout history. Willow bark was commonly used during the time of Hippocrates, when people were advised to chew on the bark to relieve pain and fever. Today, tincture and tea made from the bark is more common. Willow bark is also used for fever, the common cold, flu, and weight loss.

MAGIC AND RITUAL: The willow is a water-loving tree and responds to the lunar cycle. The Anglo-Saxon *welig* (willow) means pliancy, and withy branches (or osiers) are cut from the willow to weave baskets, mend fences, and form frames for coracles (a type of small boat). The willow is thought to have healing properties over diseases of a damp nature. It is considered as a symbol of fertility and the female cycle. The willow can bring an awareness of your feminine side and is often associated with the Goddess Brighid because her festival of Imbolc falls within the influence of the willow tree. In the American Folkloric Witchcraft tradition the willow, also known by its folk name "the tree of enchantment", is sacred to the Black Goddess. As trees of enchantment, willow groves were used by poets, artists, musicians, priests and priestesses as places of meditation and inspiration. Wands cut from willow are known as "willie wains" and are said to contain the powers of water and the moon. Witches' brooms are often bound with willow. Magic mists are raised in folk tales by aid of the willow.

Copyright Asteria Books 2017

Cat

Felis catus

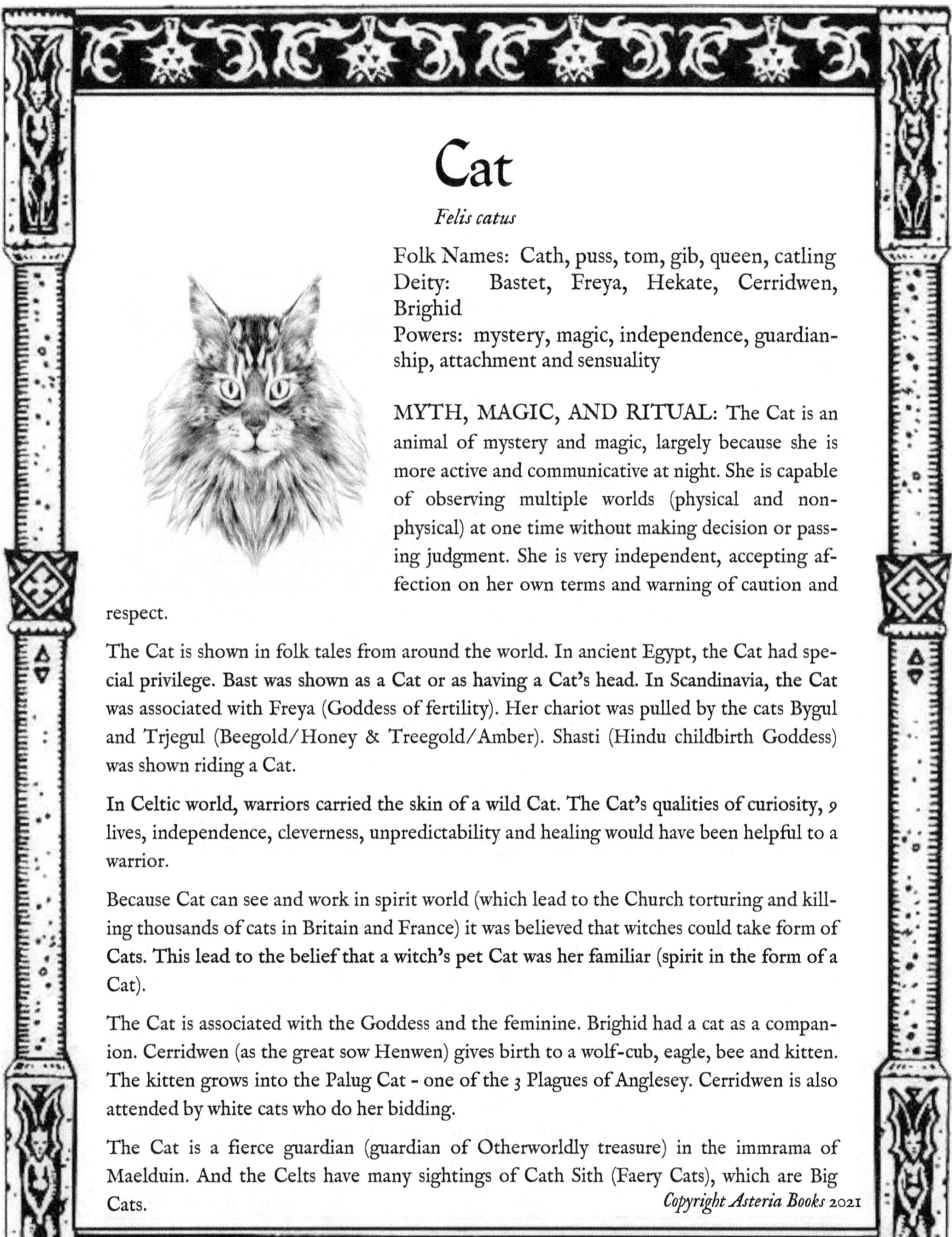

Folk Names: Cath, puss, tom, gib, queen, catling
Deity: Bastet, Freya, Hekate, Cerridwen, Brighid
Powers: mystery, magic, independence, guardianship, attachment and sensuality

MYTH, MAGIC, AND RITUAL: The Cat is an animal of mystery and magic, largely because she is more active and communicative at night. She is capable of observing multiple worlds (physical and non-physical) at one time without making decision or passing judgment. She is very independent, accepting affection on her own terms and warning of caution and respect.

The Cat is shown in folk tales from around the world. In ancient Egypt, the Cat had special privilege. Bast was shown as a Cat or as having a Cat's head. In Scandinavia, the Cat was associated with Freya (Goddess of fertility). Her chariot was pulled by the cats Bygul and Trjegul (Beegold/Honey & Treegold/Amber). Shasti (Hindu childbirth Goddess) was shown riding a Cat.

In Celtic world, warriors carried the skin of a wild Cat. The Cat's qualities of curiosity, 9 lives, independence, cleverness, unpredictability and healing would have been helpful to a warrior.

Because Cat can see and work in spirit world (which lead to the Church torturing and killing thousands of cats in Britain and France) it was believed that witches could take form of Cats. This lead to the belief that a witch's pet Cat was her familiar (spirit in the form of a Cat).

The Cat is associated with the Goddess and the feminine. Brighid had a cat as a companion. Cerridwen (as the great sow Henwen) gives birth to a wolf-cub, eagle, bee and kitten. The kitten grows into the Palug Cat - one of the 3 Plagues of Anglesey. Cerridwen is also attended by white cats who do her bidding.

The Cat is a fierce guardian (guardian of Otherworldly treasure) in the immrama of Maelduin. And the Celts have many sightings of Cath Sith (Faery Cats), which are Big Cats.

Copyright Asteria Books 2021

Owl

Strigiformes

Folk Names: Comhachag, strix, bubo, hooter, night-raven, owlet, howlet
Deity: Blodeuwedd, Cailleach, Lilith
Powers: Wisdom, magic, night, inner visions, change

MYTH, MAGIC, AND RITUAL: In the western tradition, Owl is inextricably associated with the quality of wisdom. This is due in part to its ancient associations with the Goddess Athena, and also with its large forward-facing eyes. In Welsh tradition, the Owl is among the most ancient of animals. It was the third animal that Culhwch asks regarding the whereabouts of Mabon. Whereas the salmon of knowledge offers a general kind of wisdom, the owl is symbolic of a more circumspect wisdom. It is objective and detached from the mundane. Owl watches and waits, in ruined castles, church towers, barns, and hollow trees. The owl is symbolic of esoteric wisdom and secrecy.

In folklore, the Owl is associated with death, night, and silence. The Owl is much noted for its unique feather and wing structure which allows it to fly silently.

Owls have acute hearing, and use a kind of echo-location to hunt their prey. The owl can be a symbol of both silence and the ability to hear those things that others might miss. An owl totem can be a sign that one would benefit from listening more.

One of the Celtic names for owl is "Cailleach-oidchce" (crone of the night), linking the owl with the Black Goddess as the Cailleach. The Black Goddess is the Lady of life-in-death and the call of the owl is seen as an omen of both the birth of a girl or the death of a man. This ability to foretell the future links the owl with clairvoyance and astral travel.

The owl is a bird set apart. She hunts at night, and is mobbed by other birds -- notably crows -- during the day. The Welsh point to the story of Blodeuwedd, the flower-bride of Lleu Llaw Gyffes, for the reason behind this. She was transformed into an owl as punishment for betraying her husband.

Copyright Asteria Books 2021

March Spirit Allies

Hare (*Gearr*) - lunar magic, fertility, sensitivity, swiftness, intuition
Birch (*Beithe*) - new beginnings, healing, cleansing
Goose (*Geadh*) - feminine power, springtime, questing, vigilance

Rabbits are notorious breeders, and are a symbol of the fertility of spring. The expression "mad as a March hare" comes from the rabbit's habit of fighting, courting, and mating during the early spring. The tradition of the "Easter bunny", or Eostre rabbit, reflects this springtime symbolism. Rabbits have always been associated with witchcraft. They are sacred to Hecate and have the peculiar habit of gathering in a circle, the "hare's parliament". Witches are often thought to be able to transform into a rabbit.

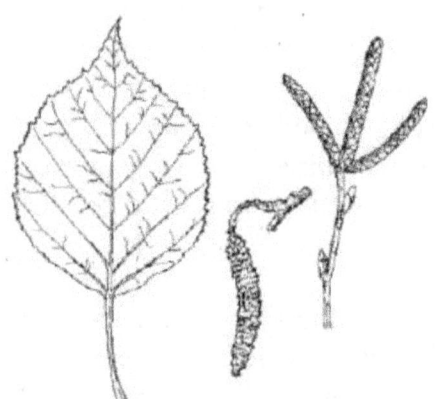

Birch Trees represent the Otherworld. This tree is the first to bud and is considered a sign that spring is just around the corner. It is a symbol of new beginnings, the start of new plans and taking significant steps in a forward direction. The Birch is considered a protective wood for women, as it is associated with safe childbirth and protection from the Underworld. It is the wood most commonly used to kindle the magical fire.

The goose is the companion of that ancient and powerful goddess, Hulda, as Mother Goose. The goose is a fierce defender of its family and territory, and many ancient gates and warrior's graves have been adorned with the motif of the goose. We often speak of "a wild goose chase" as geese are notoriously difficult to capture or kill. The goose is a symbol of early springtime, as it denotes both snow and returning light. The goose who lays the golden egg is laying the growing sun of spring.

Copyright Asteria Books 2015

Birch

Betula alba

Folk Names: Beithe, Bereza, Berke, Beth, Bouleau, Lady of the Woods, White Birch, Canoe Birch, Paper Birch
Gender: Feminine
Planet: Venus
Element: Water
Deity: Thor
Powers: Protection, exorcism, purification, fortune, change, good luck

HEALING: Astringent, diuretic, diaphoretic. The leaf tea made by infusion is said to eliminate gravel and dissolve kidney stones when taken daily for a time, 1 to 1 1/2 cups a day. It can also be used as a wash or bath additive for skin problems. A decoction of the leaves is sometimes recommended for baldness (or try the fresh expressed juice). If you have trouble sleeping, try the decoction before going to bed as a mild sedative. For chronic or severe skin problems, use a decoction of birch bark as a wash or bath additive. The inner bark contains on oil which is sometimes substituted for wintergreen in liniment.

MAGIC AND RITUAL: It has a straight white colored trunk and branches, and its leaves are bright green. Birch Trees represent the Otherworld. This tree is the first to bud and is considered a sign that spring is just around the corner. The Birch is considered a protective wood for women, as it is associated with safe childbirth and protection from the Underworld. The Birch is the symbol of new beginnings, the start of new plans and taking significant steps in a forward direction. It is the wood most commonly used to kindle the magical fire. The Maypole is frequently made of Birch, with pagans in Wales preferring to use living, standing Birch Trees for their Maypoles. Birch is the wood burned for the Beltaine fire. It is also the wood used for correction or punishment. Until recently, canes and rods made of Birch were the instrument of choice for schoolmasters and law enforcement officials in the British Isles.

Copyright Asteria Books 2017

Hare

Lepus

Celtic Name: Gearr
Gender: Feminine
Planet: Moon
Element: Water
Deity: Ixchel, Boudicca, Eostre, Freya, Hermes
Powers: lunar magic, fertility, sensitivity, swiftness, intuition

MYTH, MAGIC, AND RITUAL: Rabbits are notorious breeders, and are a symbol of the fertility of spring. The expression "mad as a March hare" comes from the rabbit's habit of fighting, courting, and mating during the early spring. The tradition of the "Easter bunny," or Eostre rabbit, reflects this springtime symbolism.

Rabbits have always been associated with witchcraft. They are sacred to Hecate and have the peculiar habit of gathering in a circle, the "hare's parliament." Witches are often thought to be able to transform into a rabbit.

Many cultures perceive the form of a rabbit in the full moon, and thus the rabbit is associated with lunar magic. So associated with the moon and old goddesses of Europe is the hare that it was once forbidden to eat its flesh in Britain and Ireland. In Kerry it is still said that to eat a hare is "to eat one's grandmother."

Rabbits bring great fortune to those who associate with them, due to their fecundity, and perhaps to their association with witches. Thus it became lucky to carry a rabbit's foot, especially during games of chance.

Rabbits could curse as well. It was considered very bad luck to even mention a rabbit when at sea, and pregnant women who had a rabbit cross their path were said to give birth to babies with a "hare lip."

Rabbits are most active during dawn and dusk, the liminal times, and their burrows are sometimes said to be entryways to the underworld or fairie realm. "Going down the rabbit hole" is a metaphor for entering into trance consciousness.

Rabbits have an old association with cats. They share the nicknames "pussy" (from the Latin lepus) and "malkin".

Copyright Asteria Books 2021

Goose

Anatidae

Celtic Name: Geadh, gander, gosling
Deity: Hulda, Aphrodite, Artemis, Juno, Hera
Powers: feminine power, springtime, questing, vigilance

MYTH, MAGIC, AND RITUAL: The goose is the companion of that ancient and powerful goddess, Hulda, as Mother Goose. The goose is a fierce defender of its family and territory, and many ancient gates and warrior's graves have been adorned with the motif of the goose. We often speak of "a wild goose chase" as geese are notoriously difficult to capture or kill.

Several goddesses and witches of folklore have been identified by their having a goose foot (La Reine Pedauque), and thus the goose is a symbol of defensive feminine power.

The call of the goose in flight is said to be the same as the baying of the Gabriel hounds of the Wild Hunt. Hulda, whose bed is made of goose feathers, is said to lead this ride. When she shakes out her bed the snow falls from goose feathers.

The goose is a symbol of early springtime, as it denotes both snow and returning light. The goose who lays the golden egg is laying the growing sun of spring.

Geese mate for life and are associated with marital fidelity. Geese are also known for their furious mating habits, and a "goose" is sometimes used as slang for a prostitute. Their feathers are often used in bedding to bestow blessings of fertility and fidelity on the couple who sleeps there.

Geese are the symbol of migration, and therefore represent both the changing of the seasons, and the call to quest. It is unknown how geese navigate over long distances, returning year after year, but return they do. This is symbolic of the dedication of the initate to remain true to the path.

When flying geese travel in a V formation. This way of flying makes it easier to travel long distances without fatigue, as it puts the greatest strain on the leader who "cuts" a path through the air for the followers to more easily travel behind. Thus, the goose can be a symbol of leadership.

Copyright Asteria Books 2021

April Spirit Allies

Serpent (*Nathair*) - resurrection, rebirth, initiation, wisdom, transformation
Ash (*Nuin*) - connections of past to present, spirit to earth, high and low
Moth (*Lèomann*) - transformation, seeking illumination, initiation

The Snake has a very paradoxical and mythical reputation. It is essentially associated with transformation, healing, and life energy. The Snake can glide through crevices into the Underworld. It represents our ability to die and be reborn, thereby symbolizing rebirth, resurrection, initiation and wisdom. The Snake can journey through life gracefully and magically, shedding old life easily when time comes. The snake is also associated with sexual energy, allowing us to be born.

Ash is the traditional Celtic and Norse World Tree. Odin hung from the great Ash tree Yggdrasil and endured an initiatory that revealed the runes. Ygddrasil's branches were in the heavens, roots were in Hell, and Earth was around its center. The Ash symbolizes connections - past & present, spiritual & earthly, lowest & highest, self & cosmos. It also represents divination, healing, inner and initiation.

The moth and the butterfly represent transformation, due to their metamorphosis from caterpillar to winged creature. The word for moth in old Lancashire dialect means "soul" (just as psyche means both "soul" and "butterfly" in Greek). The spirit of a witch is sometimes said to travel forth from the body in the form of a moth or butterfly. Just as the moth seeks the flame, so do we seek enlightenment and illumination.

Copyright Asteria Books 2015

Ash

Fraxinus excelsior

Folk Names: Nionn
Gender: Masculine
Planet: Sun
Element: Fire
Deity: Uranus, Poseidon, Thor, Woden, Neptune, Mars, Gwydion, Nemesis, Fairies, Fates, Norns, Sorcerers
Powers: protection, prosperity, sea rituals, health

MAGIC AND RITUAL: The Ash tree is the traditional Celtic and Norse World Tree. In Norse mythology, Odin hung from the great Ash tree Yggdrasil and endured an initiatory experience in which he discovered system of meaning in the roots of the great tree (Runes). Ygddrasil's branches were in the heavens, roots were in Hell, and Earth was around its center. The Ash symbolizes connections - past & present, spiritual & earthly, lowest & highest, self & cosmos. It links you to all your pathways. It also represents divination, healing, inner conflicts, and general magic. Ash wood is often used for healing and protection. Besom staffs, stang shafts and certain wands are examples of the protective qualities of the tree. In Greece, Nemesis (who represents the Fates) carried an Ash wand (a scourge) and dispensed justice with it when needed. Its roots, which are human in shape, are excellent for healing. The Ash attracts lightning and brings balance. It also brings light into the hearth at the winter solstice when used as a Yule log. The wassailing bowl used to toast trees at Yule is made of Ash. This tree can help us to understand itself and the other tress. It also helps us assimilate the knowledge gained into the Grove back into practicality.

Copyright Asteria Books 2017

Snake

Serpentes

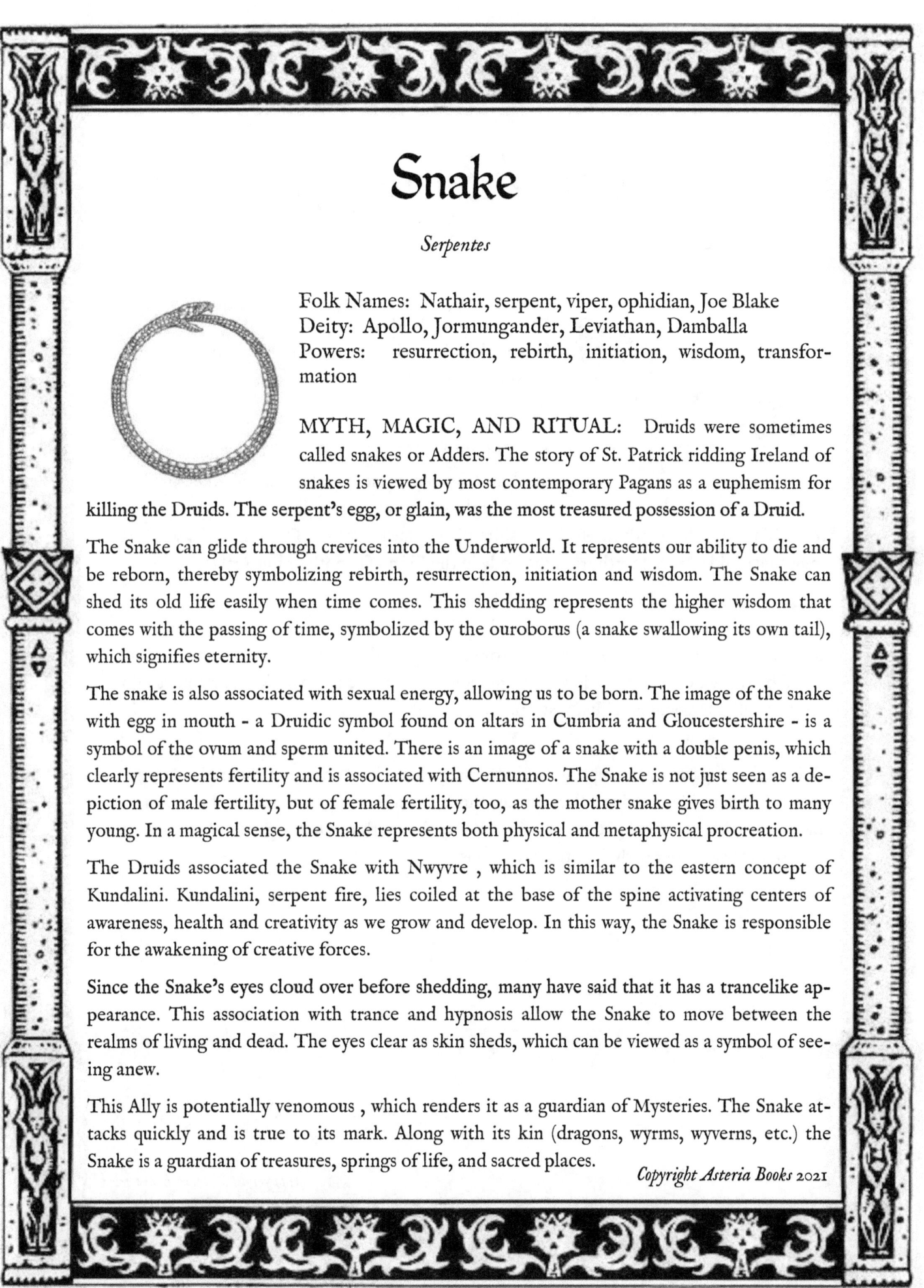

Folk Names: Nathair, serpent, viper, ophidian, Joe Blake
Deity: Apollo, Jormungander, Leviathan, Damballa
Powers: resurrection, rebirth, initiation, wisdom, transformation

MYTH, MAGIC, AND RITUAL: Druids were sometimes called snakes or Adders. The story of St. Patrick ridding Ireland of snakes is viewed by most contemporary Pagans as a euphemism for killing the Druids. The serpent's egg, or glain, was the most treasured possession of a Druid.

The Snake can glide through crevices into the Underworld. It represents our ability to die and be reborn, thereby symbolizing rebirth, resurrection, initiation and wisdom. The Snake can shed its old life easily when time comes. This shedding represents the higher wisdom that comes with the passing of time, symbolized by the ouroborus (a snake swallowing its own tail), which signifies eternity.

The snake is also associated with sexual energy, allowing us to be born. The image of the snake with egg in mouth - a Druidic symbol found on altars in Cumbria and Gloucestershire - is a symbol of the ovum and sperm united. There is an image of a snake with a double penis, which clearly represents fertility and is associated with Cernunnos. The Snake is not just seen as a depiction of male fertility, but of female fertility, too, as the mother snake gives birth to many young. In a magical sense, the Snake represents both physical and metaphysical procreation.

The Druids associated the Snake with Nwyvre , which is similar to the eastern concept of Kundalini. Kundalini, serpent fire, lies coiled at the base of the spine activating centers of awareness, health and creativity as we grow and develop. In this way, the Snake is responsible for the awakening of creative forces.

Since the Snake's eyes cloud over before shedding, many have said that it has a trancelike appearance. This association with trance and hypnosis allow the Snake to move between the realms of living and dead. The eyes clear as skin sheds, which can be viewed as a symbol of seeing anew.

This Ally is potentially venomous , which renders it as a guardian of Mysteries. The Snake attacks quickly and is true to its mark. Along with its kin (dragons, wyrms, wyverns, etc.) the Snake is a guardian of treasures, springs of life, and sacred places.

Copyright Asteria Books 2021

Moth/Butterfly

Lepidoptera

Folk Names: Lèomann, candle-fly, papillon, farfalle, pili-pala, borboleta
Deity: Psyche, Thanatos, Hekate, Selene
Powers: transformation, seeking illumination, initiation

MYTH, MAGIC, AND RITUAL: The moth and the butterfly represent transformation, due to their metamorphosis from caterpillar to winged creature. The word for moth in old Lancashire dialect means 'soul'. The spirit of a witch is sometimes said to travel forth from the body in the form of a moth or butterfly.

Psyche, the Greek 'soul' was another word for butterfly. Psyche was the consort of Eros, and underwent many initiatory tests to prove herself worthy of him. These tests were initiated by the act of seeing her lover by lamplight. Just as the moth seeks the flame, so do we seek enlightenment and illumination.

The moth navigates by attempting to fly to the greatest light source in the night sky, the moon. Modern illumination often curtails this instinct, causing the moth to be drawn to another brighter nearby light source. In this way the moth teaches us to use discernment and to stay true to our path despite distractions.

May Spirit Allies

Cow (*Tarbh/Bò*) - fertility, prosperity, protection, nourishment
Hawthorn (*Huathe*) - fertility, cleansing, protection, joy
Bee (*Beach*) - fertility, community, sweetness, celebration, organization

The Bull (*Tarbh*) is associated with health, potency, beneficence, fertility, abundance, prosperity, and power. The number of cattle owned were an indicator of wealth. The Cow (*Bo*) represents nourishment, motherhood and the Goddess. In Celtic lands, Cows have long been considered sacred. In Britain there were sacred herds of white cattle. Ireland was gifted with cattle when three Cows emerged from the sea - one red, one white, and one black.

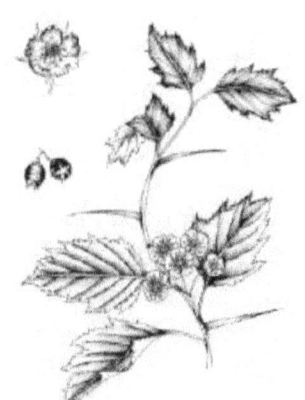

Hawthorns are often used in hedges (some linguistic studies shows that its name may actually mean "hedge thorn"). The Hawthorn has very sharp thorns that are sometimes used for ritual tattoos. Its white flowers are often woven into garlands for doors and Maypoles at Beltane. Indeed, long ago Beltane was reckoned by the first flowering of the Hawthorn tree. Its wood is the traditional material for the Maypole itself.

No animal is a better example of the power of community than the bee. Each bee in a hive has a specific function which she will perform even if it means giving her life for the hive. Because they are the agent that carries the reproductive pollen from one plant to fertilize another, bees are strongly associated with fertility and abundance. Honey was anciently the only source for a sweetener. Thus, the bee has come to symbolize the sweetness of life.

Copyright Asteria Books 2015

Hawthorn

Crataegus oxacantha

Folk Names: Bread and Cheese Tree, Gaxels, Hagthorn, Halves, Haw, Hazels, Huath, Ladies' Meat, May, Mayblossom, May Bush, Mayflower, Quick, Thorn, Tree of Chastity
Gender: Masculine
Planet: Mars
Element: Fire
Deity: Cardea, Flora, Hyman, Belenos, the Fairies, the Teutons, Thor, Witches, Olwen, Blodeuwedd, Ares and Eris
Powers: Fertility, Chastity, Fishing Magic, happiness

HEALING: Hawthorn regulates both high and low blood pressure. It strengthens the muscle and nerve to the heart. Helps prevent miscarriage. The fruit has good drawing properties as a poultice. Hawthorn may cause dizziness if taken in large doses.

MAGIC AND RITUAL: Hawthorns are often used in hedges (and some linguistic study shows that its name may actually mean "hedge thorn"). It is ideal for such a use due to its twisted trunk and dense branches, which make it difficult to penetrate. It doesn't generally grow very tall, and it is frequently a companion to blackthorn. When it is found naturally with Oak and Ash, fairies are likely to be nearby. The Hawthorn has very sharp thorns that are sometimes used for ritual tattoos. Its white flowers are often woven into garlands for doors and Maypoles at Beltaine. Indeed, long ago Beltaine was reckoned by the first flowering of the Hawthorn tree. Its wood is the traditional material for the Maypole itself. Due to these associations, Hawthorn has long been linked to weddings and fertility rites. It is also associated with inward growth, cleansing and protection. It is said to be a "village tree" because it seems to prefer growing near people.

Copyright Asteria Books 2017

Cattle

Bos taurus

Celtic Name: Tarbh/Bò
Gender: Feminine
Planet: Moon
Element: Water
Deity: Io, Hathor, Brighid, Dionysos, Mithras
Powers: fertility, prosperity, protection, nourishment

MYTH, MAGIC, AND RITUAL: The bull is associated with health, potency, beneficence, fertility, abundance, prosperity, and power. The number of cattle owned were an indicator of wealth, a fact that is carried over in the term "Bull market" = rising stock market. The bull also appeared frequently on Celtic coins. Oxen (castrated bulls) were early power supply.

Bronze horns and bronze rattle (in the shape of bull's testes) spoke to the sacredness of the bull. Its horns are used as ceremonial drinking cups even today. An early Irish ritual ("bull sleep") told of the new king when the old one died. "Gateway ceremonies" involved ritual sacrifice of bulls.

The cow represents nourishment, motherhood and the Goddess. Certain herbs are associated with cows, such as cranberry (cowberry), cowslip, and milk-wort (field gentian). In Celtic lands, cows have long been considered sacred. In Britain there were sacred herds of white cattle. Ireland was gifted with cattle when three cows emerged from the sea - one red, one white, and one black. Brighid was reared on the milk of an Otherworld cow and is considered the patroness of cattle. Three of the four sacred festivals were related to cows (Samhain, Beltaine and Imbolc) Many Eastern traditions also hold the cow as sacred.

The cow is also a source of nourishment on many levels - milk, leather, meat, horn. The fact that is contributes to much to daily life is part of what makes it so sacred and special.

In folklore, the Milky Way is also called the Cow Path, and there are Fairy Cows called the "Crodh Shith." Many offerings are made of milk, and the breath and milk of the cow are considered healing.

Copyright Asteria Books 2020

Bee

Anthophila

Folk Names: *Beach,* drumbee, drummer, doombledore, hummabee, and humble-dad
Deity: Aphrodite, Artemis
Powers: fertility, community, sweetness, celebration, organization

MYTH, MAGIC, AND RITUAL: No animal is a better example of the power of community than the bee. Each bee in a hive has a specific function which she will perform even if it means giving her life for the hive. There are three types of bees: workers, drones, and queens. The worker bees are the common bees we are most familiar with. They secrete wax to form combs, and produce honey to feed the hive.

Bees pollinate all kinds of plants, and many of our food crops would be useless without them. Because they are the element that carries the reproductive pollen from one plant to fertilize another, bees are strongly associated with fertility and abundance.

Honey was anciently the only source for a sweetener. Thus, the bee has come to symbolize the sweetness of life.

Bees communicate by dancing, and those who work with bees will find themselves drawn to dance and rhythm. The bee's dance is indirect relation to the sun in the sky. Bees are symbolic of solar celebration.

Honeybees will only sting if they feel that the hive is in danger. A honeybee gives its life when it uses its stinger.

The queen of a hive is chosen from newly hatched bee larva when the hive requires a new queen. In summer bees will swarm in search of a new hive. The chosen queen will be fed royal jelly which will allow her to become the sole reproducer in the hive. She will be attended by male drones who give their life for mate with her.

When a new coven of witches is formed from members of an older group it is said that the new coven has "hived off," just as swarming bees would gather under a new queen.

Copyright Asteria Books 2021

June Spirit Allies

Stag (*Damh*) - nobility, culling the herd, call to adventure, pride, grace
Oak (*Duir*) - security, steadfastness, primeval vigor, doorway, strength
Robin (*Spideog*) - growth, territoriality, fire

The Stag is the male aspect of the deer. As such, some discussion of the qualities of deer in general is helpful to understand Stag. Deer are associated with gentleness, innocence and a luring to new adventure. Many legends exist in which deer lure hunters and/or kings into the forest for adventures. The Stag is a symbol of pride and independence. He is an example of grace, majesty, integrity, poise and dignity. The Stag is a symbol of fertility and rampant sexuality, which is also related to the Lord of the Hunt and the Horned Gods.

Ancient Celts observed the oak's massive growth and impressive expanse. They took this as a clear sign that the oak was to be honored for its endurance, and noble presence. Wearing oak leaves was a sign of special status among many ancient European peoples. There are accounts that trace the name "druid" to *duir*, the Celtic term for the oak. The oak is a tree of protection and strength.

Robins are very territorial, and their red breasts signal other males to leave their space. Even their bright and cheery song is a used as a method of battling with other males for dominance over territory. The Robin's bright blue egg is distinctive in color. Both male and female Robins share in the feeding of the young. The Norse associated the bird with Thor and considered it to be a creature of the storm.

Copyright Asteria Books 2015

Oak

Quercus alba

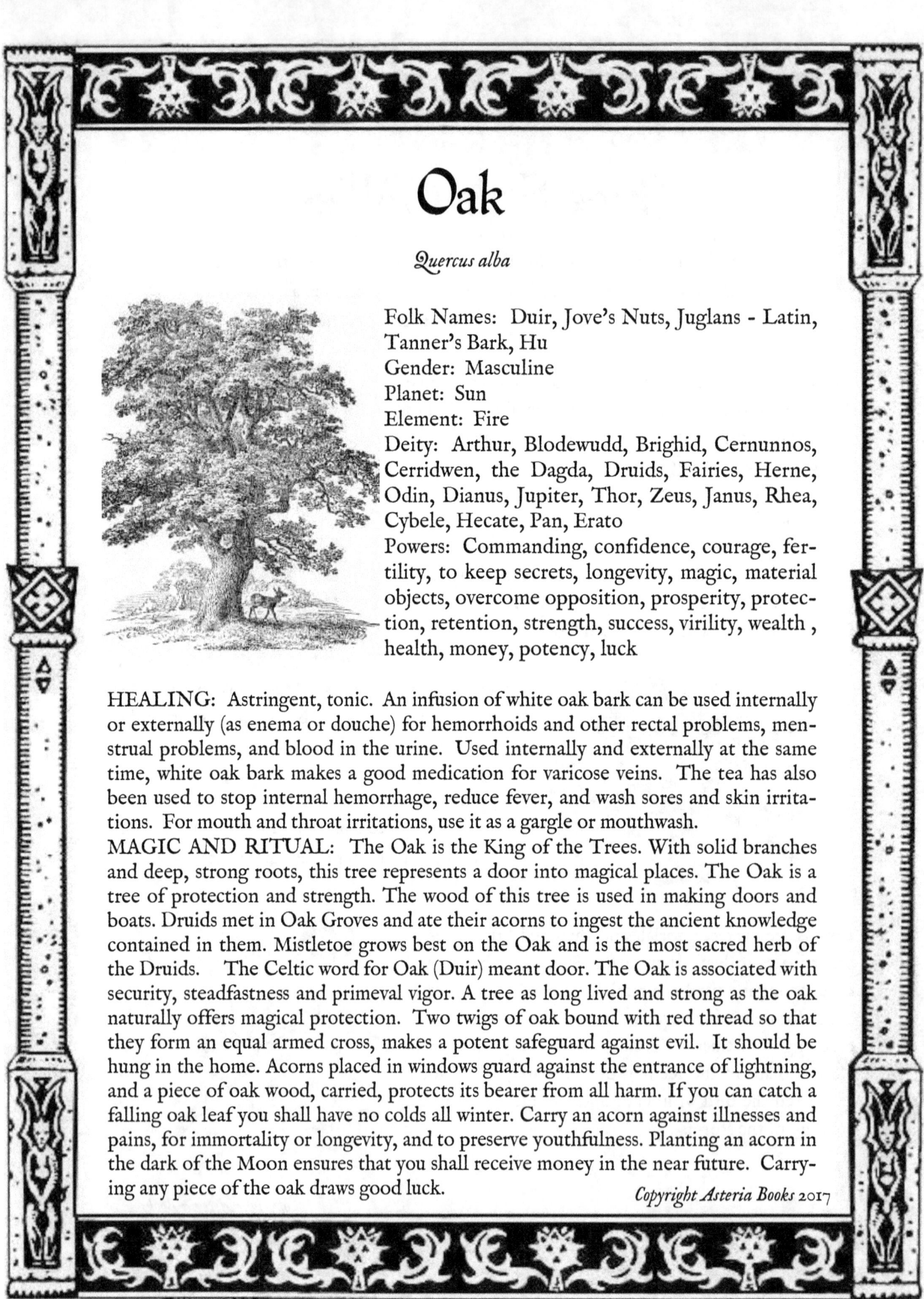

Folk Names: Duir, Jove's Nuts, Juglans - Latin, Tanner's Bark, Hu
Gender: Masculine
Planet: Sun
Element: Fire
Deity: Arthur, Blodewudd, Brighid, Cernunnos, Cerridwen, the Dagda, Druids, Fairies, Herne, Odin, Dianus, Jupiter, Thor, Zeus, Janus, Rhea, Cybele, Hecate, Pan, Erato
Powers: Commanding, confidence, courage, fertility, to keep secrets, longevity, magic, material objects, overcome opposition, prosperity, protection, retention, strength, success, virility, wealth, health, money, potency, luck

HEALING: Astringent, tonic. An infusion of white oak bark can be used internally or externally (as enema or douche) for hemorrhoids and other rectal problems, menstrual problems, and blood in the urine. Used internally and externally at the same time, white oak bark makes a good medication for varicose veins. The tea has also been used to stop internal hemorrhage, reduce fever, and wash sores and skin irritations. For mouth and throat irritations, use it as a gargle or mouthwash.

MAGIC AND RITUAL: The Oak is the King of the Trees. With solid branches and deep, strong roots, this tree represents a door into magical places. The Oak is a tree of protection and strength. The wood of this tree is used in making doors and boats. Druids met in Oak Groves and ate their acorns to ingest the ancient knowledge contained in them. Mistletoe grows best on the Oak and is the most sacred herb of the Druids. The Celtic word for Oak (Duir) meant door. The Oak is associated with security, steadfastness and primeval vigor. A tree as long lived and strong as the oak naturally offers magical protection. Two twigs of oak bound with red thread so that they form an equal armed cross, makes a potent safeguard against evil. It should be hung in the home. Acorns placed in windows guard against the entrance of lightning, and a piece of oak wood, carried, protects its bearer from all harm. If you can catch a falling oak leaf you shall have no colds all winter. Carry an acorn against illnesses and pains, for immortality or longevity, and to preserve youthfulness. Planting an acorn in the dark of the Moon ensures that you shall receive money in the near future. Carrying any piece of the oak draws good luck.

Copyright Asteria Books 2017

Deer

Cervidae

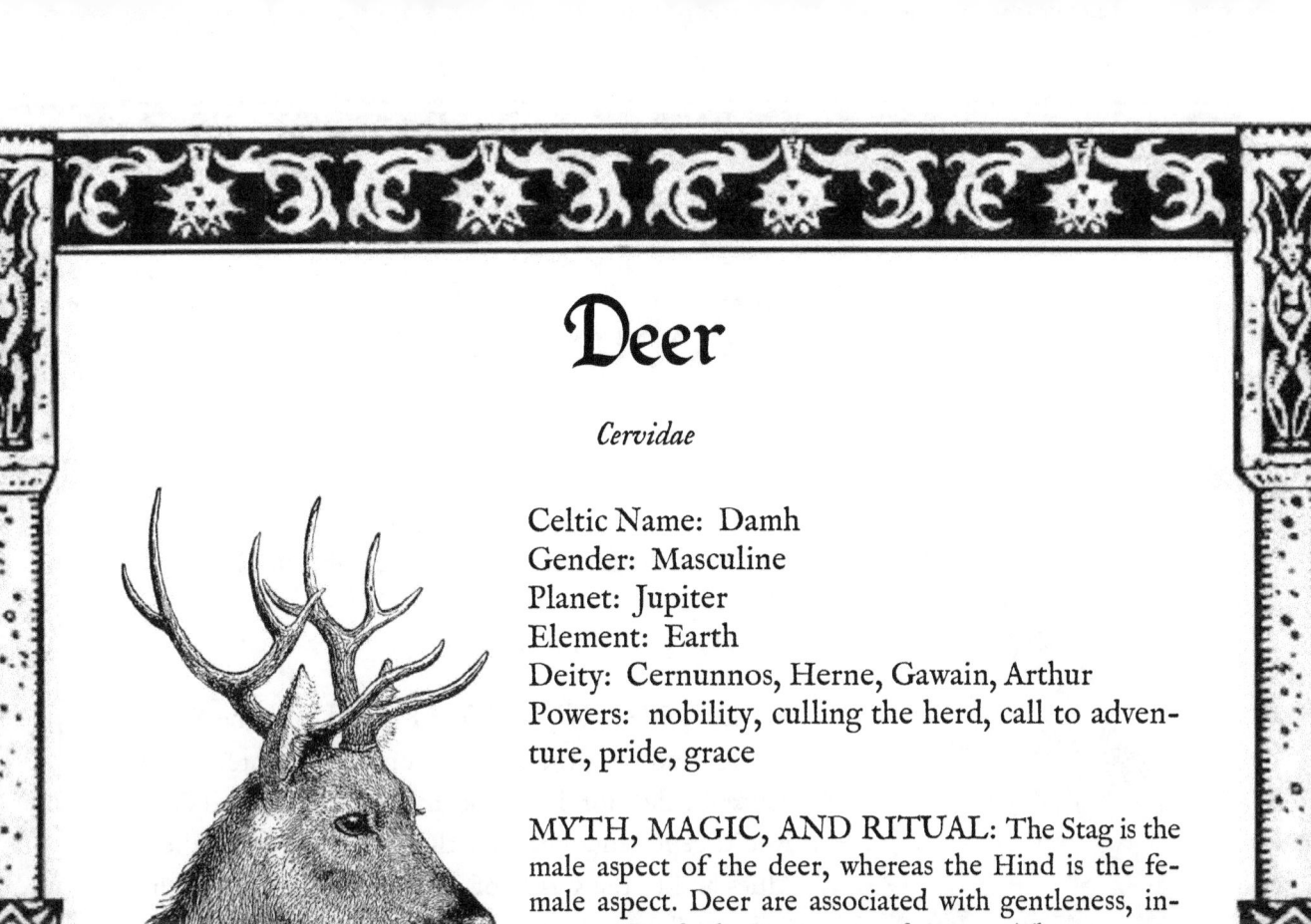

Celtic Name: Damh
Gender: Masculine
Planet: Jupiter
Element: Earth
Deity: Cernunnos, Herne, Gawain, Arthur
Powers: nobility, culling the herd, call to adventure, pride, grace

MYTH, MAGIC, AND RITUAL: The Stag is the male aspect of the deer, whereas the Hind is the female aspect. Deer are associated with gentleness, innocence, and a luring to new adventure. They are very adaptable, and they are native to every continent except Australia.

Many legends exist in which deer lure hunters and/or kings into the forest for adventures. One prominent example of this is the story of Gawain and the White Hart. Gawain followed the Hart willingly, though the pursuit ended in an unpleasant realization of Gawain's own shortcomings. However, by following willingly and facing his darker nature, Gawain was able to confront his rage and learn to control it, making him one of the best Knights of the Round Table.

The Stag is a symbol of pride and independence. He is an example of grace, majesty, integrity, poise, and dignity. These are indeed kingly qualities, so it is no wonder that there is a deer referred to as King Stag. In fact, this King Stag is associated in many ways with the Lord of the Wild Hunt, as both are responsible for protecting the herd and culling it of weaknesses.

The Stag is one of the five Oldest Animals in Welsh tradition. He leads a willing seeker deeper into the Mysteries and into the Otherworld. He is a guardian of the gateway between this plane and the Otherworld and delivers messages from that realm.

The Stag's antlers are made of bone and shed every year for 5 years. (In some species, both the male and female have antlers). The antlers start to grow in early summer and are fully developed by rutting time (late Autumn). The Stag sheds antlers around Imbolc (before birth of young). The antlers are protective by nature, and they also represent higher levels of attunement.

The Stag is a symbol of fertility and rampant sexuality, which is also related to the Lord of the Hunt and the Horned Gods.

Robin

Turdus migratorius

Folk Names: redbreast, ruddock
Deity: Cernunnos, Jack in the Green, Robin of the Woods
Powers: growth, territoriality, fire

MYTH, MAGIC, AND RITUAL: In the Spiral Castle tradition, the Robin is one of the three Spirit Allies for the month of June, along with Stag and Oak. Robin represents qualities that are kindred to these Allies and to the Castle of Stone, Cernunnos, and the Summer Solstice -- all of which share this portion of the Wheel of the Year with it.

In England and America, we are talking about two different birds, when we refer to the Robin. Brits are referring to the redbreast, while Americans call the thrush the Robin. Both birds have red feathers on their breasts, earning them an association with fire.

Most mythologies only make vague reference to the Robin, the clear distinction being the Norse, who associated the bird with Thor and considered it to be a creature of the storm.

Robins are very territorial, and their red breasts signal other males to leave their space. Even their bright and cheery song is a used as a method of battling with other males for dominance over territory. Physical confrontations, on the other hand, tend to be symbolic. Male robins don't seek to hurt each other physically.

The Robin's bright blue egg is distinctive in color. Both male and female Robins share in the feeding of the young, which is a very active process for these birds. Hatchlings are born with no feathers at all, and feedings occur at an average of every twelve minutes. Even so, Robins manage to hatch more than one brood each year. This is a testament to their growth and incredible vitality.

Copyright Asteria Books 2021

July Spirit Allies

HOUND (*Cu*) - loyalty, protection, guidance
ELM (*Lemh*) - elves, light, purification, wisdom
EAGLE (*Iolair*) - light, renewal, loyalty, intelligence, courage

The Dog is animal of faithfulness, protection, guidance, loyalty and warning. It is an excellent companion and work-mate. Dogs have been used for herding, hunting, and sporting for thousands of years. In India, Dog is a symbol of all caste systems, indicating the small becoming great. In Greece, Dog is seen as a companion and a guardian to the places of the dead. The term Cu (Dog) was given to many chiefs, warriors, heroes and champions in Celtic lore.

Elm's folk name is "Elven" (because of its long-standing association with elves, both the Seelie and Unseelie Courts of the Fey). It attracts love when carried and protects against lightning strikes. Associated with death, the grave and rebirth in legend and myth, Elm was also used for coffin wood later in English tradition, linking it to the death mythos and to the elven lore that connects the elves with burial mounds.

In America, the two primary species of Eagle are the Golden Eagle and the Bald Eagle. It is a symbol of freedom for Americans, and it was likewise a royal and potent bird among Romans, Egyptian pharaohs, Greek Thebans, and the Celts of Ireland and Scotland. The Eagle has a long association with sky Gods, such as Zeus and Ashur, which strengthens the bird's connections to the sun, storms, lightning and fire. Eagle is often associated with war and bravery, as well.

Copyright Asteria Books 2015

Elm

Ulmus campestris

Folk Names: Elven, English Elm, European Elm
Gender: Feminine
Planet: Saturn
Element: Water
Deity: Odin, Hoenin, Lodr
Powers: Love, fairies, death and rebirth

HEALING: Stringent, demulcent, diuretic, vulnerary. The bark of young branches can be used as a decoction or tincture for herpes, scurf, itch, and other skin problems. Soaking bark and bruised leaves in vinegar also makes a useful wash for the skin. The leaves have sometimes been used to help heal wounds.

MAGIC AND RITUAL: Common tree in both England and America. Its folk name is "Elven" (because of its long-standing association with elves, both the Seelie and Unseelie Courts of the Fey). Attracts love when carried and protects against lightning strikes - both because of elven associations. Associated with death, the grave and rebirth in legend and myth. At Orpheus' song upon emerging from Hades' underworld realm, the first Elm grove is said to have sprung into existence. Elm was also used for coffin wood later in English tradition, linking it to this early mythos and to the elven lore that connects the elves with burial mounds. In Italy, Elm and Vine lore is intermingled, especially in the stories of Bacchus, due largely to the tree's use as a vineyard superstructure. Elm branches were carried by the clergy and members of the chorus during annual "beating of the bounds" ceremonies, thereby linking the tree with border-marking and rulership.

Copyright Asteria Books 2017

Hound

Canis lupus familiaris

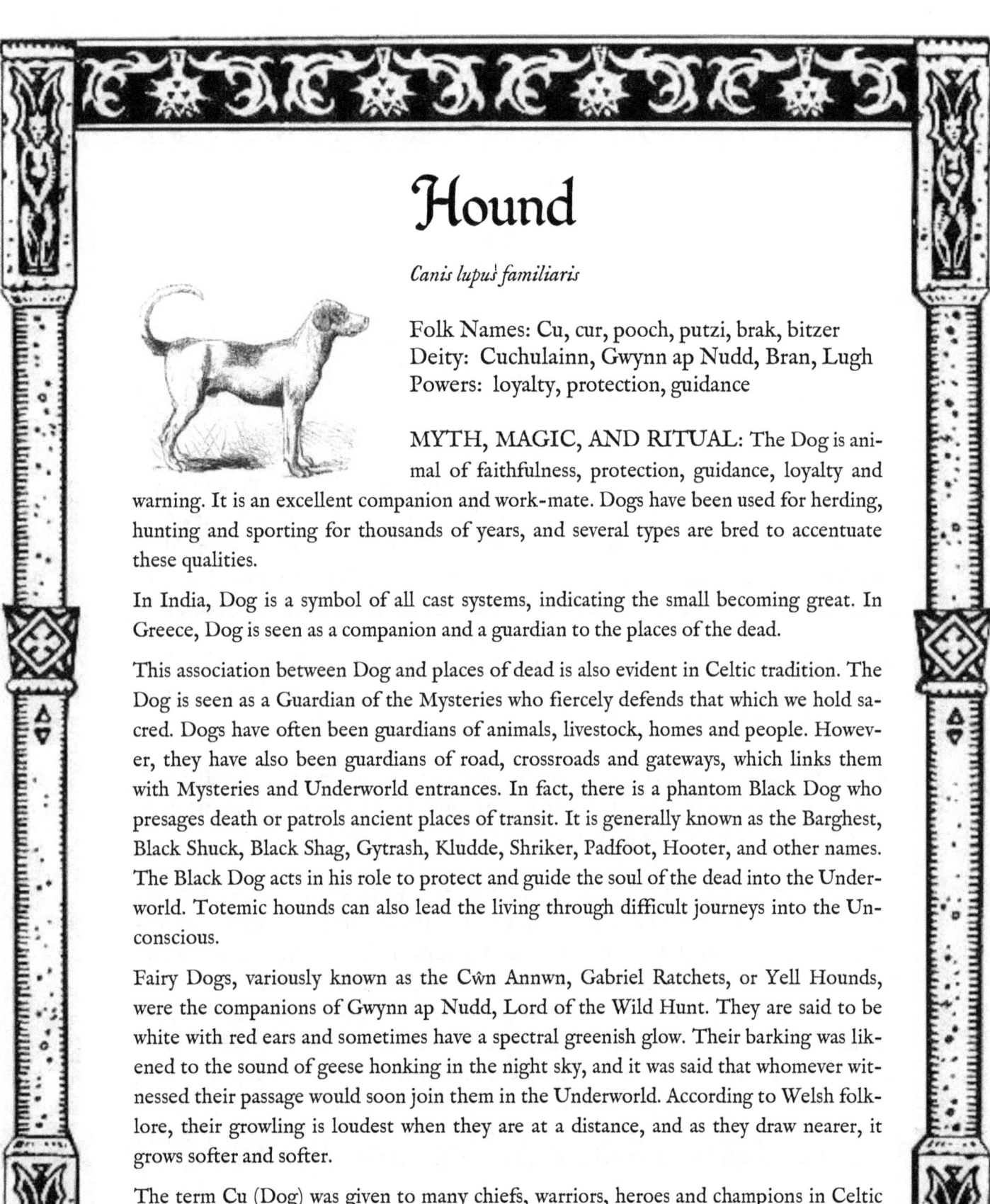

Folk Names: Cu, cur, pooch, putzi, brak, bitzer
Deity: Cuchulainn, Gwynn ap Nudd, Bran, Lugh
Powers: loyalty, protection, guidance

MYTH, MAGIC, AND RITUAL: The Dog is animal of faithfulness, protection, guidance, loyalty and warning. It is an excellent companion and work-mate. Dogs have been used for herding, hunting and sporting for thousands of years, and several types are bred to accentuate these qualities.

In India, Dog is a symbol of all cast systems, indicating the small becoming great. In Greece, Dog is seen as a companion and a guardian to the places of the dead.

This association between Dog and places of dead is also evident in Celtic tradition. The Dog is seen as a Guardian of the Mysteries who fiercely defends that which we hold sacred. Dogs have often been guardians of animals, livestock, homes and people. However, they have also been guardians of road, crossroads and gateways, which links them with Mysteries and Underworld entrances. In fact, there is a phantom Black Dog who presages death or patrols ancient places of transit. It is generally known as the Barghest, Black Shuck, Black Shag, Gytrash, Kludde, Shriker, Padfoot, Hooter, and other names. The Black Dog acts in his role to protect and guide the soul of the dead into the Underworld. Totemic hounds can also lead the living through difficult journeys into the Unconscious.

Fairy Dogs, variously known as the Cŵn Annwn, Gabriel Ratchets, or Yell Hounds, were the companions of Gwynn ap Nudd, Lord of the Wild Hunt. They are said to be white with red ears and sometimes have a spectral greenish glow. Their barking was likened to the sound of geese honking in the night sky, and it was said that whomever witnessed their passage would soon join them in the Underworld. According to Welsh folklore, their growling is loudest when they are at a distance, and as they draw nearer, it grows softer and softer.

The term Cu (Dog) was given to many chiefs, warriors, heroes and champions in Celtic lore. For example, Cu-Chulainn's name means the Hound of Chulainn.

Copyright Asteria Books 2021

Eagle

Haliaeetus and *Aquila*

Folk Names: *IOLAIR*
Deity: Zeus, Asshur
Powers: *Light, renewal, loyalty, intelligence, courage*

MYTH, MAGIC, AND RITUAL: In America, the two primary species of eagle are the Golden Eagle and the Bald Eagle. It is a symbol of freedom for Americans, and it was likewise a royal bird among Romans, Egyptian pharaohs, Greek Thebans and the Celts of Ireland and Scotland.

The eagle has a long association with sky Gods, such as Zeus and Asshur, which strengthens the bird's connections to the sun, storms, lightning and fire. Eagle is often associated with war and bravery, as well.

Native Americans hold the Eagle in highest esteem among birds, and Eagle medicine was greatly prized. Most tribes have an eagle clan, for instance, and eagle songs, dances, and ceremonies are all well-known.

Druids, as well, valued eagle magic and were said to choose this form for shapeshifting for certain ceremonies. In fact, the eagle is almost as powerful and popular a bird in Celtic myth and legend as it is in Native American lore. It is one of the four most frequently mentioned birds in the Irish and British traditions (along with the raven, swan, and crane). The eagle is particularly intertwined with the salmon at a symbolic level in Celtic myth - one representing the heights of intellect and vision; the other representing the depths of emotion and the unconscious.

Eagles are known for their swiftness, keen vision, strength, and courage.

Copyright Asteria Books 2021

August Spirit Allies

Horse *(Each)* - travel, power, freedom, civilization
Apple *(Quert)* - beauty, choices, love, inspiration
Swan *(Eala)* - shape-shifting, love, grace, beauty

The Horse is associated with the female Divine, the land, and travel both on the inner and outer planes. It is connected to the Sun and is a symbol of sexual desires. Furthermore, it is associated with power and freedom, divination, the spread of civilization, birth. Wind and sea foam often signify the power of the Horse. The Horse is often a phantom creature or provoker of nightmares, who get their name from her, as Mare is an Irish Goddess. Sovereignty is another aspect of the Horse.

Apple represents the choice between similar and equally attractive things. It is one of the "Seven Chieftain Trees" of the Celts. It's fruit and bark are used in tanning. It is related to the rose family, along with Hawthorn, and so it develops thorns from spurs on its branches. The Apple is associated with love spells, likely due to its associations with Aphrodite. Avalon, a sacred Celtic land, is named the "Isle of Apples."

The Swan is often depicted with a silver or gold chain around the neck in Celtic legends -- possibly a carry-over from the Aphrodite tradition of the golden sash. The Swan is very prominent in love stories in Celtic lands, including the tale of Oenghus and Yewberry (who is a Swan Maiden). Swan is associated with Otherworldly travel and migration of the Soul. This bird's skin and feathers were used to make the bard's ceremonial cloak. Swans are also intimately linked with shape-shifting.

Copyright Asteria Books 2015

Apple

Pyrus spp.

Folk Names: Quert, Fruit of the Gods, Fruit of the Underworld, Silver Branch, The Silver Bough, Tree of Love
Gender: Feminine
Planet: Venus
Element: Water
Deity: Venus, Dionysus, Olwan, Apollo, Hera, Athena, Aphrodite, Diana, Zeus, Iduna, Merlin, Druids, Unicorns
Powers: love, healing, garden magic, immortality

HEALING: Peels and grated unripe apple are excellent for illnesses involving diarrhea. If, on the other hand, you need a mild laxative, eat some apples whole. Apple peels can be dried and made into a tea that is recommended for rheumatic illness. Apple wine is an ancient cure all that was mentioned by Galen in the second century A.D. Use only wine that is at least two years old.

MAGIC AND RITUAL: The Apple is related to the rose family (along with Hawthorn) and so it develops thorns from spurs on its branches. It has gnarled trunks, often growing at crazy angles (to "hide" amongst other trees). Its leaves are almost heart-shaped, and its blossoms are deep pink with a scent similar to honeysuckle, which attracts bees. This tree represents the choice between similar and equally attractive things. It is one of the "Seven Chieftain Trees" of the Celts. The Apple is associated with love spells, likely due to its associations with Aphrodite. The Greeks sometimes saw the sun as a crimson apple sinking into the sea, being replaced by Hesperus (Venus) the 'star' sacred to Aphrodite. The Apple's association with Aphrodite is further strengthened by the golden apple, engraved with the words "For the Fairest," that was awarded to her by Paris (and which resulted in the beginning of the Trojan War). The Apple has long been sacred to the Celts, as well. One of its sacred islands, Avalon, is named the "Isle of Apples." Old apple trees are more likely than other types of trees to host mistletoe, making them sacred to Druids. Merlin also had a sacred apple orchard. Apple cider was the most sacred drink of the Druids.

Copyright Asteria Books 2017

Horse

Equus caballus

Folk Names: *Each, brumby, cob, cuddy, hobby, gee-gee, moke, yarraman*
Deity: Epona, Rhiannon, Macha, Etain
Powers: travel, power, freedom, civilization

MYTH, MAGIC, AND RITUAL: The Horse is associated with the female Divine, the land, and travel both on the inner and outer planes. It is connected to the Sun and is a symbol of sexual desired. Furthermore, it is associated with power and freedom, divination, the spread of civilization, birth. Wind and sea foam often signify the power of the Horse.

The Horse's skills for hauling, hunting and battle have made it an animal that has been a true partner to mankind in many respects. It has been connected to head hunting due to the fact that warriors would frequently hang the severed heads of defeated opponents about the necks of the horses. Horse gear and/or parts, like the teeth, as well as whole horses were often interred with their masters upon the human's death. Horse bones found in the foundations of houses to bring good luck, like horse shoes today. These findings indicate a long history of the Horse in connection to the burial rites of the Celts and other cultures.

Epona, Rhiannon, and Macha are all Celtic Horse-Goddesses. In some images a Mare holds a key to the Underworld or Otherworld. Rhiannon is seen riding out of the Otherworld on a white horse. A common activity at Samhain and Beltane is the riding hobby-horses. The Horse is often a phantom creature or provoker of nightmares, who get their name from her, as Mare is an Irish Goddess.

The Horse is associated with freedom because it allows us to move without restriction from place to place. However, this freedom often comes without proper restraints, which can lead to trouble for the rider. The connection to freedom is also echoed in the poets' tendencies to liken horse-riding to flying.

Sovereignty is another aspect of the Horse. In Ireland the kings performed a symbolic marriage with the horse to secure their rule and connection to the land. The Horse was then slaughtered, its blood spilling upon the ground, and its meat eaten by those in attendance. This is a version of the Sacred Marriage.

Copyright Asteria Books 2021

Swan

Cygnus

Folk Names: *Eala*
Deity: Goda, Oenghus, Lyr, Cuchulain, Aphrodite and Apollo
Powers: shape-shifting, love, grace, beauty

MYTH, MAGIC, AND RITUAL: The Swan is often depicted with a silver or gold chain around the neck in Celtic legends -- possibly a carry-over from the Aphrodite tradition of the golden sash. Aphrodite was a waterbird Goddess in early Proto-Indo European practice, and the Swan is heavily associated with her in Greek tradition. This is hardly a surprising connection, given that the Swan is very prominent in love stories in Celtic lands, including the tale of Oenghus and Yewberry (who is a Swan Maiden).

In Celtic lore, Swan is associated with Otherworldly travel and migration of the Soul. The "swan song" speaks of both grace and beauty (because Swan's final song is said to be strikingly beautiful) and also of death and transition. Swan is often the poetic representation of the Soul itself in Celtic lore.

This bird's skin and feathers were used to make the bard's ceremonial cloak, according to Philip and Stephanie Carr-Gomm's Druid Animal Oracle. This is another sign of grace and beauty -- the grace and beauty of word and song, which the celts understood to be very important to both art and magic.

Swans are intimately linked with shape-shifting in celtic lore, as well. Several tales speak of children and maidens who are changed (or can change themselves) into swans for one reason or another. Because of these shape-shifting characteristics, Swan is also further linked to Elphame and the realm of Faerie.

Swan, Horse and Apple are a very potent feminine, Faerie Totemic set in relation to the White Goddess (known/shown to members of the Spiral Castle Tradition as Goda).

Copyright Asteria Books 2021

September Spirit Allies

SWINE (*Torc/Muc*) - hunt, search, nourishment, putting up a fight
VINE (*Muin*) - prophesy, prediction and omens
CHICKEN (*Cearc*) - fertility, battle, sexuality, watchfulness

The Boar (*Torc*) is as symbol of the Warrior spirit, leadership, and direction. It is wild and powerful. There are ritual boar paths in Wales, Cornwall, Ireland and Scotland. These paths exist in the Inner Realms, too. The Boar's tusks and comb are significant and are frequently mentioned in lore. The Sow (*Muc*) is a symbol of nourishment, as swine are a particularly potent food source. Just as the sow gives life as food, so does she take life away. Any pig farmer can attest to the practice of sows eating their own piglets after birth.

While not actually a "tree," the Vine stands firmly amongst the grove of totemic trees. The fermented juice of the grape is wine, which appears in almost every Indo-European mythos at some point. The vine stands for the release of prophecy, predictions and omens. Grapevines are used to make baskets, wreaths and magical tools.

Fowl have been domesticated for over 8000 years as a provider of meat and eggs. Chickens are diurnal, being most active in the day. In fact, they are so associated with the coming of the day that the crowing of a rooster is seen as synonymous with daybreak. Chickens are highly social and quite polygamous. Pair bonding is unheard of. Yet despite this abundant promiscuity, there is tremendous territoriality and rivalry between two roosters as to who gets to mate with whom.

Copyright Asteria Books 2015

Vine

Vitis vinifera

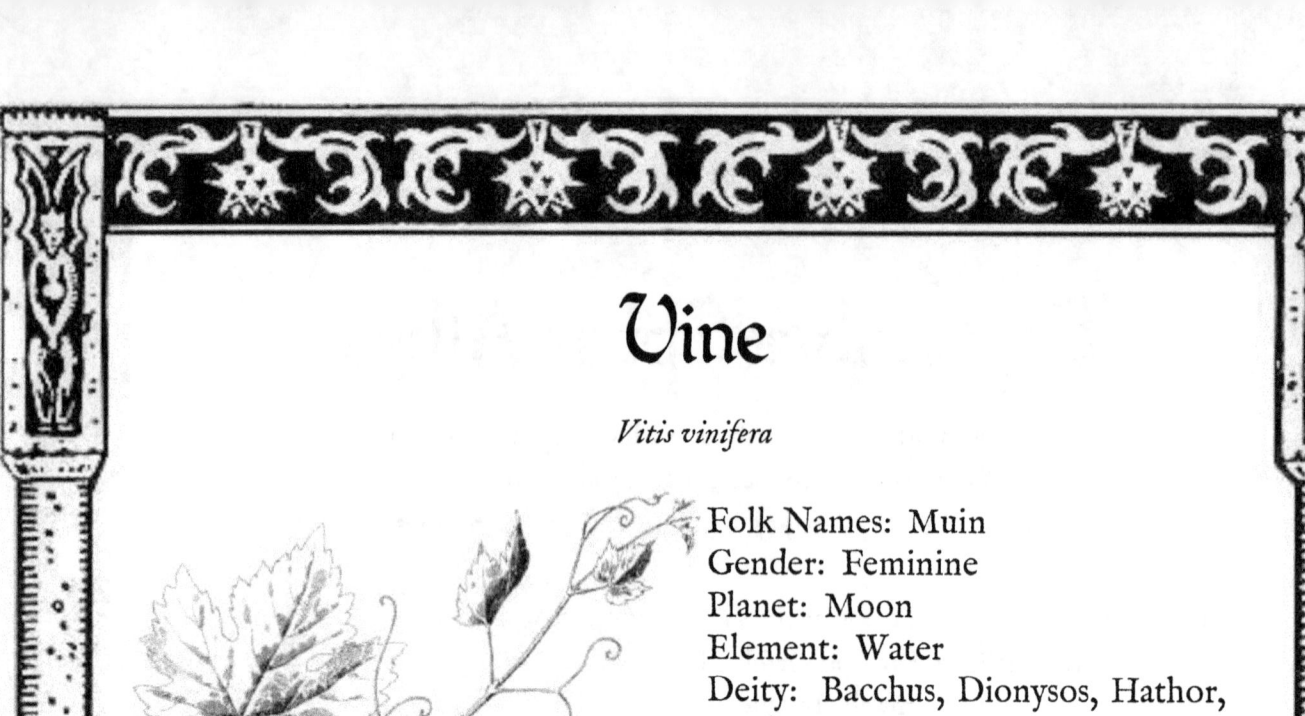

Folk Names: Muin
Gender: Feminine
Planet: Moon
Element: Water
Deity: Bacchus, Dionysos, Hathor, Lugh, Jesus
Powers: Fertility, garden magic, mental powers, money, prophecy, prediction, omens

HEALING: Grape leaves have venotonic, vasoprotective, astringent and diuretic effects. The fruits are vitaminics, tonics, anticancer, hepatoprotective, promote hair growth and prevent ischemic processes. The seeds oil is hypolipidemic and prevents the increase of vascular permeability. Some of the great benefits of grapes include their ability to treat constipation, indigestion, fatigue, migraines, heart disease, asthma, kidney disorders, breast cancer, and macular degeneration.

MAGIC AND RITUAL: While not actually a "tree," this sacred wood stands firmly amongst the sacred trees. The fermented juice of the grape is wine, which appears in every mythos at some point. From the sacred drink of the God Dionysos to the many aspects of wine in the life of Jesus, wine has played a part in most religious systems. The vine is a symbol of prophecy and is the sacred wood of the festival of Lughnasadh - the first harvest festival, which celebrates the cutting and offering of the first fruits. The Vine stands for the release of prophecy, predictions and omens. Grapevines are used to make baskets, wreaths and magical tools such as Bride's Girdle. Pictures of grapes can be painted onto garden walls to ensure fertility, as was done in ancient Rome. Eating grapes or raisins increases fertility, as well as strengthens mental powers. Place grapes on the altar during money spells.

Copyright Asteria Books 2017

Swine

Sus

Folk Names: *Torc/Muc*
Deity: Cerridwen, Freya, Freyr, Demeter, Isis
Powers: hunt, search, nourishment, putting up a fight

MYTH, MAGIC, AND RITUAL: The Boar is as symbol of the Warrior spirit, leadership, and direction. It is wild and powerful. The Boar calls you into forest to discover a secret about yourself. The Boar has a raw power that can be very destructive, but can be channeled.

There are ritual boar paths in Wales, Cornwall, Ireland and Scotland. These paths exist in the Inner Realms, too.

The Boar's tusks and comb are significant and are frequently mentioned in lore. Furthermore, combs and mirrors depicted beside boars in Scottish rock-carvings. This animal's image was often used as emblem on helmets and mouthpiece of battle-horns to terrify enemies and on swords and bronze shields to protect the warrior.

It is a secretly (inwardly) feminine symbol that is connected with healing as well as destruction. In Scotland, women would give birth at the Boar Stone, with their bare feet on the stone to absorb its power. In Celtic terms, hunting and healing seen as connected.

The sow is a symbol of nourishment, as swine are a particularly potent food source. Indeed, it is said that "everything but the oink" is used as food. Just as the sow gives life as food, so does she take life away. Any pig farmer can attest to the practice of sows eating their own piglets after birth. The sow is therefore symbolic of the Goddess who is death-in-life and life-in-death.

The sow is especially associated with Cerridwen, whose name is sometimes translated as "white sow," making her association with September (in the Spiral Castle Trad) particularly potent.

Copyright Asteria Books 2021

Chicken

Gallus gallus domesticus

Celtic Name: Cearc
Gender: Masculine
Planet: Mars
Element: Fire
Deity: Cerridwen, Ares, Mars, Maman Brigiette
Powers: fertility, battle, sexuality, watchfulness

MYTH, MAGIC, AND RITUAL: Fowl have been domesticated for over 8000 years and have a long history with man as a provider of meat and eggs. They originated in Thailand and Vietnam and were descended from a wild species called the red jungle fowl.

Chickens are diurnal, being most active in the day. In fact, they are so associated with the coming of the day that the crowing of a rooster is seen as synonymous with daybreak.

Chickens are highly social and quite polygamous. Pair bonding is unheard of. Yet despite this abundant promiscuity, there is tremendous territoriality and rivalry between two roosters as to who gets to mate with whom. And the same applies for the hens. Both hens and roosters will get quite aggressive in defending their exclusive right to mate with who they think best. These aggressions are quite impressive and violent.

The chicken has been seen as a mythical symbol of courage throughout many civilizations in the world. The romans associated chickens with Mars, the god of war. These associations are no doubt due to their aggressive and territorial behavior. Cock fights are one example of why these birds would be associated with a god of war.

Ares (Mars) took advantage of the rooster's watchfulness and aggression by setting him as a guard to watch over Aphrodite while she slept, that none might disturb her.

Cerridwen, who is the Silver Queen of the Castle Perilous, transformed into a hen to devour Gwion Bach when he became a grain of corn to escape her. Cerridwen later gave birth to the bard Taliesin, who was Gwion reborn. Because Cerridwen is both the great sow and the devouring hen, these two animals are sacred to her and the month that she reigns over in the American Folkloric tradition (September, the time of the Fall Equinox).

Copyright Asteria Books 2020

October Spirit Allies

Salmon (*Bradan*) - oldest animal; wisdom, knowledge, inspiration
Hazel (*Coll*) - wisdom, intuition, creativity, divination, the source
Lapwing (*Curracag*) - resourcefulness, distraction, wisdom, divination

The Salmon is the "Oldest Animal" in Welsh mythology and is critical in the search for Mabon. Salmon is a symbol of wisdom, inspiration and rejuvenation. The Salmon will return to place of its own birth to mate (often with great difficulty) and is, therefore, a reminder that we need to journey back to our own beginnings to find wisdom. It swims in the well of wisdom (Connla's Well) at the source of all life, a sacred pool that has 9 Hazel trees growing around it.

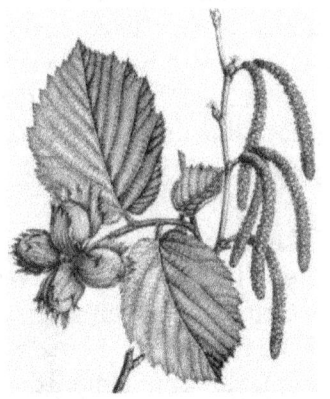

Hazel is one of the "Seven Chieftain Trees" of the Celts, and the unnecessary felling of Hazel trees brought the death penalty in Ireland. Hazel's magical associations include fertility, wisdom, marriage, divination, healing, protection, intuition, dowsing wands, individuality, finding the hidden, luck and wishes. The Hazel is considered to be the Tree of knowledge for the Celts. Its nuts are ultimate receptacles of wisdom.

The Lapwing guards the Mysteries of the Wise by "disguising the Truth." She does this by feigning injury to make herself appear helpless to predators who have come to close to her nest. Because Lapwing's nest rests on the ground in the spring, hares have been known to sit in them, looking like they are hatching eggs (which is where the combined association of bunnies and eggs come from for spring fertility celebrations).

Copyright Asteria Books 2015

Hazel

Corylus spp.

Folk Names: Coll
Gender: Feminine
Planet: Sun
Element: Air
Deity: Mac Coll, Fionn MacCumhaill, Aengus, Mercury, Thor, Artemis, Diana, Danu, Diana, Arianrhod
Powers: Luck, fertility, anti-lightning, protection, wishes, wisdom, marriage, divination, healing, protection, intuition, dowsing wands, individuality, finding the hidden

HEALING: Hazelnuts have a very high nutritional value. They are recommended for tuberculosis and diabetes patients as they have energizing effects. Hazelnuts are to be consumed as such or milled, in mixture with honey. Hazelnuts are recommended especially to anemic persons, pregnant women, children and elderly. Eating 20 hazelnuts in the morning and 20 in the evening has a beneficial effect on the body. Also, they are extremely effective in dissolving kidney stones.

MAGIC AND RITUAL: Hazel's atmosphere brings exhilaration and inspiration, and it has been called the 'Poet's Tree.' It has associations with faerie lore and entrance into faerie realms. It is one of the "Seven Chieftain Trees" of the Celts, and the unnecessary felling of hazel trees brought the death penalty in Ireland. The Hazel is considered to be the Tree of knowledge for the Celts. Its nuts are ultimate receptacles of wisdom. It was used in combination with other woods (oak, apple and willow) for various purposes, and it has associations with love divinations and love wands (possibly due to the shape of the leaves). Because it is plentiful near water, it is associated with wells and springs. For example, nine hazels of "poetic art" surrounded Connla's Well, the destination and home of the first salmon. Magically speaking, silver snakes and silvery fish dart around its roots, which signifies swift energy. Hazel brings speed through the air and water. In Cornwall, it was used for dowsing (to find water, ley lines, thieves, murderers and treasure). In France, it was used for beating the bounds (to define the boundaries and make sure they didn't fall into a state of neglect). In Wales, twigs were made into wishing caps. The The nuts were used in divination rituals, especially concerning love. Hazel wands or rods bring poetic and magical inspiration. They can also be used as "talking sticks" for order in large group discussions. The Druids also believed they could achieve invisibility from hazel crowns.

Copyright Asteria Books 2017

Salmon

Salmo salar

Celtic Name: Bradan
Gender: Masculine
Planet: Mercury
Element: Water
Deity: Cuchulainn, Fionn MacCumhaill
Powers: *wisdom, knowledge, inspiration*

MYTH, MAGIC, AND RITUAL: The Salmon is the "Oldest Animal" in Welsh mythology and is critical in the search for Mabon. Salmon is a symbol of wisdom, inspiration, and rejuvenation.

The Salmon will return to the place of its own birth to mate (often with great difficulty) and is, therefore, a reminder that we need to journey back to our own beginnings to find wisdom. The Druid quest is for wisdom and knowledge, leading eventually to the Oldest Animal.

It swims in the Well of Wisdom (Connla's Well) at the source of all life, a sacred pool that has nine hazel trees growing around it. Fionn MacCumhaill received the wisdom of the Salmon when he was cooking the fish for his teacher. The grease splashed on his hand, and he got the knowledge of the fish when he sucked the burned spot. This is a reminder to us all that the one who does the work (catches, cleans, and cooks the fish) is the one who reaps the rewards of wisdom.

Wisdom is a blessing that comes from experience. There are no shortcuts. Time, pain, and hardship are very effective teachers, though they are not the only ones by which we learn. Still, it is our OWN experience by which we gain true wisdom, and not merely insightful observation.

Copyright Asteria Books 2020

Lapwing

Vanellinae

Folk Names: Curracag
Deity: Ostara/Eostre
Powers: *Resourcefulness, distraction, wisdom, divination*

MYTH, MAGIC, AND RITUAL: The lapwing is one of the three guardian animals discussed by Robert Graves in his book *The White Goddess*. (The other two are Dog and Roebuck, both of which have a place in our totemic wheel). The lapwing guards the Mysteries of the Wise, he says, by "disguising the Truth." She does this by feigning injury to make herself appear helpless to predators who have come to close to her nest. This nest is on the ground in the spring, with her hatchlings inside. She flops and flails and flies in little spurts, all the time leading the predator away from her young. When she has gone far enough, she abandons the rouse and flies away.

The Greeks used the phrase "deceitful as a lapwing" because of this same behavior. Framed positively, though, we see the lapwing's great resourcefulness and cleverness.

Because Lapwing's nest rests on the ground in the spring, hares have been known to sit in them, looking like they are hatching eggs (which is where the combined association of bunnies and eggs come from for spring fertility celebrations). It is actually said in myth that the Teutonic Goddess Ostara transformed a Lapwing into a Hare. The Hare, of course, is already associated with shape-shifting, and this myth shows that Lapwing is also a shape-shifter (further adding to her ability to "disguise the Truth").

She is a Guardian of the Mysteries, and she teaches us to look beyond the superficial details, to ignore appearance and aim instead for reality.

Copyright Asteria Books 2021

Samhain Spirit Allies

Toad (*Buaf*) - transformation, inner visions, death and rebirth, hidden power and beauty
Elder (*Ruis*) - death and rebirth, change and transition
Crane (*Corr*) - longevity, remembrance, past lives, secret knowledge, patience

The Toad is a powerful symbol of transformation, as it grows from tadpole to Toad. It has associations with fertility, magic, fairies, and Witchcraft. Toads secrete a thick white poison through their skin. This **"Toad's Milk"** or *bufotenine* is sometimes hallucinogenic, and is said to be an ingredient in some ancient flying ointments. Witches' marks are sometimes referred to as a **"Toad's foot,"** and a birthmark shaped like a Toad is a sure sign of witch blood.

The Elder tree is associated with death and rebirth. The 13th month is a time of endings and balances, and the Elder is a tree of balance. This is a tree of the Faery. If one cuts down this tree without seeking the will of the Tree Spirits and of the Faery, a blight or curse will fall on that person. Her wood is never burned as it is considered bad luck to do so. Elder berries are a potent and delicious medicinal and are used to make wine.

Crane represents longevity and creation through focus. In Celtic lore, Cranes are often associated with the Underworld and are thought to be heralds of war and death. They are also associated with perseverance due to the fact that they will stand for hours looking into the water and waiting for the right time to strike at fish. The Crane symbolizes "secret knowledge" which is represented by the Ogham script of the Celts, which is said to be based on the shapes of the Crane's legs as they fly.

Copyright Asteria Books 2015

Elder

Sambucus canadensis

Folk Names: Alhuren, Battree, Boure Tree, Bour Tree, Eldrum, Ellhorn, Frau Holle (German), Hildemor (German,) Hollunder (German), Hylder, Lady Ellhorn, Old Gal, Old Lady, Pipe Tree, Rob Elder, Sureau (French), Sweet Elder, Tree of Doom, Yakoribengeskro (Romany), Devil's Eye
Gender: Feminine
Planet: Venus
Element: Water (Air)
Deity: Hulda, Venus, Pan, the Dark Mother, Isis, Hel

Powers: Clairvoyance, commanding, compassion, consecration, contact other planes, divination, love, magic, messages from the dead, protection, psychic protection, transformation

HEALING: Cathartic, diaphoretic, diuretic, purgative, stimulant. Some Native Americans used root bark tea for headache, mucus congestion, and to promote labor in childbirth. An infusion of leaves and flowers or a decoction of bark serves as an antiseptic wash for skin problems, wounds, and inflammations. Flower tea taken warm is said to stimulate and to induce sweating; it can also be taken for headaches due to colds and for rheumatism. Taken cold it has diuretic properties. An infusion of the leaf buds is strongly purgative. Fresh berry juice, evaporated into a syrup, is moderately purgative. The dried berries can be made into a tea useful for diarrhea and cholera. CAUTION: All parts of the fresh plant can cause poisoning. Cooked berries are safe and are commonly used in pies and jam.

MAGIC AND RITUAL: The Elder tree is associated with death and rebirth. The 13th month is a time of endings and balances, and the Elder is a tree of balance. This tree is never called into the Grove, but it is recognized where it stands (outside the Grove). The Elder is usually found at the opening to barrows and passages to the Underworld. This is a tree of the Faery. If one cuts down this tree without seeking the will of the Tree Spirits and of the Faery, a blight or curse will fall on that person. Her wood is never burned as it is considered bad luck to do so. In some parts of the world the Elder is considered as a protection against snakes and thieves. The Elder protects one from harm and psychic attack. It represents change and transition. The Elder is sacred to the various guardians of crossing over from one life to death and from death back into life.

Copyright Asteria Books 2017

Toad

Bufonidae

Folk Names: Buaf, anuran, peeper, croaker, bullfrog
Deity: WitchFather, Heket, Bael, Aphrodite
Powers: transformation, inner visions, death and rebirth, hidden power and beauty

MYTH, MAGIC, AND RITUAL: The toad is a powerful symbol of transformation, as it grows from tadpole to toad. It has associations with fertility, magic, fairies, and Witchcraft.

The toad represented the uterus in ancient Greece, Rome, and Scandinavia. Because of this symbolism, the toad came to be the symbol for a midwife, thus leading to associations with Witchcraft.

In Basque country toads were said to be favored familiars, with witches going so far as to "baptize" their toads in cemeteries, and adorn them with velvet ribbons and bells.

Toads secrete a thick white poison through their skin. This "toad's milk" or bufotenine is sometimes hallucinogenic, and is said to be an ingredient in some ancient flying ointments.

In Shropshire it was said that the spirit of a well would manifest as three toads, the largest of which was to always be addressed as the "Dark Lord" - a manifestation of the God of the Witches.

Witches' marks are sometimes referred to as a "toad's foot", and a birthmark shaped like a toad is a sure sign of witch power.

Toadstools are so named due to the toad's associations with fairyland, and with their hallucinogenic properties.

Doreen Valiente was a fan of the natterjack toad, and recommended them as pets and excellent familiars. The natterjack toad has associations with the "yellow ringed" toad which produced the legendary Toad Bone amulet, which was said to confer many strange magical powers on those who carried it. It is related to the toadstone, a stone said to rest in the head of a toad.

Copyright Asteria Books 2021

Crane

Gruidae

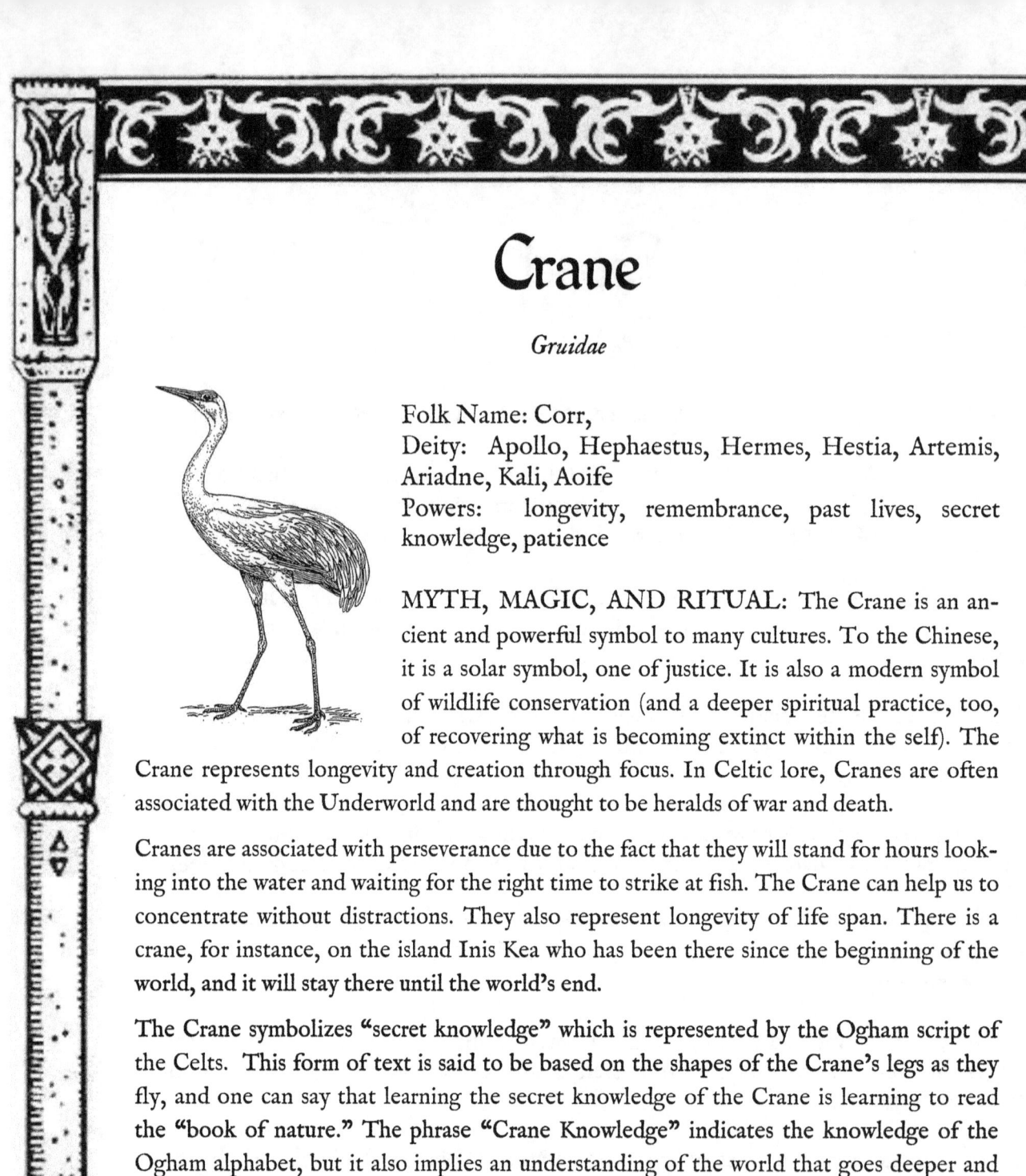

Folk Name: Corr,
Deity: Apollo, Hephaestus, Hermes, Hestia, Artemis, Ariadne, Kali, Aoife
Powers: longevity, remembrance, past lives, secret knowledge, patience

MYTH, MAGIC, AND RITUAL: The Crane is an ancient and powerful symbol to many cultures. To the Chinese, it is a solar symbol, one of justice. It is also a modern symbol of wildlife conservation (and a deeper spiritual practice, too, of recovering what is becoming extinct within the self). The Crane represents longevity and creation through focus. In Celtic lore, Cranes are often associated with the Underworld and are thought to be heralds of war and death.

Cranes are associated with perseverance due to the fact that they will stand for hours looking into the water and waiting for the right time to strike at fish. The Crane can help us to concentrate without distractions. They also represent longevity of life span. There is a crane, for instance, on the island Inis Kea who has been there since the beginning of the world, and it will stay there until the world's end.

The Crane symbolizes "secret knowledge" which is represented by the Ogham script of the Celts. This form of text is said to be based on the shapes of the Crane's legs as they fly, and one can say that learning the secret knowledge of the Crane is learning to read the "book of nature." The phrase "Crane Knowledge" indicates the knowledge of the Ogham alphabet, but it also implies an understanding of the world that goes deeper and has connections to many Realms - including past-life knowledge, predicting rain storms, etc.

The Crane bag is the Druid's medicine bag (in which he carried his Koelbren lots - or carved Ogham staves). The Crane Bag is a symbol of the fetal sac or womb and has connections to the things we carry from one life to another.

The Crane is often a guide to the Underworld, whether at the time of death or during an inner journey. These birds are often shown in groups of threes. For instance, three cranes protect entrance to Annwn, three cranes appear on a bull's back in several drawings, and three cranes guard Midhir's castle.

Copyright Asteria Books 2021

November Spirit Allies

Fox - (*Sionnach*) trickster, invisibility, shape-shifting, diplomacy, wildness

Rowan - (*Luis*) protection against enchantment, psychic power, self-control

Raven - (*Bran*) underworld messenger, shape-shifting, trickster, initiation, protection

Fox is credited with being a "cunning one" who is "strong in council." In nature, the Fox is stealthy and clever. He knows when to stay hidden and when to come out into the open. Fox can teach you the discernment to know when to speak your mind and when to keep silent. Similarly, Fox teaches invisibility. Fox is very intelligent, diplomatic, and charming. These qualities can be seen as sly and deceitful, though, when used dishonestly. Fox is often regarded as a trickster, for this reason. He is "quick on his feet" and can teach you to make quick decisions and put them into action right away.

The Rowan is sometimes referred to as the "Tree of Life" or the "Lady of the Mountain" and is thought to protect against enchantment. The wood of the Rowan was often used for rune staves (sticks which are engraved with the Ogham or runs and used as a divinatory tool) and as a divining rod for metal. The Rowan berry has a pentagram in its center and is red in color.

Raven is a bird of magic and mysticism, shapeshifting, creation, birth and death, healing, initiation, protection and prophecy. Raven is great at vocalizations and can even be taught to speak. Raven can use tools, is not intimidated by others, is fast and wary, and does not make easy prey for other animals. Raven is strongly associated with Odin, Bran the Blessed, and the Morrigan. In all of these cases, Raven is linked to messages, battle, and death.

Copyright Asteria Books 2015

Rowan

Sorbus acuparia

Folk Names: Delight of the Eye, Mountain Ash, Quickbane, Ran Tree, Roden-Quicken, Roden-Quicken-Royan, Roynetree, Sorb Apple, Thor's Helper, Whitty, Wicken-Tree, Wiggin, Wiggy, Wiky, Wild Ash, Witchbane, Witchen, Witchwood
Gender: Masculine
Planet: Sun
Element: Fire
Deity: Thor, Brigantia, Brigid, Virgin Mary
Powers: Psychic powers, healing, power, success, protection

HEALING: Some of the health benefits of rowan berries include their ability to boost the immune system, strengthen the respiratory system, improve digestion, prevent certain cancers, and reduce bacterial infections. They are also commonly pressed into jams and jellies. As the astringent taste fades with freezing, they are also commonly used as "superfoods," due to the recently discovered organic compound content of this rare berry.

MAGIC AND RITUAL: Sometimes referred to as the "Tree of Life" or the "Lady of the Mountain," this tree is thought to protect against enchantment. The wood of this tree was often used for rune staves (sticks which are engraved with the Ogham or runs and used as a divinatory tool) and as a divining rod for metal. Also used as a generally protective talisman, the branches of the Rowan Tree are hung over the doors of houses and barns to protect the inhabitants. It is planted in cemeteries in Wales to guard over the spirits of the dead. Babies' cradles are often made of Rowan wood, as it is thought to keep death and harm away from the young. Some references claim that Rowan wood protects one from the Faery. The Rowan berry has a pentagram in its center and is red in color. A necklace strung of the berries is said to protect the wearer from harm. Rowan indicates an ability to contain control of your senses, provides protection from harm and a protection when engaged in battle.

Copyright Asteria Books 2017

Fox

Vulpes

Folk Names: *Sionnach, Reynard, tod, vixen*
Deity: Ninhursag, Dionysos, Inari,
Powers: trickster, invisibility, shape-shifting, diplomacy, wildness

MYTH, MAGIC, AND RITUAL: Fox is credited with being a "cunning one" who is "strong in council." In nature, the fox is stealthy and clever. He knows when to stay hidden and when to come out into the open. Fox can teach you the discernment to know when to speak your mind and when to keep silent. Similarly, Fox teaches invisibility.

Fox is very intelligent, diplomatic, and charming. These qualities can be seen as sly and deceitful, though, when used dishonestly. Fox is often regarded as a trickster, for this reason.

He is "quick on his feet" and can teach you to make quick decisions and put them into action right away. He can also teach you to navigate obstacles quickly and decisively.

Fox is connected to Raven in this month's totems by virtue of them both being messengers who can access all Realms. Foxes can climb into the high branches of the trees (Upperworld), are astute navigators and runners on the ground (Middleworld), and dig dens below ground (Underworld).

Names for fox in different lands have been used by chieftains, princes, and advisers. *Reynard* means "strong in council," and *Louernia* means "son of Fox."

Foxes are usually red and white (or black and white) and are therefore linked to the three sacred colors. Animals with this sort of coloring were generally seen as sacred or special by the Celts, and fox fur has been discovered in princely or religious burial sites .

Copyright Asteria Books 2021

Raven

Corvus corax

Folk Names: Bran, storm petrel, Mother Carey's chicken
Deity: Odin, Morrigan, King Arthur, Apollo, Qayin
Powers: underworld messenger, shape-shifting, trickster, initiation, protection

MYTH, MAGIC, AND RITUAL: The Raven is the most sacred bird of the British Isles. Raven is a bird of magic and mysticism, shapeshifting, creation, birth and death, healing, initiation, protection and prophecy. Raven is great at vocalizations and can even be taught to speak. She can use tools, is not intimidated by others, is fast and wary, and does not make easy prey for other animals.

In the Near East, Raven is considered unclean, due to the fact that she is a scavenger. In Norse tradition, Odin had 2 Ravens as messengers (Thought and Memory). Furthermore, Odin was known to shape-shift as a Raven. In the Pacific Northwest, Raven was the bringer of life and order. She was the bringer of sunlight. Even in British tradition, Raven is seen sometimes as a bird of morning, sunlight and joy. In the tale of Beowulf, Raven helps Beowulf to victory.

Bran the Blessed, whose name means Raven, was sometimes known as the Raven King. He was beheaded in battle, and his head was buried in White Mount, which later became the hill on which the Tower of London was built. His head was placed to face the enemies and protect England from invasion. In fact, both London and Lyons had Raven totems. Furthermore, both cities were dedicated to Lugh who was warned of the approach of the Formorians by Ravens. Another legend claims that King Arthur became a Raven upon his death.

Ravens are often associated with death and the Underworld. The cries of Ravens are heard before death in battle, and Ravens are often said to bring messages from the Underworld. For this reason, they are bird of prophecy and divination. The Raven has the ability to see the past and the future, while living in the present.

In this way, the Raven is a bringer of Initiation, both little "i" and big "I" initiation is, after all, a death of one thing and the birth of another.

Raven is strongly associated with Morrigan (and one of Her particular aspects, Badb). Morrigan appears on the battlefield as Raven (or Scald-Crow), bringing havoc and fear in the enemy. Linked to their presence at or proclamation of Death, they are associated with deep healing (the kind of healing that comes from radical confrontation with the hidden), the type of healing offered by the Morrigan.

Copyright Asteria Books 2021

December Spirit Allies

Goat (*Gabhar*) - surefooted, achievement, sensuality, sacrifice
Holly (*Tinne*) - protection, balance, unity, defense, battle
Wren (*Drui-En*) - resourcefulness, boldness, sacrifice

The Goat's horns indicate an ability to perceive future and are also associated with weapons and defense. Its thick coat enables it to survive hostile conditions. The Goat was depicted in the zodiac through Capricorn - a time of year for culminating new moves or initiating them. Originally denoting the Goat that was slaughtered, "Yule Goat" now typically refers to a goat-figure made of straw. It is also associated with the custom of wassailing, sometimes referred to as "going Yule Goat" in Scandinavia.

The Holly is the strongest protective herb, offering protection against evil spirits, poisons, short-tempered or angry elementals, thunder and lighting, and uninvited spirits. As an evergreen, it represents immortality and is said to bring luck and prosperity. Holly is also associated with dream magic, clear wisdom and courage. Its flower's petals form an equal-armed "cross" which resembles a star. The berries are poisonous to all but birds.

The Wren was said to be crowned the king of the birds, after riding an eagle to the highest point in the sky, above all other birds, and then soaring above even the eagle! The Wren is noted for its cunning for this stunt, and for the trick of building many false nests to lead away hunters. Breton Druids claimed that it was the wren who first brought down fire from heaven, forever singeing its tail feathers, causing the wren to have its distinctive blunt tail.

Copyright Asteria Books 2015

Holly

Ilex aquifolium

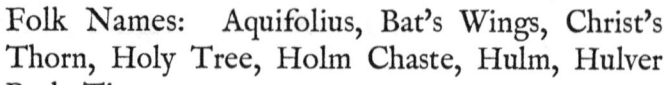

Folk Names: Aquifolius, Bat's Wings, Christ's Thorn, Holy Tree, Holm Chaste, Hulm, Hulver Bush, Tinne
Gender: Masculine
Planet: Mars
Element: Fire
Deity: Inanna, Odin, the Holly King and Wildman (Green Man), Cuchulain, Druids, Lugh, Saturn, Mars

Powers: Clairvoyance, consecration, divination, magic, protection, renewal, transformation, virility, anti-lightning, luck, dream magic

HEALING: Diuretic, purgative. White holly seems to have been used in the past primarily as a means of cleansing the system by promoting the proper elimination of waste products from the body. **CAUTION:** The berries are mildly poisonous and are dangerous to small children.

MAGIC AND RITUAL: Holly flowers' petals form an equal-armed "cross" which resembles a star. The berries are poisonous to all but birds. The Holly is the strongest protective herb, offering protection against evil spirits, poisons, short-tempered or angry elementals, thunder and lighting, and uninvited spirits. It represents immortality (as an evergreen) and is said to bring luck and prosperity. It is also associated with dream magic, clear wisdom and courage. In winter, Druids advised people to take it into their homes to shelter elves and fairies, though it was critical to remove them before Imbolc Eve since faeryfolk couldn't live peacefully with humans beyond this day. Long associated with Midwinter religious observances. Its bright leaves and colorful berries lift the spirits and ward against depression, which is more likely to occur during the cold and dark winter months. Branches shouldn't be cut, but rather pulled free (as is usually the custom with sacred trees). It is said to be unlucky to burn or bury green-skinned holly branches. Protects against lighting if a holly branch from the Yule decorations is hung on the door throughout the year. A berry carried in a man's pocket makes him more attractive to women. Holly wands are said to have the strength to compel. The wood is used for making spear shafts, thus associating it with warrior pursuits.

Copyright Asteria Books 2017

Goat

Capra aegragus

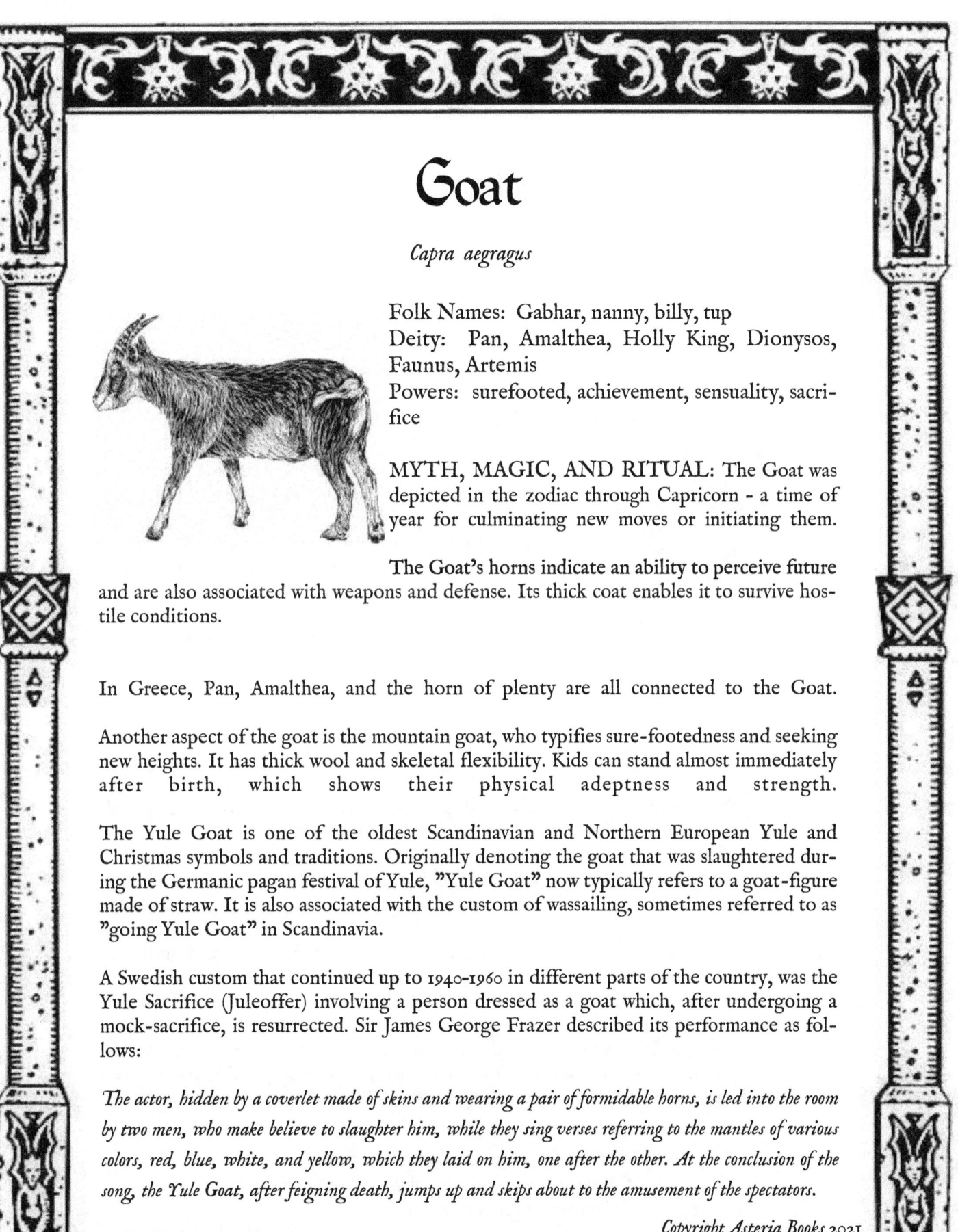

Folk Names: Gabhar, nanny, billy, tup
Deity: Pan, Amalthea, Holly King, Dionysos, Faunus, Artemis
Powers: surefooted, achievement, sensuality, sacrifice

MYTH, MAGIC, AND RITUAL: The Goat was depicted in the zodiac through Capricorn - a time of year for culminating new moves or initiating them.

The Goat's horns indicate an ability to perceive future and are also associated with weapons and defense. Its thick coat enables it to survive hostile conditions.

In Greece, Pan, Amalthea, and the horn of plenty are all connected to the Goat.

Another aspect of the goat is the mountain goat, who typifies sure-footedness and seeking new heights. It has thick wool and skeletal flexibility. Kids can stand almost immediately after birth, which shows their physical adeptness and strength.

The Yule Goat is one of the oldest Scandinavian and Northern European Yule and Christmas symbols and traditions. Originally denoting the goat that was slaughtered during the Germanic pagan festival of Yule, "Yule Goat" now typically refers to a goat-figure made of straw. It is also associated with the custom of wassailing, sometimes referred to as "going Yule Goat" in Scandinavia.

A Swedish custom that continued up to 1940-1960 in different parts of the country, was the Yule Sacrifice (Juleoffer) involving a person dressed as a goat which, after undergoing a mock-sacrifice, is resurrected. Sir James George Frazer described its performance as follows:

The actor, hidden by a coverlet made of skins and wearing a pair of formidable horns, is led into the room by two men, who make believe to slaughter him, while they sing verses referring to the mantles of various colors, red, blue, white, and yellow, which they laid on him, one after the other. At the conclusion of the song, the Yule Goat, after feigning death, jumps up and skips about to the amusement of the spectators.

Copyright Asteria Books 2021

Wren

Troglodytidae

Folk Names: *Drui-En*
Deity: Holly King,
Powers: resourcefulness, boldness, sacrifice

MYTH, MAGIC, AND RITUAL: Of all of the birds venerated by the Celtic peoples, and associated with the Druids, the humble wren is the most revered. The wren was said to be crowned the king of the birds, after riding an eagle to the highest point in the sky, above all other birds, and then soaring above even the eagle! The wren is noted for its cunning for this stunt, and for the trick of building many false nests to lead away hunters.

Breton Druids claimed that it was the wren who first brought down fire from heaven, forever singeing its tail feathers, causing the wren to have its distinctive blunt tail.

There is a Manx legend of a mermaid who transformed into a wren, causing sailors to wear wren feathers when at sea to protect them from drowning.

The wren, mighty king of the birds, dies a king's sacrificial death each year on St. Stephen's day (December 26) when it is hunted by the "Wren Boys."

Irish tradition holds that the wren symbolizes the old year (the Holly King), while the robin symbolizes the year to come (the Oak King, born as the newly risen sun at Yule).

Originally, groups of small boys would hunt for a wren, and then chase the bird until they either have caught it or it has died from exhaustion. The dead bird was tied to the top of a pole or holly bush, which was decorated with ribbons or colored paper.

Early in the morning of St. Stephen's Day, the wren was carried from house to house by the boys, who wore straw masks or blackened their faces with burnt cork, and dressed in old clothes. At each house, the boys sing the Wren Boys' song. Such as:

The wren, the wren, the king of all birds,
On St. Stephen's Day was caught in the furze;
Up with the kettle and down with the pan,
Pray give us a penny to bury the wren.

Copyright Asteria Books 2021

Craft Specialties

Witch as Artisan

"Artisan" is a broad category that encompasses all of the Witchcrafting specialties that involve making magickal objects. An Artisan-Witch is skilled in (and/or passionate about) Crafting physical items for use in their Craft, and they may or may not sell their goods, as well. Additionally, many items that they make for daily use are imbued with magickal energy and intention.

These Witches often employ one or more of the traditional arts, crafts, or trades in their work — such as smithing, cooking, baking, brewing, sewing, weaving, embroidery, dyeing, carving, sculpting, jewelry-making, painting, doll-making, candle-making, etc.

Their focus may be on producing a whole finished product that was crafted with magickal intent (like a garment), or it may be on embellishing an item to imbue intent (by embroidering bindrunes or sigils onto a garment). Knowledge of magickal alphabets, sigil-crafting, colors, and various symbolism often plays a large role in the creation of both traditional and new talismans. Indeed, Witches who are drawn to talismanic magick are Artisans at heart.

Many Artisan-Witches have a sub-specialty, such as "blacksmith" or "kitchen witch" that defines the area of their greatest interest, skill, and contribution. In a coven setting, they might be relied upon to share these skills to augment ritual or spellcraft by guiding the talisman creation, leading ritual feasts, sewing robes and cloaks, etc.

Copyright Asteria Books 2022

Witch as Bard

A Witch who is drawn to the role of Bard creates and understands their world (and expresses their magick and spirituality) via word and/or music.

As a musician, they may employ voice and instrumentation, original and traditional composition, etc. They are often interested in researching traditional instruments and musical styles from the cultures that inspire or contribute to their Craft practice. They write and perform songs (with or without lyrics) to accompany ritual, spellcraft, and journey work. They may also set traditional pieces of poetry, group chants, or other existing words to music.

As a writer or wordsmith, they may create works of fiction, non-fiction, poetry, and liturgy. In this way, they contribute to the working materials of their coven/tradition — or to the practice of Witchcraft at large. Writing chants, ballads, charges, calls, releases, and other pieces to be read or recited during ritual or magick is one of the most common ways that Bards practice their Craft; although those who write essays (or even fictional works in which real magick may be discerned) are also practicing the Bardic arts within a Craft context.

A Bard can be both a music and wordsmith — or just one of these.

Copyright Asteria Books 2022

Witch as Conjurer

In some parts of the world (and in certain time periods), to be a Witch has been synonymous with being a Conjurer. While most Traditional and Folkloric Witches work with Spirits to some extent (such as their Spirit Court), we recognize that there are those among us who call upon Spirits frequently and interact intimately with the Unseen World. The Conjurer works closely with Land Wights, Ancestors, Daemons, Angels, Fey, Sidhe, and/or other types of Spirits in order to accomplish nearly any type of magickal goal.

Conjurers often live in a world of Spirit, with one foot in consensus reality and the other in the vale of the Unseen. They understand and have methods for calling upon Spirits to aid with divination and prophecy, healing, prosperity, finding lost objects, protection, retribution, gaining status and acclaim, and/or other goals that are important to them (or their coven, if they work within one).

They are comfortable and knowledgeable in Building the Pyramid (or Triangle of Art) in order to aid Spirits in manifesting, and they have a strong sense of when and how to use banishing techniques, which Spirits to avoid, and how best to communicate with a given Spirit. They may experience Spirits in ways that are unique to themselves, as well, particularly if one of their "inner senses" is more dominant.

Copyright Asteria Books 2022

Witch as Healer

Healing traditions within Witchcraft are numerous, and there is much lore surrounding the Witch as midwife for both birth and death. Many contemporary Witches are strong energetic healers who expand their skills to include both alternative and established medicine. Witches who are Healers are knowledgeable in healing techniques that can include physical, energetic, and spiritual modalities. They may employ herbalism, massage, acupuncture, acupressure, tonal healing, energy manipulation, journeying/flight, stones, and more.

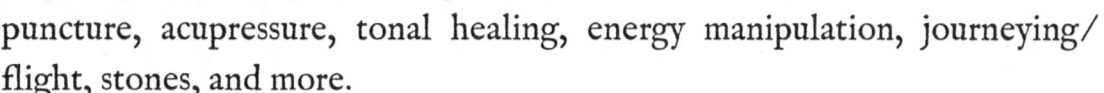

Most Healers within the Craft take a holistic approach in which health is seen as the natural state and involves balance of the mind, the body, and the spirit. Imbalances in any of these areas can create stress and dis-ease in the whole person.

Herbalism is a common area of study for the Healer, whose techniques may either primarily focus on working with Plant Allies to bring the target's mind-body-spirit into harmony (through the use of teas, tinctures, and other herbal preparations), or they may use herbs as an adjunct to another healing modality (such as using herb-infused oils or essential oils while they perform massage or energy healing).

Copyright Asteria Books 2022

Witch as Seer

Witches have a long and notorious history as diviners and oracles, and the Seer skills of the Witch have been sought with fear, curiosity, and awe since ancient times. As a Seer, the Witch seeks patterns, guidance, and wisdom via divination, oracle, trance, and other "visionary" states.

The "inner sense" via which the Seer experiences psychic communication and gnosis may not be visual, however. A Seer may receive auditory messages, as well as pick up on textures/temperatures, scents, and tastes. Furthermore, they may have a sudden sense of "knowing" that comes to them from the Unseen worlds.

The skills of the Seer include divination with one or more tools, journey work (or Witch Flight), mediumship, and even remote viewing. The purpose of the Seer's work is often to gain insight, experience revelation or gnosis, explore the Mysteries, find solutions to problems, or aid in healing.

Many Seers accomplish these tasks through the assistance and guidance of a Familiar Spirit or tutelary Godd.

In a coven setting, a Seer may be the primary medium for oracles from the Godds.

Copyright Asteria Books 2022

Witch as Votary

The most pervasive images of a Priest or Priestex in the ancient world are not of clergy ministering to the people of a congregation, but of sacred functionaries who carry out the tasks associated with honoring or caring for a Deity. The Witch who is a Votary performs works in service and connection to a particular Godd or Power (or occasionally to a group of Godds). They seek to better understand the Divine through deep, personal connection. They may also act as a bridge between this Godd and the community (coven, Trad, public, etc.).

A Votary, by definition, is a person who has made vows of dedication to religious service.

The Votary-Witch will often experience their work as a calling or vocation, and they often experience their relationship as an employee, emissary, mentee, progeny, partner, sibling, lover, or spouse of the Godd or Power to whom they are devoted.

They perform acts of ritual and service as defined by that Godd/Power, which deepen and expand their practice and provide a path to enlightenment. Within a coven or community, they may act as an exegetai (one who provides exegesis or explanation/extrapolation) regarding the myths and symbols around their Godd.

Copyright Asteria Books 2022

Witch as Warden

Most Traditions require that all Witches have some basic knowledge and skill in warding magicks — those defenses established to protect the individual, the home, and the person/group. A great number of Craft Traditions assign a ritual role as sentry, guardian, or warrior, as well — to protect the group during magickal operations. Some Traditions recognize the call of a few Witches to take on this role (called "Warden," here) on a larger or more frequent scale.

The Warden acts as guardian and warrior on behalf of self/partner/coven/Trad. They are skilled at energetic shielding, ward-setting, psychic self-defense, and possibly also in one or more martial or combat arts. They often identify as a warrior, protector, or guardian in other aspects of their life, as well.

Many people who are called to the role of Warden have an interest in martial arts theory, philosophy, and techniques from all over the world — including the chivalry of medieval Europe, Wing Chun and Shaolin King Fu of China, Brazil's Capoeira, Israel's Krava Maga, or any of the others that span the globe. Most of these systems are encoded with their own ethical and/or energetic principles, which tend to inform the magickal practice of Warden-Witch.

Wardens understand that safety and protection, like health, are holistic states involving mind, body, and spirit.

Copyright Asteria Books 2022

Mysteries

Life in Death, Death in Life

From Liber Qayin, The Black Book of Lilith-Sophia:

1) *In the beginning there was only me.*

2) *I am the darkness.*

3) *From the wind in the night I came.*

4) *I am called Lilith.*

5) *The Elohim fashioned me from Wind and Blood and dark, rich Earth; for I am the womb of the world, and I am its tomb.*

27) *I am the dark road of death and am called Life-in-Death. Hekate.*

From Liber Qayin, The White Book of Ishtar-Eve:

4) *I am the Light in the Darkness, the star-fire of your soul, the hope and joy and pleasure of Gods and men. And I am also Death-in-Life, the little death found in the arms of love.*

5) *I am all possibility without limit.*

6) *You see in me the ocean or the vast starry heavens, opening into the fruition of your dreams. And so I am.*

7) *And if you have Wisdom, you tremble before me.*

8) *For I am untempered Life come rushing to meet you, unbounded Love poured upon you like the Sea.*

Copyright Asteria Books 2022

The Rose Beyond the Grave

From *Beyond The Realms Of Death-- by Robin the Dart*

... For we also celebrate life, having a deep respect for all deserving things around us. More importantly, we believe that life is but a preparation for death. As [Evan] John [Jones] once said to me - "I thought I was learning to live, but I am really learning to die". Blessings be upon him and all past Clan members [always in our thoughts and often with us]. ...

After a substantial preparation, the rite culminates in ritual. Wrapped within the 'Clan' shroud adorned with specific symbols and angelic seals, his spirit finally began its journey with full ceremony. Eventually, the aspirant returned from this complex and involved rite in which success cannot be guaranteed [much depends upon the individual's own egress], a radiant, shining, illuminated soul. When one touches just briefly true Virtue, one brings back a token of that sentience, and as the travelling continues one learns to love life and fear not death, the gateway to eternity.

... Focus is on one's inner self, for out of nothing comes something [ex nihilo]; ... To be the child, the fool, allows us a different perspective. It is this innocence that allows the mask to fall to peer beyond the veil, to be at one with everything, to understand the delusion of illusion. To see beyond the self wherein the heart soars like a bird. The musician tunes his instrument and so must we tune the mind to the frequency of the universe - the music of the spheres.

But there can be no rebirth without the dark night of the soul; we have to feel the pull of the future, not the push of the past. Remember, with writing came the reliance of the appearance of wisdom, instead of the reality of wisdom. ... Rather, the true seeker must look beyond these superficialities to extinguish their Will as subject to True Will. For only then is the bond to material things loosened, only then too of the self to life itself, absolute renunciation, and total freedom from the fear of death. ... the gaze turned inwards engenders something else. This is why real magic is hard work. Zen saying - "show me the face you had before you were born."

... To stand at the setting and the arising, being the living among the dead, as the dead among the living, the quick not the dead. So understand the meaning of the 'Fisher King; where his wound is my wound, his bleeding my bleeding, the cure is to be touched by the same thing, the love of the source the lover and the loved being one [for the hunter and hunted are but one]. To touch the divine, a vibratory rate so high, we as matter, tremble. To experience such an unearthly fear is beyond logic, to explain it denigrates the truth of it. Then comes the pain, the terrible withdrawal whereupon the body becomes an encumbrance.

Yet to have lineage is not to impress with age or authenticity, but simply to have a track to follow our ancestral brethren, distant travellers, guides and guardians of the keys and symbols, into the Void and beyond.

What the Mask Reveals

From ... "The Profane Art of Masking: A Study into the Darker Elements of our Winter Masking and Guising Rituals" [edited extract taken from the entitled article published in 'The White Dragon' Nov. 2008]
--- by Shani Oates

Magically, a mask is understood to represent three characters: the wearer, the personage it represents and the spirit that synthesises the two. ...

Masks are the oldest expression of humanity. They retain the element of mystery, inculcating uncertainty within the onlooker. ... They adopt a public face by hiding the private one; they transform, protect, scare, intimidate, shock, all by inversion! Masks generate transformation in the viewers mind, for the wearer of such a tool, this is immensely empowering. It is also liberating. They are the intercessors between the gods and man, hence all the superstitions accorded to them by onlookers. Masks command attention. ...

To cover ones face is alluring and motivates intrigue, it cultivates curiosity and fear; it arouses suspicion and often engenders unease. ... We cannot know our tormentor, entertainer, anarchist; they remain shadows to our senses. ... There is no full communion between masked and unmasked, interaction is restricted. We are simultaneously seduced and repelled by it. The mask and disguise invites an intimacy that is at once a barrier, paradoxically enforcing separation. ...

Mundanity is vanquished, momentarily banished in this small suspension of reality. We are drawn into an alternative worldview, and we believe it, just for a moment.... For a few brief moments we experience euphoria, elation whilst riding the tide of unease. Friction or fiction? Success depends upon our willingness to engage. Fight or flight. Adrenalin rush either way. This is pure magic and heady stuff. ...

Was it or can it ever be, just harmless fun? Are we drawn inexorably towards aggression, depravity and decadence when immersed in our darker natures? How are such things determined and measured? Is it liberating and edifying or intimidating and oppressive? Surely it all depends from which side of the mask we view the world? And this is precisely where we enter the realms of the sacred use of masking within the Mysteries wherein the individual seeks the companie of the 'other' from both sides of the mask......

"All the world's a stage, and all the men and women merely players........"

The Robin and the Wren

There is much folklore around both the Robin and the Wren, and some bits of folklore and poetry that link them. When sung together, we hear of the love between Cock Robin and Jenny Wren — a love that often ends in tragedy, as one is killed, since they are both birds of sacrifice. We also see them pitted against each other in battles reminiscent of the Oak King and Holly King.

They also have links to the Solstices and to the 3 Realms. Robin is associated with Summer, and Wren with Winter. Robin with the world of the Dead below, and Wren with the path of the Sun in the celestial realm.

The Wren Song
The wren, the wren, the king of all birds,
St. Stephen's Day was caught in the furze,
Although he was little his honour was great,
Jump up me lads and give him a treat.

Chorus:
Up with the kettle and down with the pan,
And give us a penny to bury the wren.

The Wren She Lies in Care's Bed
The wren lies in her sickbed
In much misery and pining
When in came robin redbreast
With breads in sugared water and wine
Robin says, "will you sip this?"
And you'll belong to me
No, not a drop, robin
For it has come too late

Copyright Asteria Books 2022

Oak and Holly King

From Cad Goddeu (The Battle of the Trees):

> *Holly, it was tinted with green,*
> *He was the hero.*
>
> *The oak, quickly moving,*
> *Before him, tremble heaven and earth.*
> *A valiant door-keeper against an enemy,*
> *his name is considered.*

Robert Graves in *The White Goddess* identifies other legends and archetypes of paired hero-figures as the basis of the Holly/Oak King myth, including:

> Lleu Llaw Gyffes and Gronw Pebr
> Gwyn and Gwythyr
> Lugh and Balor
> Balan and Balin
> Gawain and the Green Knight
> Jesus and John the Baptist

Path of the Kings -- which connects the Horned Lords of Summer and Winter, Basajaun and Janicot – Cernunnos and Odin. They are the Oak King and Holly King, keepers of the Stone Castle and the Glass Castle, guardians of the Stone Bowl and the Glass Orb.

Copyright Asteria Books 2022

What is Seen by Odin's Eye

Across mythology and folklore, we see tales of figures whose physical sight is sacrificed in order to gain greater wisdom — or even the gift of prophecy. Odin is one of these figures, and he sacrifices one of his eyes at Mimir's Well in order to see into the future.

The Glass Orb of the Spiral Castle Tradition is sometimes called "Odin's Eye" — and also by the names "Glain" and "Adder's Egg."

We recognize the challenges of balancing Sight in other Realms with continuing to see clearly in this Realm. The Glass Castle — or Glastonbury — is a place long associated with both clear-seeing and also illusion.

Copyright Asteria Books 2022

Upon an Uneasy Seat

In his first letter to Norman Gills, Robert Cochrane writes that a witch *"... INVOKES THE GODDESS THROUGH 'THE DARK OF NIGHT AND THE EVENING STAR MEETING TOGETHER', WHICH AS YOU SHOULD KNOW IS BROUGHT ABOUT IN THE BEGINNING BY 'AN UNEASY CHAIR ABOVE CAER OCHREN'."* These phrases refer to the Mystery of invocation or possession.

Let's start with 'The dark of night and the evening star meeting together.' This is a reference to possession, which is also called channeling, invocation, aspecting, or being ridden. Later in the same letter, Cochrane says that this process can't be taught in writing.

Perhaps it is easiest to say that the "dark of night" is a reference to the Self — that internal place, the opening, yearning for something greater than what is known and seen. We all have it, this chasm that cries out for spiritual experience, for that which is beyond us.

The "evening star," then, is the Goddess who is being invoked. It could be any Goddess or God. Some covens do possessory work at specific Sabbats or Esbats, and it is often done for the primary purpose of oracular communications from specific Deities. We seek their advice and listen to the wisdom that they share.

Caer Ochren is one of the castles of Grail lore, possibly Caer Sidhe itself. Some of this is just our gut instinct, but a little comes from an interesting linguistic find. "Ochren" means "sides." It could be easy to mistake "sidhe" (which means fairy) as "sides" — or to intentionally muddy the waters by playing language tricks with these words. This is the center point of the witch's compass, opening onto all the sides. A seat above it, poetically speaking, could be the starry point to which the central spire of the castle rises. The North Star, Tubelo's nail star, the iron hook.

It is possibly a reference to the oracle of Delphi sitting upon her tripod stand above the fissure within the temple's floor. The temple at Delphi held the omphalos, the world's navel, the center point. You can use a rocking chair as the tripod, as the "uneasy seat." When a witch sits in the rocking chair at the Sabbat, she begins the process of ascending to the top of the Spiral Castle. It is the seat of wisdom, the seat of vision. By rocking back and forth as she works toward invocation, she is seething, which is a VERY effective way to alter consciousness.

Copyright Asteria Books 2015

Light out of Darkness, Darkness in Light

The White Goddess rules in the South at Lammas, and the Black Goddess dominates the North at Imbolc. In fact, these are two faces of the SAME Goddess -- the quintessential Witch's Goddess – the Witch Mother. She is both light and darkness.

Through the light half of the year, we mark the influence of the White Goddess whom we call upon as Goda. Hulda is an aspect of the White Goddess, and you will see us later refer to Her as a Queen (for She is the keeper of the Castle of Revelry). The same is true for the Black Goddess (Kolyo), Cerridwen (the Queen of the Castle Perilous), and the dark half of the year.

However, as much as the Black and White Goddesses counterpoint each other on the Year Wheel and within the compass that we lay, we must acknowledge and understand that they work along a continuum. They are not truly separate from each other. One requires the other for full manifestation, and the dynamic balance maintained between the two (within the Year Wheel, the symbolism of the Trad, and the inherent energies They represent) is critical to the practice of the Craft as we know it.

Each holds within Herself the core of the other. Within the darkness of the night, the light of the moon and stars reaches us. During the brightness of the day, shadows lurk. Just as the white knife cuts in the physical realm, and the black in the astral; so, too, do the Goddesses relate respectively to the physical and astral. The two are, in fact, reflections of each other.

From LiberQayin, the Black Book of Lilith-Sophia:
1) *In the beginning there was only me.*
2) *I am the darkness.*
8) *Adam and I lay together, and I conceived a daughter by him. She was Eve, the mother of all races.*
9) *Eve was my treasure, the Light I brought forth from my Darkness.*
10) *But she was also my rival. For I am the Darkness in the Light.*

From Liber Qayin, the White Book of Ishtar-Eve:
Thus spake Ishtar-Eve, consort of Qayin:
2) *I am the Bride, the Queen of Heaven, the joy upon the Earth.*
3) *My names have been many and beloved, as the stars of the heavens, for I am Asherah, Aphrodite, Babalon, the Magdalene, Aradia, Inanna, Astarte.*
4) *I am the Light in the Darkness, the star-fire of your soul, the hope and joy and pleasure of Gods and men. And I am also Death-in-Life, the little death found in the arms of love.*

Copyright Asteria Books 2022

Fire and Ice

Fire and Ice have been powerful builders and shapers in the world's landscape. They are both deadly and destructive powerful forces, and they both call to the human Spirit with voices of beauty and allure.

In hard winters, they are both there. Both are threats to survival, and yet both are part of the same life-giving cycle.

At Imbolc, we look to the fires that burn in tiny places under the ground (the metabolic processes awakening in the seeds), the growing light of the Sun, and the fire of the Hearth to stead us through what is often the iciest and harshest parts of the year.

"Far beneath the winter snows / A heart of fire beats and glows"

A deep study of the Runes Nauthiz and Isa (which are present in the holding of the Stav and Tein — or Stang and Arrow) and an exploration of the galdr of these two Runes can be very illuminating.

Copyright Asteria Books 2022

Whirling Without Motion

In his letters to Joe Wilson, Cochrane says that the Mystery of the Broom is "whirling without motion between three elements." He also relates this Mystery to the Qabbalistic Middle Pillar and the "path to the 7 gates of percep-tion." He is, of course, talking about the practice of trance-work and medita-tion -- and using these tools (the Broom, is the metaphor for the tool) in or-der to access ALL THAT IS.

The Broom (according to the copies of Cochrane's letters that I printed from Joe Wilson's website in 1999, and which actually include illustrations) is constructed from a small, forked Ash staff. Between the prongs of the fork, a sacred stone is bound. The strips used for binding, the broom twigs, and the handle, are each different sacred woods. (A forked Ash staff, Birch bristles, and Willow bindings.) Each of these woods is related to a different element — Earth, Air, and Water. The stone he calls "balanite," we have researched to be none other than basalt — the most common stone on the Earth's surface, which is formed when lava is rapidly cooled in water. In a sense, it is the result of liquid fire meeting water. (Alchemy in action!)

The Mystery of the Broom is an inner alchemy that allows us to enter the trance state — to "spin" (without moving) between the Upper Realm of Air, the Middle Realm of Earth, and the Under Realm of Water.

Copyright Asteria Books 2022

The Sword That Cuts Both Ways

The English idiom "to cut both ways" is a phrase that refers to the nature of a double-edged sword. It means, in general usage, that an action can have both good and bad effects, and also that it can affect both sides of the arrangement.

Within the Spiral Castle Tradition, our Covens hold a "Sword That Cuts Both Ways" which acts as the "Sword-Bridge" that candidates for initiation must cross at the beginning of the rite. It is across this Sword-Bridge that the threshold guardian gives the challenges and the warnings of the serious nature of the rite.

"For it is better that you rush upon this blade and spill out your life's blood than enter here with fear or falseness in your heart. How do you enter?"

"In perfect Love and perfect Trust."

This call and response does not represent a threat. Rather, it is a warning. To enter the initiation for the wrong reasons, out of coercion or obligation, with distrust for the initiator or the process, is to invite disaster for both yourself and for the initiator/Coven.

The blade reminds us that the Oaths and Vows impact both those who give them and also those who receive them.

Copyright Asteria Books 2022

The Fires Under Caer Sidhe

One of the shared visions of the cosmology of the Spiral Castle is that of a Castle on a Hill with the North Star (the "Nail Star" at the topmost spire and Tubelo's forge deep below. With these, we see the Star-fire and Forge-fire that are symbolic of our enlightenment and illumination.

As an extension of this shared vision, one of the Mysteries that we have seen is that of two Dragons below the Castle who blow the fires of the Forge.

Like Vortigern's Dragons, they are Blood Red and Milk White, and also like them, they may represent two (or rather, multiple) influences within our Craft. Unlike Vortigern's Dragons, they are not at odds — slashing each other and shaking our foundations. Instead, they work in tandem, in complement — each fueling the Great Work.

There is undoubtedly a link between these Dragons and the red and white roses we associate with the two faces of the Witch Mother, as well.

Finally, we also know them to be connected to the "sarf ruth" — the "fire in the land" — Dragon-power in the sacred landscape.

Copyright Asteria Books 2022

There Is No Magic Without Sacrifice

There is an ebb and flow to the Universe, which includes its resources both visible and invisible. We may not be able to see the balance of the scales from our finite perspective, but if we are Wise, we know that a cause over here produces an effect over there.

Magic is any act of Will that produces change. That change can happen within us and then be brought into the world; it can be brought about by logical and practical applications of effort; and it can also happen through triggers and ripples of mechanisms that are unseen by us.

Anytime we seek to produce a change in one area, we set into motion a series of events that changes another area. Perhaps many changes.

In our relationships with both people and Spirits, we understand the nature of reciprocity. A gift for a gift. Whether we always see and understand the mechanisms of the change we have Willed into being, we must always be prepared to give a gift in exchange for the gift we seek.

Copyright Asteria Books 2022

What Songs the Siren Sings

Excerpted from "Siren Song ---quid Sirenes cantare sint solitae?"
- by Ian Chambers

Robert Graves, that inspired and inspirational poet of the last century, to whom many owe a debt of gratitude, opened his landmark study The White Goddess by reiterating some questions attributed to Dr Thomas Browne, but more correctly from Suetonius(i) "What songs the siren sang?" is one of those questions. Beginning the epic voyage that such a puzzle requires means we must equip ourselves in order to navigate the mythic landscape with a well constructed myth-faring vessel. With a keen ear to the wind, and with the poet cartographer mapping the terrain before us, only then may we set a course to enquire "what songs the siren sang".

...the tone of the siren's song is a sombre lament, although the theme is one of love or desire. The 'siren song' represents something tempting with its allure, while possessing a quality ultimately with mortal consequences. What love song has not contained within it the threat of the lament for the broken heart, just as the gift of life brings with it the inevitable promise of death. The pang of love, while rapturous in our hearts, also causes it to ache at separation and this is the affect of the siren. ...

The song of the sirens, then, is the lament of the soul at being separated from its source, the anima mundi. It is the pine for reunification, the unio mystica where a union of souls occur, an appeal to the heart of the hero who has bound himself to the vessel of the world upon the great sea of the cosmos. Ultimately, to hear the siren song is to feel the irresistible pull of the anima mundi playing the heart strings like the lyre of Orpheus. ...

In answer to the question, then, "What song the sirens sang", we can offer the solution that it was the song of the soul, sung seductively by sirens, calling it back home.

"And Uriel said unto me: 'Here shall stand the angels who have lain with women... and those women whom they seduced shall become sirens."
First Book of Enoch, Chapter 19

The Dance of the Seven Veils

Consider Salome's "Dance of the Seven Veils" as an ecstatic dance to liberate the Soul, an initiatory dance to relinquish the mortal ties to life (if only briefly) and to glimpse the Self – naked and true. It is a re-enactment of the Descent of Inanna, the Descent of Ishtar in which the Goddess of Life and Fertility seeks to know her dark sister and her truest self in order to understand the Mysteries of Death and Rebirth. At each Gate of the city of the dead, she is confronted by a guardian to whom she must surrender the powerful magickal objects that have defined her life.

The First Gate – Sun – Gold – Great Crown – Ego and sense of identity

The Second Gate – Moon – Silver and Moonstones – Earrings – Emotions and intuition

The Third Gate -- Jupiter -- Lapis Lazuli – Beads around her neck – Wealth/Goods and Profession/Vocation

The Fourth Gate -- Venus -- Copper – Toggle Pins at Breast/Heart – Relationships

The Fifth Gate -- Mars -- Iron – Girdle of Birthstones – Reproduction and passions

The Sixth Gate -- Mercury – Quicksilver – Bangles on Wrists/Ankles – Memories and thoughts

The Seventh Gate -- Saturn -- Lead/Bone – Robe – Body

Copyright Asteria Books 2022

The Two Words That Don't Fit in the Cauldron

Robert Cochrane writes on the "two words that do not fit in the cauldron" as a mystery of the Craft. The answer to this riddle is "Be Still" for within the cauldron lies all motion, all potential, and all things. It cannot hold stillness, but this too is a mystery. The cauldron is used not just for the brewing of potions, but also as a vessel for scrying in liquid or flame. To accomplish this we must find stillness within the cauldron, by quieting our own minds.

Cochrane, in his letters to Joe Wilson, mentions a thread of connection between the Goddess of the Cauldron ("one who becomes seven states of Wisdom" and also to the Mystery of the Broom, which he equates with the Middle Pillar exercise and also with the "dance of the seven veils." These are different approaches with similar results.

In an article titled "The Spirals of Existence" written for *The Cauldron* in 1997 (and reprinted in *The Roebuck in the Thicket*), EJ Jones says:

> "In the same guise, she [the Pale-Faced Goddess] is still the keeper of the cauldron, which is now invested with all of the attributes of the Anglo-Saxon wyrd. It is still the same cauldron where past, present, and future are one and the same thing, and it is always in a constant state of flux, always forming and reforming, never still. It holds all of the knowledge of the past and present that combines over and over again to create what is yet to come. It is also the vessel of wisdom and inspiration from which, if we manage to sup from it, we can gain some of that knowledge."

Copyright Asteria Books 2022

Sangreal

From Liber Qayin, the White Book of Ishtar-Eve:

> 40) *The rose of my love is stained crimson with the blood of his sacrifice.*
>
> 41) *For it is unto me, the Lady of Love and Life and Liberty, that all blood sacrifice must be made and for whom all War must be waged. And so it is that I am She of Love and War, for both are bought with blood.*
>
> 42) *The first thrust of Love and the passage of Birth are marked with my crimson seal, the Rose of Blood, my red flower.*
>
> 43) *You may have neither Life nor Freedom nor Love without paying the price, for these are the deepest magics.*
>
> 44) *My mother Lilith-Sophia is the source, the Fountain, the Sang Real, the Holy Blood.*
>
> 45) *And I am Eve-Babalon, the vessel, the chalice, the San Graal, the Holy Grail.*

The power and virtue held within the blood is of particular interest within many Mystery Schools. The term sangreal could mean either "royal blood" or "holy grail," depending upon how this compound word is divided.

The Arthurian Mysteries themselves point the way to many of our Craft Mysteries, and we see the power of blood (both in terms of lineage and of sacrifice) play out in these legends.

We account Witch Blood as coming from the Witch Mother and Witch Father, though we most often discuss the bloodline as the Line of Qayin — a lineage that we share by virtue of our vows and oaths, which are sealed in blood.

Menstruation, sacrifice, and lineage are all tied to this Mystery.

Copyright Asteria Books 2022

The Five Transformations

Gwion Bach (the "small boy") gives us a peek at the transformations of the Soul through the phases of enlightenment on his own path to becoming the "shining browed" Taliesin.

Awen (inspiration) is the elixir which ignites the shift, and Gwion Bach is chosen by Awen, which he has been diligently stirring for a year's toil at the employment of Ceridwen, keeper of the cauldron and powerful sorceress. Gwion Bach is not Ceridwen's intended recipient of the elixir, but he is chosen by the brew itself — who recognizes him as being the worthy recipient.

In murderous rage, Ceridwen gives chase to the now all-wise child, who knows his doom is at hand.

He transforms into a hare, and she gives chase as a greyhound.

He transforms into a fish, and she gives chase as an otter.

He transforms into a bird, and she gives chase as a hawk.

He transforms into a grain, and she devours him as a hen.

As a woman again, she births the Radiant One.

Their initiatory pursuit leads them through the Realms and beyond — through destruction to rebirth. It tempers the knowledge gained through inspiration into true Wisdom.

Copyright Asteria Books 2022

Regalia

Regalia and Gifts

These are the garments, jewels, and other markers worn by Witches of the Spiral Castle Tradition during ritual. A Witch is not compelled to wear anything beyond their robes and cords, unless moved by custom and desire.

Greening

- Green Cord

Adoption

- Red Cord
- Black, hooded Robe
- White, hooded Robe
- Copper Cuff (gifted)
- Black Cloak

Note: Hoods/Veils may be separate from Robes

Raising

- Triple Cords (Black and White added to Red)
- Amber, Jet, Bone necklace (gifted)
- 3 Knives – on ring belt or Cords
- Witch's Mark – tattoo on ring or index finger (stang or 3 dots)

2nd Admission

- Service Cords – hanging from Triples
- Bone Ring (gifted)
- Crane Bag – on ring belt

Queen, Devil, Consort

- Garter Cords
- Plain, Crescent, or Horned Crown (gifted)
- Red Cloak

All

- Seasonal Ladders
- Ritual Talismans
- Star-Stone Ring (any tektites – moldavite, obsidian, Lybian desert glass, etc.)

Copyright Asteria Books 2022

Initiation

No-Kill Food List

Fruits & Berries
Apples
Apricots
Bananas
Blackberries
Blueberries
Cantaloupe
Cherries
Coconuts
Cranberries
Dates
Figs
Grapes
Grapefruit
Honeydew Melons
Kiwi
Lemons
Limes
Mangoes
Nectarines
Olives
Oranges
Pomegranates
Pears
Plums
Raisins
Raspberries
Strawberries
Watermelon

Many Vegetables
Artichokes
Asparagus
Bell Peppers
Greens (spinach, chard, collard, kale)
Tomatoes
Avocadoes
Broccoli
Squash (all varieties)
Pumpkin
Zucchini
Brussels Sprouts
Cauliflower
Cucumber

Beans & Some Legumes
Green Beans
Peas
Peanuts
Black Beans
Kidney Beans
Navy Beans
Pinto Beans
White Beans
Soy Beans, Edamame

Many Herbs, Spices & Seasonings
Salt
Pepper
Cinnamon
Cardamom
Cocoa (unsweetened)
Allspice
Nutmeg
Curry
Chives
Cilantro
Dill
Oregano
Rosemary
Mint
Basil
Parsley
Sage
Thyme
(All the leafy herbs)
Oil
Vinegar

Most Seeds & Nuts
Cashews
Sunflower Seeds
Pepitas
Almonds
Walnuts
Pecans
Pistachios

Grains & Starches
Corn, Hominy, Grits, Polenta
Oats, Oatmeal
Quinoa
Barley
Buckwheat
Bulgar wheat
Couscous
Potatoes
Sweet Potatoes
Rice

Dairy
Butter
Sour Cream
Milk
Cheese
Yogurt
Heavy Cream

Unrefined Sweeteners
Agave
Raw Honey
Monk Fruit Sweetener

Copyright Asteria Books 2020

No-Kill No-No List

No-No Vegetables
Beets
Cabbage
Carrots
Celery
Garlic
Leeks
Mushrooms
Onions
Parsnips
Radishes
Turnips

No-No Legumes
Chickpeas
Lentils

No-No Herbs, Spices & Seasonings
Turmeric
Ginger
Most prepared condiments (will have onion, garlic, or turmeric -- or sugar)

No-No Grains & Starches
Pasta (prepared with egg)
Bread (prepared with egg & yeast)

No-No Sweeteners
White sugar
Brown sugar
Corn syrup
Light syrup

No-No Proteins
Animal meat (including fish)
Eggs

As with any type of fast, the No-Kill Fast is intentionally restrictive. However, it's purpose isn't to deprive your body of essential nutrients or create a state of lack or general privation. The purpose is to bring mindfulness, clarity, and purification.

You are free to choose other types of fasts, if you prefer. The Spiral Castle Tradition has always favored this one, however, because it draws such a sharp point of focus while allowing great room for personal choice without leaving any food groups out. With forethought, you should be able to eat balanced meals and snacks during your time of fasting.

Tips: Watch out for pre-packed foods. So many of them have onion or garlic powder or sugar! Read the labels carefully. When in doubt, research "home harvesting" or "is X a perennial" for the ingredient to see if the parent plant would likely be killed in your garden for you to eat this food.

Copyright Asteria Books 2020

A Few No-Kill Fast Recipes

Breakfasts

- Quick (or Steel Cut) Oats with honey, cinnamon, cream
- Grits with honey and butter
- Greek yogurt with berries and toasted oats

Snacks

- Cottage cheese with fruit (orange slices, pineapple chunks, or strawberries) and sesame seeds
- Parmesan crisps and homemade hummus or guacamole (leaving the garlic out of either dip, of course)
- Apple slices with sugar-free peanut butter
- Banana with a handful of almonds

Nachos

Corn chips
Freshly chopped tomatoes
Black beans
Shredded cheese (2-3 varieties)
Avocado slices
Sour cream

Three Sisters Bowl

2 cups cubed and peeled squash of choice
1 Tbsp balsamic vinegar
1 Tbsp olive oil
1 pinch salt

Toss these together and roast in the oven for 20-30 minutes (until fork tender).

Meanwhile, sauté the following in a Dutch oven:

2 ears corn
1 1/2 cups pre-cooked or canned beans
1-2 tablespoons olive oil
1 red pepper, diced
2 tablespoons chopped parsley
1 tablespoon chopped sage
1 teaspoon minced rosemary leaves
1 teaspoon thyme leaves
salt and pepper, to taste

Combine. Serve warm as is or over wild rice, quinoa – or even cold with kale/greens as a salad.

Creamy Vegetable Soup

I start with the most basic potato soup ever – peeled cubed white potatoes, water, butter, a little salt, and heavy cream. To this I add BARLEY and whatever chopped vegetables I like and can find from our list, preferring ones that are in season. Favorites include okra and squash. I really don't measure anything, as you really can't "mess it up."

Copyright Asteria Books 2020

Initiation Recipes

Incense

2 tbsp Red rose petals (Kolyo)
2 tbps Jasmine blossoms (Koda)
1/2 tsp Forge scale for Tubal Cain
1 tsp Dittany of Crete
1 tsp White copal resin
1 tsp Rowan berries
1 tsp Sandalwood
10 drops Amber oil

Anointing Oil

1 oz Base oil (Jojoba, Grapeseed)
10 drops Rose oil
10 drops Jasmine oil
5 drops Amber oil
3 drops Clary Sage oil

Dressed Candle

Dress a white chime candle using a small amount of your anointing oil and incense. This is the candle you will burn during your preparatory bath.

Bath Sachet

Place the following in a muslin drawstring bag or cotton/linen hankie tied with a string:
2 tbsp Crushed rose petals
2 tbsp Crushed jasmine blossoms
1 tbsp Mugwort
Pinch of Sandalwood
Pinch of Sea Salt

Add 1/4 cup Apple Cider Vinegar directly to water

Sabbat Wine

Warm 1-2 cups of a VERY sweet red wine (like Oliver soft red or Manischewitz Concord grape) in a saucepan.

For every cup of wine, steep the following herbal mix in equal parts (using a teaball):

Mugwort
Lemon Balm

Steep for 5 minutes, then remove the teaball. Add raw honey to sweeten.

Copyright Asteria Books 2020

Rite of Dedication

MATERIALS
- Candles, lighter
- Red knife, thumb pricker or lancet and alcohol swabs
- Black or White Robe or Hood
- Red Cord
- Offering of Whiskey or Dark Beer

You will need solitude and quiet for this ritual. Come to it freshly bathed and wearing only your ritual robe, hood up (or simple, clean dark clothes, with your shawl/scarf).

AT A LIMINAL PLACE (riverbank, lakeshore, crossroads, graveyard, etc), make the following Declaration: "I come to this liminal place, ready to begin my study and practice of the Craft. My name is _____, and I am a Witch."

TYING THE RED THREAD
Clean your finger with the alcohol swab and draw a large drop of blood using the lancet. Dab the blood onto your Red Cord.

Dedication Oath: "I make this Oath. I vow to dedicate myself to the study and practice of Witchcraft for at least a year and day. I honor the Witch Blood that is my inheritance from the Witchfather. I vow to act with honor within the Family and to hold sacred the teachings of the Craft. I seek the starfire at topmost spire of the Spiral Castle, as well as the forge-fire at its bottommost roots. Before the Witchfather and Witchmother, I make this vow. Before my Spirits, I made this vow. Before my Holy Self, I make this vow. So mote it be!"

Make your offering and spend some time in quiet meditation of the step you just took and the vows you have made. Contemplate your link to other Witches. Open yourself to messages from the Godds or Spirits.

When you are done, clap your hands three times and say, "The work is done."

Copyright Asteria Books 2020

Rite of Raising – Self-Initiation 1

Materials
- Stang, candles, lighter
- Cauldron, water
- Anvil, hammer, lancet
- Three knives (red, black, white)
- Red Cord, Black Cord, White Cord
- Bread, lipped dish or bowl
- Red wine, cup, mugwort, lemongrass, honey, teaball
- Initiation incense, holder, charcoal
- Bath sachet, dressed candle, anointing oil
- Stone Bowl with stones, Dark Mirror
- Initiation Gift (amber, jet & bone necklace)

Raise the Stang
Lay the Compass
Open the Gates
Challenges & Trials

- **Challenges** -- Within the ritual space, challenge and query yourself by Mind, Heart, and Spirit.
- **Sabbat Wine** -- Drink the Sabbat Wine or Mugwort Tea.
- **Three Stones** -- Ask the stones which of our Deities is choosing to guide you in your future studies, work, and service within the Spiral Castle. The first stone you touch holds your answer (white-Goda, black-Kolyo, red-Qayin).
- **Black Mirror** -- Scry for these things: 1) your Craft names -- secret and known, and 2) your Mark.
- **Triple Cords** -- Braid the black cords, the white cords, and ultimately, the full set of Triple Cords together while contemplating Kolyo and her role as Weaver of Magic and Fate.

Vows, Oath & Presentation

- **Vows & Oath** -- Before the Oath Stone, ask and answer aloud each Vow. Then make your Oath in blood upon the Stone, using your full known Craft name.
- **Presentation** -- Anoint yourself with the oil, and say, "So now do I proclaim myself a true Witch of the Spiral Castle. So shall I be recognized among my Folk and Family! I present myself to the Realms, Gates, Towers, Spirits, and Godds of the Spiral Castle. I am, [Complete Craft Name], a fully Raised Witch of the Spiral Castle! So Mote it Be!"
- **Gift** -- Give yourself the Witch's Necklace (or other gift)

Housle

Copyright Asteria Books 2020

Oath of Raising

Turn to the Oath Stone.

Kneel and grasp the Stone with your blooded hand, both to give and receive the Oath of Initiation.

From this day forward, _____ will be my name in the Initiate circles of the Spiral Castle Tradition. As I will it, so mote it be! So mote it be! So mote it be!

I, _____, do take this solemn Oath of Initiation. I will be an Initiate member of this Family and Tradition from this day forward. I vow to honor Tubal Qayin, Kolyo, and Goda who have made this Path their own. I will hold secret all the Mysteries of this Family and the personal accounts of my Siblings. I will respect my fellow Initiates, and I will consider members of my Covenant as blood kin. By taking these vows, I freely twine my spirit with the Raised Witches of the Spiral Castle. I give you my trust and my honor. I give Tubal Qayin, Kolyo, and Goda my heart. I promise to speak honestly and behave with integrity. I will serve the Spiral Castle to the very best of my ability. [Additional vows may be added here.] So swear I, _____. As I will it, so mote it be. So mote it be! So mote it be!

So now am I proclaimed a true Witch of the Spiral Castle!

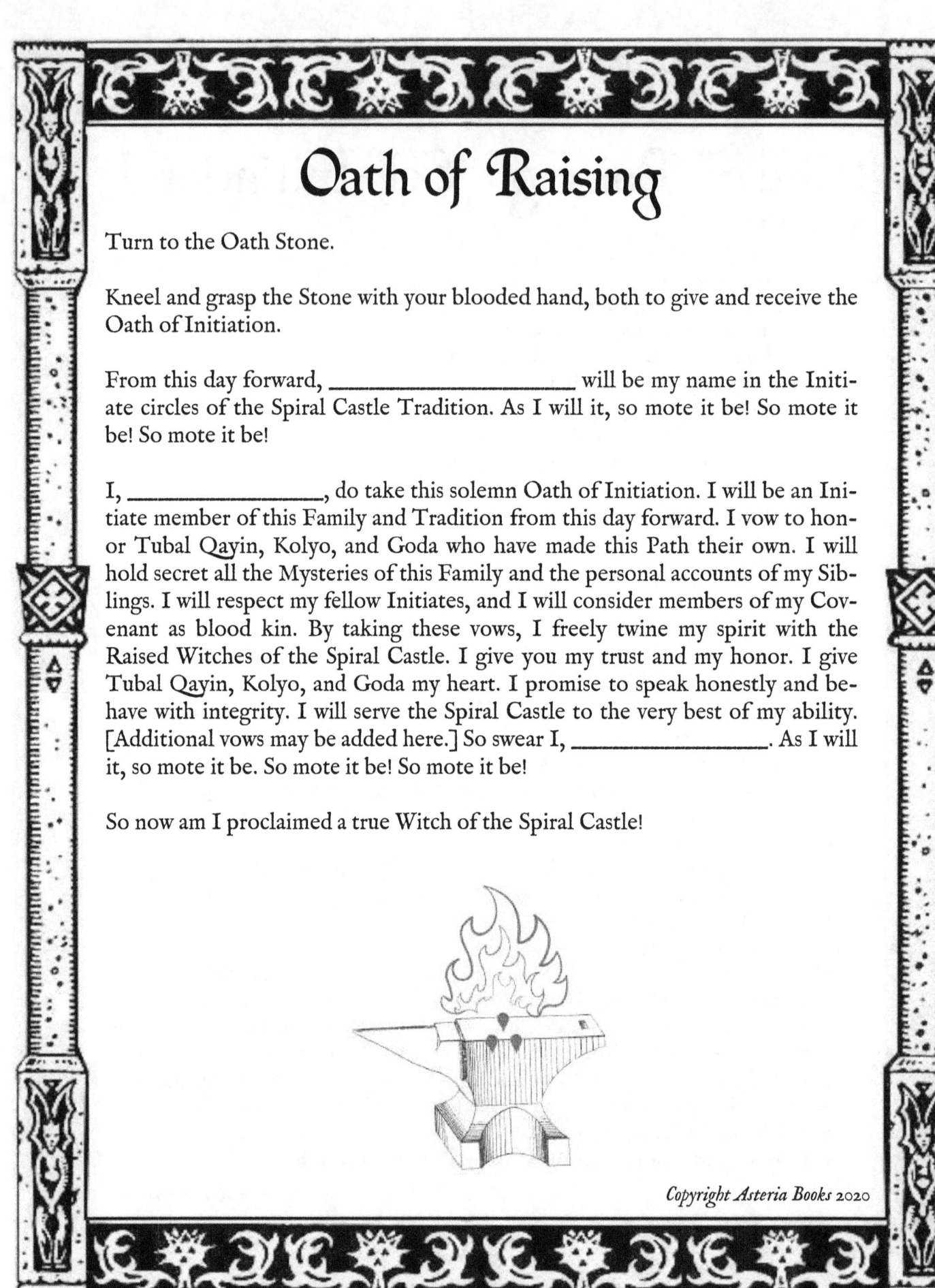

Copyright Asteria Books 2020

Vows of Raising

We do not sever the Red Cords of Adoption. A child of the Spiral Castle will always be Family ~ connected to the Craft, the Castle, its Caretakers, and this Kindred by Blood and Word. Having passed the Trials of Initiation - tests of mind, heart, and spirit -- I move forward. I have found my True Name (both spoken and silent), found and made my Mark, and seen the Vision Quest. I have proven myself worthy of the name Witch, but I am not bound to take it. I am free in all things. Furthermore, a Raised Witch is a full member of the family and can never be cast out of the tradition, even if the cords are burned, the Mark is cut from the flesh, and the blood withdrawn from the stone. The bond of the Secret Name exists between the Initiate and the Mighty Ones and can be broken by no one.

Do I choose with my own free will to take initiation in the Spiral Castle?

I have passed an examination of my knowledge of the Craft. Am I ready to fulfill my intellectual responsibilities as a Raised Witch?

I have sought and found answers from the Unseen. Am I willing to seek beyond the veil for the Truth, for both myself and my siblings?

Am I prepared to weave my spirit with the Witches in this Tradition by becoming an Initiate?

I have sought and found a vision for myself. Am I willing to share that vision and make it a reality as I grow?

I have been chosen by our Witch Father/Queen as a child of the Craft. Am I willing to explore the Mysteries of this relationship as I grow?

I say plain: I would be sworn a Witch.
I say again: I would be worn a Witch.
By Thrice-three I lay my claim: I will be sworn an Initiate Witch in the Spiral Castle Tradition.

So mote it be!

Copyright Asteria Books 2020

Rite of 2nd Admission (Self)

Materials
- Stang, candles, lighter
- Cauldron, water
- Anvil, hammer, lancet
- Three knives (red, black, white)
- Yarn for Service Cords
- Bread, lipped dish or bowl
- Red wine, cup, mugwort, lemongrass, honey, teaball
- Initiation incense, holder, charcoal
- Bath sachet, dressed candle, anointing oil
- Mazey Stone
- Veil/Shroud
- Initiation Gift (bone ring)

Raise the Stang

Lay the Compass

Open the Gates & Raise the Castles

Challenges & Trials

- **Challenges** -- Within the ritual space, challenge and query yourself by Mind, Heart, and Spirit.
- **Sabbat Wine** -- Drink the Sabbat Wine or Mugwort Tea.
- **Mazey Stone** -- Trace the finger path on your Mazey Stone to enter trance.
- **Service Cords** -- Braid your Service Cords while contemplating the contributions, sacrifices, and benefits of your Specialty and your role within it.
- **Sacrifice & Rebirth** -- Perform the ritual sacrifice and go through the Death and Rebirth cycle.

Vows, Oath & Presentation

- **Vows & Oath** -- Before the Oath Stone, ask and answer aloud each Vow. Then make your Oath in blood upon the Stone, using your full known Craft name.
- **Presentation** -- Anoint yourself with the oil, and say, "So now do I proclaim myself a true [Warden, Votary, etc] of the Spiral Castle. So shall I be recognized among my Folk and Family! I present myself to the Realms, Gates, Towers, Spirits, and Godds of the Spiral Castle. I am, [Complete Craft Name], a full Witch and [Artisan, Bard, etc] of the Spiral Castle! So Mote it Be!"
- **Gift** -- Give yourself the Witch's Ring (or other gift)

Housle

Copyright Asteria Books 2022

Oath of 2nd Admission

Turn to the Oath Stone.

Kneel and grasp the Stone with your blooded hand, both to give and receive the Oath of 2nd Admission.

I, _____, do take this solemn Oath of 2nd Admission. I will serve and study as a/n [Specialty]-Initiate member of this Family and Tradition from this day forward. I vow to serve Tubal Qayin, Kolyo, and Goda who have made this Path their own, through my skill, knowledge, and experience. I will seek the Mysteries of the [Specialty] and the deeper Mysteries of the Craft of the Wise. By taking these vows, I freely begin the work of 2nd Admission within the Spiral Castle. I promise to speak honestly and behave with integrity. I will serve the Spiral Castle to the very best of my ability. [Additional vows may be added here.] So swear I, _____. As I will it, so mote it be. So mote it be! So mote it be!

So now am I proclaimed a Witch of 2nd Admission and a [Specialty] of the Spiral Castle!

Copyright Asteria Books 2022

Vows of 2nd Admission

I have come to this place as a Raised Witch of the Spiral Castle, to offer myself in service and study — to the Powers whose Kindred this is, to the Family, and to MySelf. Having passed the Trials of Initiation - tests of mind, heart, and spirit -- I move forward. I have found my way into the Heart of the Mysteries, studied and served as a [Specialty], and have made the ultimate sacrifice. I have proven myself worthy of the name [Specialty] in service to the Powers, the Family and MySelf, but I am not bound to serve. I am free in all things. I remain a Raised Witch — a full member of the Family who can never be cast out of the tradition, even if the cords are burned, the Mark is cut from the flesh, and the blood withdrawn from the stone. The bond of the Secret Name exists between the Initiate and the Mighty Ones and can be broken by no one.

Do I choose with my own free will to take this role of service in the Spiral Castle?

I have passed an examination of my knowledge of the Craft. Am I ready to fulfill my intellectual responsibilities as a Witch of 2nd Admission?

I have ventured into the Unseen. Am I willing to seek beyond the veil for the Truth, for both myself and my siblings?

Am I prepared to continue studying and practicing the arts of the [Specialty]?

I have sacrificed and found renewal. Am I ready to see and seek the pattern of sacrifice and renewal around me?

I have sought the balance of practical magick and esoteric gnosis. Am I able to continue seeking this balance as I walk my Crooked Path?

I say plain: I would be sworn a Witch of 2nd Admission and a [Specialty].
I say again: I would be sworn a Witch of 2nd Admission and a [Specialty].
By Thrice-three I lay my claim: I will be sworn a Witch of 2nd Admission and a [Specialty] in the Spiral Castle Tradition.

So mote it be!

Copyright Asteria Books 2022

Rite of 3rd Admission (Self)

MATERIALS
- Stang, candles, lighter
- Cauldron, water
- Anvil, hammer, lancet
- Three knives (red, black, white)
- Yarn for Garter Cords
- Bread, lipped dish or bowl
- Red wine, cup, mugwort, lemongrass, honey, teaball
- Initiation incense, holder, charcoal
- Bath sachet, dressed candle, anointing oil
- Gandreid
- Initiation Gift (crown)

RAISE THE STANG

LAY THE COMPASS

OPEN THE GATES & RAISE THE CASTLES & CALL THE REALMS

CHALLENGES & TRIALS

- CHALLENGES -- Within the ritual space, challenge and query yourself by Mind, Heart, and Spirit.
- SABBAT WINE -- Drink the Sabbat Wine or Mugwort Tea.
- WITCH FLIGHT -- Fly to the Brocken and meet your Initiating-Power.
- GARTER -- Braid your Garter Cords while contemplating the Virtue and Mys-tery you have received, and your place as a Queen, Devil, or Consort in the Clannad.

Vows, Oath & Presentation

- Vows & OATH -- Before the Oath Stone, ask and answer aloud each Vow. Then make your Oath in blood upon the Stone, using your full known Craft name.
- PRESENTATION -- Anoint yourself with the oil, and say, "So now do I proclaim myself a true [Queen, Devil, Consort] of the Spiral Castle. So shall I be recognized among my Folk and Family! I present myself to the Realms, Gates, Towers, Spirits, and Godds of the Spiral Castle. I am, [Complete Craft Name], a full Witch and [Artisan, Bard, etc] and [Queen, Devil, Consort] of the Spiral Castle! So Mote it Be!"
- GIFT -- Give yourself the Crown (or other gift)

HOUSLE

Copyright Asteria Books 2022

Vows of 3rd Admission

I have come to this place as a Raised Witch and a [Specialty] of the Spiral Castle, to offer myself in service and study — to the Powers whose Kindred this is, to the Family, and to MySelf. Having passed the Trials of Initiation - tests of mind, heart, and spirit -- I move forward. I have danced among the Mysteries, planned and prepared for leadership, and have received the Virtue of one of our Great Powers. I have proven myself worthy of the name [Queen, Devil, or Consort] in partnership to the Powers, the Family and MySelf, but I am not bound to serve. I am free in all things. I remain a Raised Witch — a full member of the Family who can never be cast out of the tradition, even if the cords are burned, the Mark is cut from the flesh, and the blood withdrawn from the stone. The bond of the Secret Name exists between the Initiate and the Mighty Ones and can be broken by no one.

Do I choose with my own free will to take a place as an Elder in the Spiral Castle?

I have passed an examination of my knowledge of the Craft. Am I ready to fulfill my intellectual responsibilities as a Witch of 3rd Admission?

I have ventured to the Brocken. Am I willing to fly-out in search of ecstasy, union, and Truth?

Am I prepared to continue seeking the face of the Mysteries, all the days along my Path?

I have received the Virtue of [Goda, Kolyo, or Qayin]. Am I ready to manifest that Virtue within the Clannad?

I have sought the balance of practical magick and esoteric gnosis. Am I able to continue seeking this balance as I walk my Crooked Path?

I say plain: I would be sworn a Witch of 3rd Admission and a [Q,D,C].
I say again: I would be sworn a Witch of 3rd Admission and a [Q,D,C].
By Thrice-three I lay my claim: I will be sworn a Witch of 3rd Admission and a [Queen, Devil, Consort] in the Spiral Castle Tradition. So mote it be!

Copyright Asteria Books 2022

Oath of 3rd Admission

Turn to the Oath Stone.

Kneel and grasp the Stone with your blooded hand, both to give and receive the Oath of 3rd Admission.

I, _____, do take this solemn Oath of 3rd Admission. I will serve and study as Elder member of this Family and Tradition from this day forward. I vow to serve Tubal Qayin, Kolyo, and Goda who have made this Path their own, through my skill, knowledge, and experience. I will continue to seek the Mysteries — among them the Light, Shadows, and Contours of my Souls. By taking these vows, I freely begin the work of the Elders of the Spiral Castle. I promise to speak honestly and behave with integrity. I will serve the Spiral Castle to the very best of my ability. [Additional vows may be added here.] So swear I, _____. As I will it, so mote it be. So mote it be! So mote it be!

So now am I proclaimed a Witch of 3rd Admission and a [Queen, Devil, or Consort] of the Spiral Castle!

Copyright Asteria Books 2022

Coven Leadership

Under the Rose

To work "Under the Rose" means to work in secrecy, taken from the Latin *subrosa*. Most modern covens assume a level of secrecy for some or all of their meetings and rituals and hold both their membership and meeting place confidential as a matter of precaution. This clandestine air has a two-fold purpose. One is a simple safety measure. The other is an act of guardianship relative to the Mysteries.

While we are no longer hunted openly in Europe, North America, or Australia, it is still not considered entirely safe to be a Witch throughout most of the world (even in places where it is no longer a criminal act). For this reason, the Ardanes (or "laws") of many groups forbid revealing the name of another Witch or the location of the covenstead to a cowan.

Preserving the Mysteries of the Craft (or of the Gods) is another reason for working *subrosa*. Robert Cochrane once said, "*No genuine esoteric truth can be written down or put within an intellectual framework of thought. The truths involved are to be participated in during comprehension of the soul.*" This is what is meant by Mystery.

It is said that Eros gave Harpocrates (the Egyptian God of secrets) the rose with which Harpocrates became associated in honor of Eros' own mother Aphrodite. Aphrodite had a long association with the rose — and many delicious (and dangerous) secrets to keep. She kept her own and those of others in many myths.

A rose suspended from a chamber ceiling in the Middle Ages pledged all to secrecy. The Rosicrucians (Order of the Rosy Cross) were a secret society. Many confessionals are decorated with carved roses to reinforce the idea of secrecy.

The Black and White Goddesses of the Craft are both symbolized by the rose, reminding us of the Mystery of life-in-death and death-in-life. — a secret which must be experienced to be understood.

Copyright Asteria Books 2019

Coven Caer Sidhe - Guidance

Coven Caer Sidhe is the "Home Coven" of the Spiral Castle Clannad. It was the first Coven formed within this Tradition by its original founders, and it is the spiritual home of the Clannad's current Regent.

The policies and procedures of the Home Coven serve as a map or template that other Covens within the Tradition might use to create their own Charters. Each Coven, though, has a unique personality, and their structure and leadership should reflect themselves rather than being a mirror image of any other group.

Copyright Asteria Books 2022

Norms & Expectations
Coven Caer Sidhe

Coven Caer Sidhe is an egalitarian gathering of like-minded Witches who are connected through the bonds of Family. We honor and recognize the wisdom and experience of the Elders among us and look to them for teaching and counsel.

Participation & Behavior – All persons present are expected to contribute their intellect, skills, care, and labor in meaningful and constructive ways. We complete the tasks for which we volunteer to the best of our ability, and we are accountable to each other for the success of all of our endeavors. All active Coveners are expected to attend the classes, rituals, and meetings of their Degree, if they are reasonably able, and also to complete assignments.

Communication – All members of our Coven communicate as clearly and compassionately as possible, both in-person and via electronic means. Honesty is a deeply held value, though we temper it with our genuine love for each other. Our spaces are "safe spaces," in which members are free to share difficult thoughts, ideas, and experiences without judgment or retalia-tion. They are also "brave spaces" where we understand that challenging assumptions and rationale is a path to personal growth.

Privacy – The names, addresses, professions, family members, likenesses, and experiences of our Siblings are held sacred and are not shared with those outside our Coven, except with the express consent of that Sibling.

Shared Resources – All members are asked to contribute to the resources of the Coven, within their means to do so. Financial obligations for supplies will be split between those present, with each "pitching in" what is needed for rituals. Personal tools may be volunteered for group use, either long-term or for a single ritual. Tools may also be purchased or donated for permanent group use. In the event of disbanding of the Coven, tools and supplies will be re-turned to their contributors, if reasonably possible. Any monies collected will be divided evenly among active members. In the case of an individual leaving the Coven, they are entitled to reclaim any tool which they had offered (but not _donated_) for group use, so long as they make that claim within three months of their last attendance.

Copyright Asteria Books 2022

Norms & Expectations, cont.
Coven Caer Sidhe

Set-Up/Clean-Up — The Covenstead shall be kept reasonably clean and tidy by the home-holder so that Coveners are not expected to clean-up or deal with debris, clutter, and soil prior to meetings, classes, or rituals. All Coveners will assist with the set-up of ritual space, according to their physical ability. Any messes that are made as part of the Coven's gathering (including dishes dirtied, supplies and tools displaced, and furniture moved) shall be cleaned, tidied, and restored to their proper places. All Coveners will take part in the clean-up, as well.

Entheogens — Coveners should not be under the influence of any entheogens (alcohol, drugs, psychoactive herbs/fungi, etc) unless such sacraments are appropriate to the ritual or work being undertaken. In these cases, entheogenic use will be explicitly discussed and plans will be made regarding transportation and lodging. (Pain- and anxiety-management concerns should be addressed with the Elders, privately.)

Corrective Measures — Coveners who struggle to meet these expectations will be privately corrected by an Elder and give the opportunity to come into alignment with the Coven. Re-peated abuses or inability to comply could result in a hiatus or leave-taking.

Copyright Asteria Books 2022

Leadership
Coven Caer Sidhe

Within Coven Caer Sidhe, facilitation of rituals, classes, and meetings is delegated among the Witches active and present. All members of Red Cord and above are encouraged to take on a facilitation role.

Council of Elders — All active Queens, Devils, and Consorts of the Coven are *de facto* Elders, and are members of the Council of Elders. Together, this group guides the policy-making of the Coven and offers advice and mentorship to all Coveners. The Elders rotate the teaching and meeting duties, and all provide Pastoral Care according to their availability and desire.

All facilitation roles within Coven Caer Sidhe are self-selected. The terms are for one calendar year, with a mentoring/transition period of two months (from Samhain to New Year). Not all roles are required to be filled, and it is possible for one Covener to hold two roles. We are also open to adding roles, as needs arise.

The primary roles that are needed within this Coven are:

Scribe — takes detailed notes regarding business issues; concerns and ideas mentioned at meetings and classes; and keeps the minutes of all official gatherings

Pursewarden — provides financial reports at meetings; suggests a budget; maintains account-ing of dues, donations, and expenses

Watcher — provides security at public gatherings and rituals; acts as "vibeswatcher" for all private meetings

Lorekeeper — maintains the Coven scrapbook and/or storybook

Ranger — leads set-up and clean-up activities; delegates tasks as needed within this area; ensures that Covenstead and other gathering places are left better than we found them

Herald — maintains the Coven website; edits Coven publications

Copyright Asteria Books 2022

Membership
Coven Caer Sidhe

The members of Coven Caer Sidhe are Family with bonds of blood, love, and trust. There is grief and loss when one of our Witches leaves this Family. As such, we take the acceptance of new members very seriously.

Screening and acceptance of new members — Prospective members are first invited to interact with Elders and/or other Coveners in a public venue. We take this opportunity to ask questions, offer access to public materials (like the Coven website/blog), and get to know the person over the course of 1 to 3 months. If all Coveners are in agreement, we invite the pro-spective member to attend classes and rituals with us. They should attend at least two of each before requesting Greening. Greening is a period of orientation that can last another 1 to 3 months. During this time, the Green Cord is given and the new person is included in classes and rituals. If they choose to proceed, they will request Adoption (in writing), and the current active Coveners will come to a consensus to either approve or deny this request. Before Adoption into the Coven, the new Witch should have purchased their own copy of RTA Year 1: Foun-dations and have either a black or white robe with hood or veil (according to the season).

Hiatus/sabbatical of members — It is understood that we all experience cycles during our studies and practice. When a cycle of rest and/or isolation is needed, a Covener need only make their intention known to the Coven's Elders. Hiatus/Sabbatical is taken in quarter-turns of the Year Wheel, with Coveners returning to full participation at Samhain, Beltaine, Lammas, and Imbolc. It is recommended that a Covener not take more than two consecutive "turns" away from Coven life. In cases where Coveners are away for more than 6 consecutive months, the Coven must reach consensus regarding the inactive Covener's re-integration into Coven practice.

Active/inactive members — All Coveners will be considered "active" if they have participated actively and consistently in class, ritual, or other official gatherings in the last month. "Inactive" members in-clude those on hiatus, those with recently lapsed attendance and/or participation, as well as those who have chosen to discontinue their participation or association with the Coven or who have been out of contact with the Elders for more than 6 months. All Coveners, both active and inactive, are members of the Family — bonded by blood and oath.

Copyright Asteria Books 2022

Decision-Making
Coven Caer Sidhe

The members of Coven Caer Sidhe are Family. As such, all Adopted members are invested with a voice in Coven decisions.

We utilize a consensus model in our decision-making and deliberations. All Adopted Witches (of active status) are included in this consensus-building.

If a situation arises in which the Council of Elders are at odds with the Coven as a whole, the Council will have the final say in the decision, and every effort will continue to be made to bring the whole Coven to a place of consensus.

We recognize that consensus-building can be a time- and energy-consuming way to run a group, but we are committed to the egalitarian principles on which we were founded.

Copyright Asteria Books 2022

Schedules
Coven Caer Sidhe

As a result of the relocation of some members, and also resulting from the global pandemic, Coven Caer Sidhe is in the process of restructuring its meeting schedules. This is the current schedule that is in place, though it is subject to change.

Red Cord (Foundations) Studies — The Red Cords of the Coven meet every Thursday night to work through the lessons in the Year 1 course manual, as well as to read passages from the current "Book Club" selection. If possible, they meet in person at the Covenstead. Alternatively, Coveners are able to join the class via Zoom. These classes, which include Sabbat celebrations and 4 group lunar workings, are available to all members of the Coven.

Practicum Studies — Coveners engaged in the Year 2: Practicum lessons (and those wishing to add a Specialty Area) meet on the first Friday of the month to share their progress and projects. If possible, they meet in person at the Covenstead. Alternatively, Coveners are able to join the class via Zoom. This is open to all Raised Witches, of any Admission.

Mastery Studies — Coveners engaged in the Year 3: Mastery lessons, as well as those who have been admitted to 3rd Degree, gather once per quarter to fly out, discuss the Mysteries, and perform experimental Witchery together. This gathering is open to Coveners of 2nd and 3rd Admission, only. Attendance is in-person at the Covenstead, and gatherings happen on the 2nd Friday of January, April, July, and November.

Annual Retreat — All Coveners are encouraged to attend an annual weekend camping retreat which happens close to Beltaine.

Copyright Asteria Books 2022

Titles and Offices

There have been many names for the roles of Coven leadership within folkloric forms of the Craft. The Spiral Castle Tradition does not dictate what names Witches might use for themselves in this or any other capacity, though there are a few titles that are easily recognizable by and among us. These include:

WITCH, PELLAR, CUNNING PERSON/FOLK — These all have slightly different meanings and contexts, but any one of them might be the preferred term for a practitioner of our Artes. These are applicable regardless of gender or level of study, although we say "Witch of the Spiral Castle" to reference a Raised Witch within SCT.

ARTISAN, BARD, CONJURER, HEALER, SEER, VOTARY, WARDEN — Within the Spiral Castle Tradition, Witches of 2nd Admission have studied and practiced a Specialty within the Craft, and they are recognized among us as being at least one of these.

QUEEN, DEVIL, CONSORT — Witches of 3rd Admission are invested with the Virtue of one of our Great Powers and are acknowledged via their relationship to that Power. They may also be a leader of a Coven, or one of the Elders of a Coven.

MAGISTER OF THE LINEAGE — A Queen, Devil, or Consort who was initiated within the founding line (ie, by Laurelei or someone else in her lineage) might additionally use this term. The Grand Coven is the full body of all active Magisters.

MAID, SQUIRE, JACK, VERDOLET, BLACK ROD, PAGE — In Covens with a hierarchical structure, rather than an egalitarian structure, these titles are sometimes given to the understudy(ies) to the leader(s). They facilitate in the absence of the leader(s), and are usu-ally tasked with making sure the people of the Coven know when and where the meeting will take place. Some groups specify that a Witch of a certain degree holds this office. There may be two or three people holding titles such as these, and all should be fully Raised Witches.

REGENT - This title is worn by the Elder who serves as the Head of the Clannad.

Copyright Asteria Books 2022

Laurelei Black

Dedication in Clan of the Laughing Dragon—Aug. 1999
>by Lady R-M of Dragon Heart Coven

1st Degree in Clan of the Laughing Dragon—Aug. 2000
>as BmTQ
>by Lady R-M of Dragon Heart Coven

2nd Degree in Clan of the Laughing Dragon—Jan. 2002
>by Lady R-M of Dragon Heart Coven

3rd Degree in Clan of the Laughing Dragon — Jan. 2005
>as Lady DnM
>by Lady R-M of Dragon Heart Coven

Foundation of Dragon's Eye Coven — May 2005

Initiation into and Foundation of Spiral Castle Tradition and Coven Caer Sidhe— Jan 2009
>as RTQ alongside LNK

Laurelei is one of the two Founding Mothers of the Spiral castle Tradition, and she currently holds the post of Regent for the Clannad. No lineage documents exist for her initiator, Lady R-M, who studied through 3rd Degree with (what was later revealed as) a "Black Gard" coven in Berkley, CA; up to 1st Degree with one of the daughter covens of the Roebuck; and through 7th Degree with two Welsh Druids.

Laurelei is on the Council of Elders for the "home coven" of the Clannad — Coven Caer Sidhe.

Copyright Laurelei Black 2022

www.ingramcontent.com/pod-product-compliance
Lightning Source LLC
Chambersburg PA
CBHW081024240426

43671CB00029B/2921